# CHRISTOPHER CAUDWELL

CRITICS OF THE TWENTIETH CENTURY
Edited by Christopher Norris, University of Wales
Institute of Science and Technology

A.J. Greimas and the Nature of Meaning: Linguistics, Semiotics
and Discourse Theory
*Ronald Schleifer*

Titles in preparation:

Raymond Williams
*John Higgins*

# Christopher Caudwell

ROBERT SULLIVAN

CROOM HELM
London & Sydney

© 1987 Robert J. Sullivan
Croom Helm Ltd, Provident House,
Burrell Row, Beckenham, Kent BR3 1AT
Croom Helm Australia, 44–50 Waterloo Road,
North Ryde, 2113, New South Wales

Published in the USA by
Croom Helm
in association with Methuen, Inc.
29 West 35th Street,
New York, NY 10001

British Library Cataloguing in Publication Data

Sullivan, Robert J.
    Christopher Caudwell. — (Critics of the
    twentieth century).
    1. Caudwell, Christopher
    I. Title   II. Series
    192       B1618.C364

ISBN 0-7099-3881-0
ISBN 0-7099-3882-9 pbk

Printed and bound in Great Britain by Mackays of Chatham Ltd, Kent

For the Unfallen
Those men and women who died
Fighting fascism in Spain

It will be evident, then, that the world has long dreamed of something of which it only has to become conscious in order to possess it in actuality.

*Karl Marx: letter to Arnold Ruge*

# Contents

# Editor's Foreword

In his essay 'Components of the national culture' (1972) Perry Anderson advanced some influential theses concerning what he saw as the peculiarities of British intellectual tradition.[1] More specifically, Anderson set out to give reasons for the failure of Marxist sociology and criticism to make any appreciable impact in this country, at least before the advent of those Continental theorists whose work Anderson himself did so much to promote through his editorship of *New Left Review*. Briefly stated, his argument went as follows. British intellectuals had long been wedded to an ideology of homespun common-sense empiricism which rendered them impervious or deeply resistant to the claims of systematic theory. This resistance took a more overtly political turn in the closing years of the eighteenth century, when it was raised to a high point of principle by Burke and other such right-wing ideologues. It was (Burke argued) all their talk of theory and abstract principles that had got the French into their current revolutionary mess. The British should be thankful that they possessed an unwritten Constitution based on a tacit consensus of values, one which stood in no need of theory or justifying grounds since its roots went deep into the national character. To expose these values to any kind of ideological critique was to side with the zealots like Robespierre who had brought their own country to ruin by wilfully ignoring the inherited wisdom of the ages. The great virtue of the British Constitution (according to Burke) was its inbuilt resistance to the forms of intemperate, destructive will-to-change brought about by this attachment to abstract ideas. It reposed upon a sense of shared cultural identity, a feeling that transcended those mere local differences of class and material interest that ideologues could wilfully exploit so as to stir up radical sentiment. The best remedy against such disorders was an inculcation of the common-sense attitude which fostered a healthy respect for tradition and a strong mistrust of all theoretical debate.

This attitude is still with us — so Anderson argues — and has even left its mark on the development of Marxist and other oppositional forms of discourse. One result of the British 'resistance to theory' was the absence of any strong tradition of bourgeois sociological critique, such as flourished on the Continent through the influence of large-scale systematising thinkers like Durkheim, Weber and Simmel. Whatever their political orientation, these theorists provided a framework of ideas and (above all) a sense of critical engagement which was lacking in the British tradition. In its place there developed two main forms of native socio-cultural discourse. One was the kind of meticulous empirical research that stuck to the facts and made a rule of avoiding any large theoretical commitments. The other, more unlikely development was a shift of interest toward literary criticism as an oblique means of expression for those dissenting ideas and values that found no alternative outlet. From Coleridge, through Arnold to Eliot and Leavis, these thinkers criticised existing social relationships from the standpoint of a broadly organicist ethos rooted in aesthetic models and metaphors. For Coleridge, this led from the idea of poetry as a language that reconciled manifold conflicting impulses ('unity in multiplicity') to the theme of an idealised communal life in which class divisions would not so much fall away as appear insignificant by comparison with our shared humanity. In Arnold, the pursuit of 'disinterested' knowledge — of cultural sweetness and light — goes along with a desire to transcend mere politics in the name of universal values.[2] By Eliot's time this vision had receded into a mythical past age when poetry and culture were as yet untouched by that 'dissociation of sensibility' which supposedly set in with the English Civil War and whose symptoms were everywhere to be read in the subsequent history of secular decline. For one brief moment — prototypically the age of Shakespeare, Donne and the Jacobean dramatists — there existed the conditions of a perfect harmonious relationship between 'thought' and 'emotion'.[3] Thereafter poets could only look back and strive (like the Imagists) to recreate that moment through a self-denying ordinance of disciplined technique and a willed forgetting of history and politics.

In the work of F. R. Leavis this elaborate mythology assumes its most articulate and influential form. Criticism is fixed in a permanent gesture of regret for times past, for that age of 'organic' sensibility and culture which has long been overtaken by the dislocating forces of modern mass-civilisation. The best one can do in this worsening predicament is maintain an attitude of principled intransigence, affirming the values timelessly embodied in the Great Tradition from Shakespeare to Lawrence, and denouncing the symptoms of latter-day decline from a standpoint of beleaguered minority culture.[4] Thus literary criticism takes up the burden of sociological critique, but without (as Anderson argues) any kind of informing theoretical vision or systematic framework of ideas. Leavis of course had absolutely no use for literary theory, regarding it as a tedious irrelevance, a mere distraction from the critic's proper business of intuitive judgement and response.[5] Such is the nature of that potent aesthetic ideology which runs all the way from Coleridge to Leavis. It substitutes mythology for history and – instrumental to this process — a mystified organicist notion of art for the activity of reasoned theoretical critique. One might add that Anderson's diagnosis finds striking confirmation in some late essays by Paul de Man on the discourse of post-Kantian aesthetic philosophy.[6] For de Man, it is through their habit of misreading certain crucial texts in Kant — notably those that negotiate the passage from sensuous apprehension to concepts of pure understanding — that aestheticians have managed to side-step these critical implications. And in so doing they have fostered, like Eliot, a myth of aesthetic transcendence — a nostalgic mystique of 'unified sensibility' — which works to promote a willed disregard for the actual, historical conditions of artistic production.[7]

It is here that Christopher Caudwell enters the picture, along with other pioneering spirits of British Marxist and left-wing criticism. For their work is also marked — as Anderson sees it — by this deep-grained empiricist cast of mind and resultant lack of theoretical rigour. Terry Eagleton pursued much the same line of argument in his book *Criticism and ideology* (1976). Here Caudwell figures as the main exemplar of an isolated, homespun and premature attempt to graft Marxist thinking onto the barren heritage of British common-sense philosophy. What Caudwell's theorising notably lacked was any sense of the complex mediations involved in working a passage from the material determinants to the cultural or socio-political forms of existence. Hobbled by his crudely literal acceptance of the base/superstructure metaphor, Caudwell resorted to the kind of all-purpose analogical thinking which sought (for instance) to 'explain' the growth of lyric poetry entirely in terms of an emergent bourgeois individualism, or indeed the rise of the novel in much the same way. Thus the sheer ambitiousness of his project — taking in not only literature and art but *inter alia* philosophy, anthropology and the crisis in modern physics — is for Eagleton a sign of Caudwell's confusion, his failure to observe (in Althusserian parlance) the 'relative autonomy' of discourses belonging to the cultural sphere. 'Specu-lative and erratic, studded with random insights, punctuated by hectic forays into and out of alien territories and strewn with hair-raising theoretical vulgarities'[8] — there seems almost nothing to be salvaged for the purposes of present-day critical thought.

If Caudwell is the prime exemplar of this underdeveloped Marxist tradition, Eagleton discovers the same disabling tendencies manifest just about everywhere on the British intellectual left. Following Anderson, he situates the work of Raymond Williams in that line of 'culture and society' debate which came down from Coleridge to Leavis. Although Williams very clearly distanced himself from the overt conservatism present in most of these ideologues, he nevertheless continued to think of 'culture' in broadly organicist terms, as a fund of communal ideas and values which could always be summoned to memory against the distorting pressures of modern civilised existence. In this respect Williams can be seen to pursue a strain of 'left-Leavisite' cultural critique whose limitations show up in its failure to break with the empiricist appeal to experience and common-sense knowledge. The only way beyond this deadlocked tradition (according to Anderson and Eagleton) is the path of an Althusserian Marxist 'science' which would clearly distinguish the discourse of theory from the elements of pre-critical humanist ideology. Such at least was the message conveyed by those New Left thinkers of the mid-1970s who discovered no work of real (theoretical) merit in British Marxist criticism of an earlier generation.

Since then the situation has changed so much as to warrant a complete reassessment of Caudwell's standing and historical importance. Althusserian Marxism has run into various problems, not least on account of that hardline distinction between science and ideology, the belief that theory could provide some kind of ultimate conceptual grounding, untouched by the messy contingencies of lived experience. Eagleton himself has virtually abandoned the quest for a full-scale, rigorous Marxist aesthetic, coming round (in his recent book *Literary theory*) to what appears a well-nigh pragmatist position: that theories are good for what one is able to get out of them in this or that context, and not for any intrinsic reason of explanatory grasp or superior cognitive power.[9] So his book takes the form of a quickfire narrative history, linking up the various schools and movements with a lively sense of their ongoing dialogue. And it ends with a chapter recommending that we now leave off this delusory search for better theories and return to the age-old tradition of *rhetoric* — the study of language in its practical, persuasive uses — as a means of putting criticism back in touch with political realities. Nothing could be further from the high theoreticist ambitions of Eagleton's earlier work.

In Anderson likewise, the critique of common-sense empiricism has now given way to a polemical engagement with the avatars of French post-structuralist theory, directed in the main against Derrida and Foucault, but clearly encompassing certain aspects of Althusser's work.[10] What Anderson now sets out to rebut is post-structuralism's bracketing of the real — of lived history and language in its material, referential aspect — brought about by its retreat into a solipsistic world of unanchored signifying systems. There is no room here for a detailed review of Anderson's arguments. Suffice it to say that, coming from an erstwhile protagonist of new French theory, they force some fairly drastic re-thinking of the whole post-structuralist diagnostic line on critics like Williams and Caudwell.

Sullivan's book is in part a response to this present, unsettled situation in the discourse of literary theory. It is also (remarkably) the first treatment of Caudwell's work to have taken full account of its sheer imposing bulk, from detective novels to books on aerodynamics and aviation history, as well as the studies of aesthetics and literary history on which his reputation will surely come to rest. Yet Sullivan is far from presenting all this in a spirit of uncritical adulation. While properly impressed by the extraordinary burst of productivity which marked the few months before Caudwell's death in the Spanish Civil War, he is also conscious of the very real problems and theoretical shortcuts pointed out by a critic like Eagleton. Nevertheless the effect of Sullivan's work can only be to stimulate much wider interest in a figure whose cardinal importance for the history of British Marxist debate has up to now been obscured by a complex of ideological motives and circumstances. 'Who is the major English Marxist critic? Christopher Caudwell, *hélas*.'[11] Thus Eagleton, placing his Althusserian stamp on what seemed pretty much the definitive verdict. It is the great merit of Sullivan's book to reopen this enquiry with more adequate evidence and a sharpened sense of historical hindsight.

Christopher Norris

## Notes

1. See Perry Anderson, 'Components of the national culture', *New Left Review*, no. 50 (May/June, 1968).
2. On this tradition and its ideological background, see Chris Baldick, *The social mission of English criticism* (Oxford, Clarendon Press, 1983).
3. Eliot lays out his view of literary history in the two early essays, 'Tradition and the individual talent' and 'The metaphysical poets', in T. S. Eliot, *Selected Essays* (London, Faber & Faber, 1964), pp. 3–11 and 241–50.
4. See for instance F. R. Leavis, *Revaluation: tradition and development in English poetry* (London, Chatto & Windus, 1936) and *The great tradition: George Eliot, Henry James, Joseph Conrad* (London, Chatto & Windus, 1948).
5. Notably in Leavis's reply to René Wellek, 'Literary criticism and philosophy', *Scrutiny*, vol. VI (1937), pp. 59–70.
6. See Paul de Man, 'The resistance to theory', in Barbara Johnson (ed.), *The pedagogical imperative*, Yale French Studies, no. 63 (1982), pp. 3–20.
7. See Roger Scruton, *The aesthetic understanding* (London, Methuen, 1983) for some striking examples of this mystifying process at work.
8. Terry Eagleton, *Criticism and ideology* (London, New Left Books, 1976), p. 21.
9. See the closing chapter of Terry Eagleton's *Literary theory: an introduction* (Oxford, Basil Blackwell, 1983).
10. Perry Anderson, *In the tracks of historical materialism* (London, New Left Books, 1983).
11. Eagleton, *Criticism and ideology*, p. 21.

# Preface

Although I had read Caudwell's *Illusion and reality* in the early sixties, the genesis of the present study dates from a seminar at Brown University in 1979. Most of the participants remarked on the disorganisation, the labyrinthine argument of the book, while I found myself highlighting what seemed to me Caudwell's crucial insights on poetry's 'characteristics' and its function within society. Nevertheless, the convoluted organisation of the book, with its five-hundred plus bibliography, intrigued me and this led to an investigation of the book's sources and composition. I spent a considerable time researching numerous titles in Caudwell's bibliography and a picture of the book's evolution began to emerge. After reading the various manuscripts and biographical materials at the Humanities Research Center, University of Texas, Austin, my suspicions about the composition and structural fractures of *Illusion and reality* were confirmed for me; that the writing of the *Studies and further studies in a dying culture* (carried out while Caudwell was revising *Illusion and reality*) was responsible for the latter book's disorganisation. Evidence for such a belief is offered in Chapter 4 and the Appendix, which together form the heart of this book; that is, an explication of the genesis and construction of the hurried project entitled *Illusion and reality*, the solidity of the central insights of that volume, and an explanation of its irritating inconsistencies.

The biographical materials at Austin revealed to me how intricately intertwined Caudwell's life and work were in those frantically busy few years between 1934 and 1936, when he wrote all of the work for which he is known. It is for this reason that Chapter 2 is taken up with Caudwell's activities during this period. His *theory*, written mostly during the 'breaks' he could manage from his daily Party work and his involvement in Poplar's fight against fascism, is more clearly understood in the light of this *practice*. In the 'Introduction' I have tried to place Caudwell in his historical milieu, setting out to differentiate him from most of the usual stereotypes associated with the 'Auden generation'. In Chapter 3 I have concentrated on Caudwell's novel *This my hand*, a psycho-social study of murder, and the only creative work he allowed to appear under the pseudonym. This work, although revealing strains of Caudwell's attempt to align his creative work with his new world-view, is of interest if only because of the amalgamation of psychoanalytic material with social issues, the dual concerns

7

of *Illusion and reality*.

In the fifth chapter I explore the central concerns of *Studies and further studies in a dying culture*, explicating them in the light of Caudwell's two abiding epistemological positions — the separation of subject and object in bourgeois philosophy and social relations, and its concomitant result, a false conception of freedom. In this chapter I also plot the genesis of many of Caudwell's discourses, showing how he as subject was reacting to the object of his own historical time. Chapter 6, the final postscript, is meant to be read as a prologomena to a re-reading of Caudwell in the light of more contemporary cultural theory. Rather than seeing Caudwell as a pioneer in British Marxist theory, a footnoted historical monument, this summary seeks to suggest his contemporaneity. Although his work was hardly 'finished' (as he himself remarked) and although we must recognise some of its 'vulgarities', we should also seek out its very palpable strengths, especially some of Caudwell's shrewd remarks on the ideological matrices of form.

For example, Terry Eagleton, reviewing *Romance and realism* (which was intended as one of the 'studies' and not a separate book), remarks that Caudwell has 'nothing whatever to say' concerning the 'complex relations between class, ideology, language, and literary form'. This observation seems all the more inexcusable if we consider that Eagleton had recently completed a book that concerned itself with some of the issues Caudwell addresses in *Romance and realism*. Eagleton's *Exiles and emigrés* deals with those modern writers who were aliens in one sense or another (Conrad, James, etc.), writers whose experiment with point of view (Caudwell argues) was an *effect* of their exile and alienation. Caudwell was one of the first commentators to point out how Conrad and James attempt to solve the 'epistemological problem' of the novel, and relates this to analogous problems of the 'observer' in physics. In *Criticism and ideology* Eagleton refers, in terms very similar to Caudwell's, to how Conrad's narrative technique is an attempt to solve that very same 'epistemological problem'.[1] This is not a plea to excuse what Eagleton in the same review terms Caudwell's 'hectic, hair-raising gallop through English literature since 1600', but an invitation to recognise some of the insights on form that are still meaningful for us.

Caudwell was also concerned with the nature of the 'subject', the search for a social psychology and the nature of perception and reality, areas of obvious concern in contemporary debate. In

Chapter 6 I suggest that Caudwell's viewpoint on these matters is essentially that of classical Marxism, an emphasis on the unity of theory and practice and a mutually determining relation between the subject and object, self and world. Such a position is compared and contrasted with Lacan's metaphysical notion of the subject and Althusser's version of ideology as an essentially subjective entity (as opposed to a class construct), which leads inevitably to a state of *political* stasis. These problems are discussed within the rubric of Fredric Jameson's *The political unconscious* which, in its attempts to synthesise various aspects of contemporary theory, offers itself as a paradigm for examining Caudwell's own attempt at a synthetic account of cultural creations. I conclude this last chapter with the suggestion that at this juncture in history, when Marx is being rewritten, we need to re-read Caudwell in this light, because his endeavour (no matter how fleeting) was analogous to Marx's own: 'If the construction and preparation of the future is not our business, then it is the more certain what we do have to consummate — I mean the ruthless criticism of all that exists.' In *Illusion and reality*, Caudwell felt he was offering, a manifesto for a 'preparing of the future'; and in the *Studies* a 'ruthless criticism' ('destructively analysing all bourgeois culture' as he put it) of his own historical time.

Many people contributed to the making of this book, and those that I forget to mention will know who they are. I owe a great many thanks to Jo Ann and Bob Scholes for their extensive hospitality and friendship during most of the writing of the manuscript. Sally Richmond was a friend and partner during much of the writing and contributed to the book's making in more ways than she realises. My friends Kieran O'Hara and Chuck McBride offered support when support was needed. My tutors and colleagues at Brown University, most especially Robert Scholes (who encouraged the project from the beginning), Roger Henkle and Mark Spilka, had the misfortune to read early drafts and offer advice — for this I give thanks. Robert Coover and Michael Harper offered advice and enthusiasm when enthusiasm flagged and I am grateful to them as friends. Finally, I owe a debt to E. P. Thompson who took time from his own hectic schedule to read my manuscript and offer encouragement as well as severe criticism. The advice I have neglected to take (from Thompson as from all the others) is my own responsibility, as is, of course, the final responsibility for the pages which follow.

Robert Sullivan, Providence, Rhode Island

# Notes

1. Terry Eagleton, Review of *Romance and realism* in *Review of English Studies*, vol. XXIII, No. 92 (1972), pp. 499–500; *Exiles and emigrés* (New York, Schocken Books, 1972), especially the introduction; *Criticism and ideology: a study in Marxist literary theory* (London, Verso Editions, 1978), p. 137. Caudwell's remarks on the ideological matrices of the novel's form are discussed at the end of Chapter 5.

# Acknowledgements

I have several individuals and institutions to thank for their help in the making of this book. The English department's secretarial staff at Brown University persevered over many years with my many requests as did the librarians at the same institution. While on a Fellowship kindly awarded by Brown, the librarians at Yale University were most helpful in supplying me with a great deal of research materials as well as a place to store and read them. At the Humanities Research Center, the University of Texas, Austin, the librarians extended to me not only their vast holdings of the Caudwell manuscripts, but also the warm hospitality for which the state is known.

All this research, however, could not have been offered in its present form without the aid of Rosemary Sprigg, Caudwell's half-sister and executor, who gave permission as well as support. Finally, the title of one of Geoffrey Hill's volumes of poetry supplied me with the wording which virtually dictated itself as the epigraph to the book, a contribution which seems only fitting from an old teacher.

# 1

# Introduction

*The Marxist tradition is* not — *and it is lamentable that it needs even to be said at this point* — *is not a tradition of 'theoreticians'. By the Marxist tradition we mean a tradition that has for one and a half centuries involved literally millions of men and women in life and death struggles. And whatever we mean by Marxist theory, unless from the beginning we put it in that context, then we are no more than idealists.*

Terry Eagleton

*It might be argued that the real thirties was that of John Cornford, Christopher Caudwell, Tom Wintringham, Ralph Fox and Julian Bell.*

Stephen Spender

Christopher Caudwell was a remarkable human being. Not yet thirty years old, he left a huge volume of manuscript behind him before he died fighting with the International Brigades in Spain on 12 February 1937. He had already published seven detective novels, one 'serious' novel, books on the art and technique of aviation, and his most ambitious project, *Illusion and reality*, was being set up in type when he left for Spain. His *Studies in a dying culture* (1938), *The crisis in physics* (1939), *Poems* (1939), *Further studies in a dying culture* (1949) and *Romance and realism* (1970) have all been published posthumously. He left unpublished, two volumes of short stories, a science fiction novel, two dramas, enough poetry for several volumes, and an important study on the ideological bases of biological theories.[1] Apart from the sheer volume of his work, one is confronted by an enormous diversity of interest. These concerns range from the problematic of modern physics, through biology and psychoanalytic theory, to the attempt to establish a Marxist aesthetics. Most of the work that we know him for, *Illusion and reality*, *Studies and further studies in a dying culture* and the *The crisis in physics*, was written, incredible as it may seem, in just over one year: from August 1935 until his departure for Spain early in December, 1936.

Caudwell's writings, in all their diversity, demonstrate an erudition and sophistication that make us wonder just how great a thinker and influence he would have become had he survived the Spanish Civil War. Nevertheless, despite this unique contribution to a wide area of discourse — indeed *because* of it — Caudwell's work needs to be considered in the historical context in which he wrote. In the final analysis, the only way to explicate such an extended and disparate set of discourses is to consider them as an individual response to the cultural concerns of the epoch. It should be noted at the outset, however, that such an approach does not deny Caudwell his unique contribution. On the contrary, in this introductory chapter, and at further length in the chapters that follow, I suggest that Caudwell's response, both in his life and in his writings, invites us to re-evaluate many of the events and texts of his time. In Piaget's sense of the term, Caudwell 'transforms' that cultural structure that commentators have imposed on the intellectual, social and literary life of the 1930s. Caudwell, who had read Piaget and who had in part derived his 'interactionist' philosophy from this thinker, believed that through the poetic process man both changes reality and transforms himself in the one dialectical process. In a similar way, Caudwell as a subject reacting to the reality of the 1930s, changes our comprehension of that reality, while at the same time we see him transform himself.[2] One of the 'deep' structural motifs shared by almost all the literary intelligentsia of the period was the search for a system of belief in what seemed an irredeemable world of fragmentation. Such was Caudwell's quest also, but as this intro-duction hopes to document, his was less an unconscious desire for 'communion' than a recognition of the necessity of historical events.

In one of the first studies of English intellectuals during this time, the Russian emigré Dmitri Mirsky notes that the 'principal result of 1931 for the intelligentsia was its return to politics'. He goes on:

> That revival of interest in politics was accompanied by an
> increased need for a world view, for a system. The purpose
> of this system was to save an intellectual from being isolated,
> to provide him with a group, to enable him to feel part of
> some greater whole, to elaborate a system of arguments to
> justify the aims of the whole, and in short to provide him
> with a key to the chaos, the so puzzling confusion into which
> reality seemed to have moved. I purposely describe it in
> this abstract way – that is to say, as an abstract general
> need to free themselves from an individualist, rootless
> position, and come to an understanding of a reality which
> seems incomprehensible.[3]

Paradigmatic of this search for a system within the literary 'revolutionary' movement was the publication in 1933 of the collection edited by Michael Roberts and entitled *New country: prose and poetry by the authors of New Signatures*.[4] This anthology when compared with *New Signatures* of the previous year is important as an index of how a radical movement that was 'literary in its manifestations' turned inexorably to the left. If Eliot's *The waste land* imaginatively captured the vision of a fragmented post-war world, then we can consider *New country* as a comprehensive analysis of that social ethos. It is worth considering here just how the contributors to this volume (sometimes unconsciously using leitmotifs from *The waste land*) offer a condensed version of how the literary intelligentsia viewed the fragments of their 'dying culture'.

The contributions are rife with the 'noise of history' and the sanctity of revolution: the prose pieces include Day Lewis's 'Letter to a young revolutionary', Spender's 'Poetry and revolution' and Edward Upward's stories of conversion to socialism, 'The colleagues' and 'Sunday'. Significantly, and indicative of the ever-increasing search among the younger intellectuals for a synthesis that would account for all the aspects of the 'dying culture', there is in this 'literary' anthology an essay by G. F. Brett·entitled 'Science marking time'. In the poetry section Auden contributed, among other poems, 'A communist to others', which warns the various elements of English society, including the poet, that 'salvation' does not lie in 'personal regeneration', but, rather,

'Love outside our own election/Holds us in unseen connection'. A good deal of the poetry is conspicuously (to adapt some words of Wilfred Owen) 'in the propaganda', as evidenced by this refrain from Rex Warner's 'Hymn': 'Come then, companions. This is the spring of blood,/heart's heyday, movement of masses, beginning of good.'[5] The introductory 'Preface' by Roberts is in the form of a manifesto urging the intelligentsia to unite, in the sort of tone that led one commentator to devise the term 'Revolutionary Council'.

That a great deal of the 'revolutionary' fervour among the intellectuals was literary in flavour has been well documented. More than a few of the studies of the period have on their title page the conjunction of 'politics and literature'. Christopher St John Sprigg thought of himself as a poet during these years and was no doubt aware of the literary propagandists, the practitioners of what Caudwell was later to call 'rhyming Marxism'. But Sprigg had left school at the age of fifteen, did not attend any university, let alone Oxford or Cambridge, and he belonged to no literary coterie. Indeed, he was caught up in the busy round of Fleet Street and the writing of poetry was for him an activity snatched from the labours of office work. Nevertheless, Sprigg's conscious-ness was formed by the same historical circumstances, the same 'ideological pressure', as Caudwell was to term it, as others of his generation: the same years and historical circumstances as those of Auden, Spender, Day Lewis, MacNeice and Upward. Indeed they were all born within three years of one another, Caudwell in 1907, the same year as Auden and MacNeice.

In this sense the metamorphosis of Christopher St John Sprigg, middle-class poet, into Christopher Caudwell, communist and cultural theorist, is very much a product of the epoch. However, although he shared in the hopes and frustrations that characterised his generation (I mean here 'generation' in the purely chrono-logical sense), his move toward socialism was more conscious than those literary contemporaries who affected a similar path. From the very beginning Caudwell's motives were practical as well as theoretical and never 'literary' in their genesis.

When Caudwell wrote to a friend in 1935, he indicated that his adoption of his new-found *Weltanschauung* would require more than a 'mere polishing-up of prose'. Rather, it would necessitate the coming 'to terms with both [him]self and [his] environment'. As always (and this is a hallmark of his life and work), the subject could not be considered without the object, nor could theory be considered without practice. Typically enough, he had chosen to embark on his theoretical enterprise (the writing of *Studies* and the final version of *Illusion and reality*) while living in the militantly working-class area of Poplar. Among his 'practical' activities were those of selling the *Daily Worker* at an underground station and getting beaten up and jailed for protesting at a Mosley meeting. While Auden wrote of the 'boring [communist] meeting', Caudwell acted as secretary to his local branch, even though he disliked the job. Conversely, in the midst of action theory could not be forgotten. In Spain, engaged in what Spender called 'a poet's war', Caudwell wrote no poems. His letters from training camp demonstrate a continuing interest in the prosaic business of Party organisation, the theoretical struggle to get the arms ban lifted in England.

Caudwell, aware of the difficulty of writing the kind of poetry that seemed necessary for an age such as his — the kind of difficulty remarked upon by Roberts and the contributors to *New country* — gave up the practice of writing verse and turned to theory. Unlike the majority of his contemporaries, who found in Marx and Freud sources for a secular mythology to impose on their art, Caudwell used the two great influences on his generation to form a synthetic *Weltanschauung* that would help explain art's social function. Of the two works for which he is best known, *Illusion and reality* and *Studies and further studies in a dying culture*, the former can be seen, in part, as setting out to answer a crucial question of the epoch: Can art, especially poetry, actually help shape social reality? The *Studies*, on the other hand, are more concerned with the various distortions or rationalisations implanted in the bourgeois psyche by ideology, and especially, how such distortions were affecting the contemporary intelligentsia — the artist, the scientist, the philosopher, those very figures who had contributed to *New country*.

The fact that there were ideological and historical pressures that helped produce Caudwell's texts does not mean that they are mere period pieces. In his search to document his belief in the social determination of consciousness, he read swiftly and widely in biology, anthropology, psychology and (in the last few years of his life) Marxism. His vast project led him toward the basis for a social psychology which, in its implications, is strikingly modern. His remarks on the social nature of the sign, that consciousness only realises itself through the intermediacy of social signs, and his stress on the key role which language plays in the structure of the psyche — these observations are of obvious contemporary relevance.

Yet, above all his innovations in poetic theory, Caudwell may well find his true place in intellectual history as a twentieth-century *philosophe* who was fascinated by ideology in all its guises. This interest ranged from the role of the imagination in human evolution to the construction of class consciousness. In short, he was interested in the interrelationship of all aspects of the super-structure, and his work in that last hurried year of his life can be seen as an attempt to explicate the 'crisis in every aspect of art and culture' that so many of the intelligentsia commented upon, but in Caudwell's opinion, little understood. It was his opinion that the only world view that would explain the circumstances that he and his generation faced was that of dialectical materialism, a point of view that stresses the causal relationship of all phenomena in a process of becoming. In his Foreword to the *Studies in a dying culture*, Caudwell put it like this: 'Either the Devil has come amongst us having great power, or there is a causal explanation for a disease common to economics, science, and art.' He was to attempt a comprehensive analysis of the 'decay' of contemporary culture and relate his findings to social relations themselves.

Ortega y Gasset, in his book *Man and crisis*, considers the philosophical parameters underlying such periods as that under discussion, and his remarks afford a fitting appraisal of the 1930s in England and Caudwell's position within the decade. He defines an historical crisis as a time when the 'system of convictions' held by a previous generation is no longer tenable. This situation results in the lack of a world-view, a period of nihilism, in which 'one feels a profound disdain for everything or almost everything, which was believed yesterday'. As the situation worsens from crisis to catastrophe, men (especially younger men), without the 'map' of the system of convictions which had allowed the previous generation to 'move within [their] environment with a certain security', find themselves totally disorientated. In desperation they attempt to persuade themselves to be 'convinced of this or that'. Ortega y Gasset summarises his argument thus:

> During periods of crisis, positions which are false or feigned are very common. Entire generations falsify themselves to themselves; that is to say, they wrap themselves up in artistic styles, in doctrines, in political movements which are insincere and which fill the lack of genuine convictions.[6]

It was just such a 'genuine conviction' that marked Caudwell off from his contemporaries and set him apart from the 'literary revolution' as represented by *New country*. Nowhere in his work is such a stance more prominent, and pertinent to one of the central dilemmas of the age, as in the final pages of *Romance and realism*. Here Caudwell addresses the 'role of the artist in a revolutionary situation' and warns those who would both 'betray art and social change' because the styles 'they wrap themselves up in' are insincere. The role of the poet in times such as his is of singular importance:

> What, then, is the proper position for a bourgeois poet today who finds himself arrived at the situation of Auden, Spender, and Lewis? To be a revolutionary, certainly, but a real revolutionary, not a free-lance agitator; to be a member of a revolutionary party and to carry out a common party line, not his own line; to be a revolutionary not only in blank verse but in every activity which he can carry out and his party suggests. Agitation is necessary certainly, so is propaganda, but let the poet be a genuine propagandist, not a blank-verse propagandist. Is the proletariat made conscious of its goal by rhymed economics? No, verse is not, and never was, the instrument of propaganda in this sense... Notice that not only does this attempt not revitalise poetry, but it gives rise to a perversion of poetry, self-consciously propagandist poetry. Poetry can be revitalised only by a change of the economic relations on which it rests, and a corresponding change and synthesis of the dissolving culture of today.[7]

If the 'real thirties' (as Spender suggests in the epigraph to this introduction) belonged to men of genuine conviction, those who could not countenance theory without practice, thought without action, then the decade cannot be understood without a full appreciation of Christopher Caudwell. But perhaps the 'real thirties' belonged to Caudwell in a more theoretical sense. Compared with many of the other intellectuals, including Auden, Day Lewis, and Spender himself, he seemed most aware, most conscious, of how (to use Ortega y Gasset's terminology) 'generations falsify themselves to themselves'. Many of the better-known figures have, with hindsight, analysed their attraction to the workers' movement in similar terms: the 'quasi-religious' motive, a sense of guilt in a world of rising unemployment, the need for a system of belief. But Caudwell documented these motifs of what he called the '*Zeitgeist*' of the time in a short story he wrote almost a year *before* he himself became involved in the workers' cause.

'We all try' is the narrative of a young, upper-middle-class malcontent who, bereft of any religious conscience and sick of his parasitic existence, becomes a working man and flirts with communism for a time. There are tensions within this unpublished story which suggest that Caudwell was scrutinising not only the current intellectual trend, but his own motivations. He wrote to a friend describing the story as a depiction of 'the failure of idealism, as long as it is really only a selfish longing for self-fulfilment, and has no social roots'. And when he dramatised the story for possible performance (under the title of *The way the wind blows*), the message for his fellow writers and intellectuals (and, one imagines, to himself) is unequivocal. A Jewish communist, Levy, is talking to the would-be converted, middle-class Brian Mainwaring:

> Oh, we don't want you. Not down here. The workers distrust your sort, deboshed intellectuals trying to save their souls! If you really want to do propaganda, go back to your Mayfair drawing-room and carry on with your old life.

The 'down here' referred to in this extract is the working-class East End of London. Caudwell, unlike his creation, Brian Mainwaring, was to remain in this area and, it seemed, was resolved never to go back to his 'old life'. Unlike a great many figures in the 1930s who adopted 'feigned positions', there is evidence to suggest that Caudwell had rediscovered, for the short time remaining to him, his true self. He was, in essence, a poet and a philosopher who had become temporarily involved in business. Sensing the inappropriateness of his own poetry, and eschewing what he saw as 'rhyming Marxism', he turned to the study of poetry's function. This in turn led him to consider other products of consciousness, and especially an investigation of what he saw as the ideological anarchy of his era. The result is a large body of writing which, as he himself admitted, is hardly 'finished', but which contains numerous insights into man's social and artistic evolution that remain crucial to contemporary thought.

As early as 1948, Stanley Hyman remarked on the extensive bibliography that documents Caudwell's reading, calling it a 'catalogue of the best of twentieth-century thought'. I have extensively traced the evolution of Caudwell's response to that thought; not only the grand synthesis of biology, psychology and sociology that went into the making *Illusion and reality*, but the historical and cultural matrices that were the genesis of the *Studies in a dying culture*. This has involved a thorough investigation of the manuscripts, resulting in what I believe to be a definitive chronology of their composition. In the chapters that follow this introduction, I consider Caudwell's life and work, including his uncomfortable role as poet and novelist, in their interrelationship. I have tried to show how the poet, the novelist and the theorist shed light on one another.

Caudwell's central epistemological position was a belief in the causal nexus between all phenomena, both material and spiritual. This study of the man and his work, immeasurably more modest, has an analogical goal. It seeks to connect Caudwell, so often treated as a peripheral or enigmatic figure, to the vital intellectual issues of his time.

## Notes

1. Parts of this unpublished work have recently been published in two volumes: the prose in *Scenes and actions*, ed. Jean Duparc and David Margolies (London, Routledge & Kegan Paul, 1986), and the unpublished poetry in Christopher Caudwell, *Collected poems*, ed. Alan Young (Manchester, Carcanet Press, 1986).

2. The decade, and what almost amounts to a synchronic structure of agents and events, has been, to use Hayden White's terminology, 'motifically encoded' by numerous commentators. Of the many titles dealing with the 1930s, I have found the following particularly helpful: Bernard Bergonzi, *Reading the thirties* (Pittsburgh, University of Pittsburgh Press, 1978); Richard Crossman (ed.), *The god that failed* (New York, Harper & Bros, 1949, repr. New York, Bantam Books, 1965); Robert Graves and Alan Hodge, *The long week-end: a social history of Great Britain 1918–1939* (New York, W. W. Norton, 1963); Samuel Hynes, *The Auden generation* (London, The Bodley Head, 1976); D. E. S. Maxwell, *Poets of the thirties* (London, Routledge & Kegan Paul, 1969); Peter Stansky and William Abrahams, *Journey to the Frontier: Julian Bell and John Cornford: their lives and the 1930's* (London, Constable, 1966); Julian Symons, *The thirties: a dream revolved* (London, Cresset Press, 1960); Neal Wood, *Communism and British intellectuals* (New York, Columbia University Press, 1959).

3. Dmitri Mirsky, *The intelligentsia of Great Britain* (London, Gollancz, 1935), p. 40–1.

4. Michael Roberts (ed.), *New country: prose and poetry by the authors of New Signatures* (London, Hogarth Press, 1933).

5. *New country*, p. 254.

6. José Ortega y Gasset, *Man and crisis* (New York, W. W. Norton, 1962), p. 86. It was partly such attitudes which no doubt prompted W. H. Auden, himself so adept at assuming 'feigned' positions, to describe the 1930s as that 'low dishonest decade'.

7. *Romance and realism*, pp. 135–6.

# 2

## Caudwell in the Thirties

*Seriously, I think my weakness has been the lack of an integrated Weltanschauung, I mean one that includes my emotional, scientific, and artistic needs.*

Caudwell

*Just as, therefore, at an earlier period, a section of the nobility went over to the bourgeoisie, so now a portion of the bourgeoisie goes over to the proletariat, and in particular, a portion of the bourgeois ideologists, who have raised themselves to the level of comprehending theoretically the historical movement as a whole.*

Marx and Engels

*And next day took the boat*
*  For home, forgetting Spain, not realising*
*That Spain would soon denote*
*  Our grief, our aspirations;*
*Not knowing that our blunt*
*  Ideals would find their whetstone, that our spirit*
*Would find its frontier on the Spanish front,*
*  Its body in a rag-tag army.*

Louis MacNeice

On 9 December 1936, writing from his East End address where he had been living for just over a year, Christopher St John Sprigg addressed his brother, Theo, as follows:

> I expect it will be a surprise to you, but I am leaving for Spain on Friday. I did not know there was any chance of this till yesterday afternoon. They are badly in need of drivers who are in the Party or close to it. I have passports, & I therefore volunteered.

On the same day he wrote to his friends and frequent correspondents, Paul and Elizabeth Beard, with the same news, mentioning the urgency of his decision 'in view of Franco's big push with German and Italian troops'. Despite the 'present rush' he takes the trouble in this letter to explain his motives for writing the recently composed 'Studies', and although he considers them incomplete — needing 'refining, balancing ... ripening and humanising' — he feels that they contain 'some good ideas'. Although considering it a 'contingency', he proceeds to set out a table of his manuscripts: 'There is always a possibility that I may not come back from Spain, in which case I shall leave behind me a mass of manuscript some of which may be worth publishing.' He goes on to set out the list of the last few years' work with marginal comments for his friend Paul Beard, who was, with Christopher's brother, to become his literary executor.

The short stories and 'various poems', parts of which might be worth publishing, 'all belong to [his] dishonest sentimental past'. *The crisis in physics* is 'just half ready for press', but the plays, novels, etc. are 'all completely worthless'. He doesn't mention *Illusion and reality* because that book was being set up in print by Macmillan.

Thus it was that Christopher St John Sprigg left for Spain; and through some of the manuscripts mentioned above, which he had 'accumulated', he was to become known posthumously as 'Christopher Caudwell'. Caudwell's work was known only among a few friends and the very small number of the public who had bought *This my hand*. It was only after Sprigg's death that the works of Caudwell became better known than those of Christopher St John Sprigg. Some indication of his 'identity' may be gleaned from the following obituaries.

*The Surrey Comet* (13 March 1937):

News has just reached England of the death, while fighting with the International Brigade outside Madrid, of Mr. Christopher St John Sprigg, the promising young author and poet, who had lived for a number of years with his brother, Mr. T. S. Sprigg, at Addacoom, Mount View, Ruxley, Claygate, Surrey.

And the London *Evening News* (11 March 1937):

Mr. Christopher St John Sprigg, a well-known British airman and journalist has been killed while fighting as a soldier with the International Brigade near Madrid, it was announced today.[1]

He was killed in the battle for Madrid on 12 February 1937, some few months after his twenty-ninth birthday.

Although his brother, Theo, was aware, and at times alarmed by Christopher's recent activities within the working-class movement, it *would* have come as a 'surprise' to learn just how far his younger brother's commitment had taken him. Their relationship had been a very close one, both in business and in their personal lives, until the late summer of 1935 when Christopher wrote from Cornwall to say that when he returned to London he would no longer live with Theo and his wife, but would instead move to the Poplar district in the East End of the city, to get, as he put it, some 'local colour' for his writing. It was here, in this vehemently working-class area, that 'John Sprigg' (the name by which he was known to his comrades), in just over one year wrote most of the work that secured for 'Christopher Caudwell' his reputation as the most controversial of English Marxists.[2]

Christopher St John Sprigg was born on 20 October 1907 in Putney, which then must have been a quiet, middle-class suburb of London. His mother, Jessica Caudwell, came from an old family out of Berkshire; she was a black and white miniaturist and died in 1916 when Christopher was only eight years old. It was his mother's maiden name that Sprigg was to adopt for what he considered to be his serious work, although the novel *This my hand*, published in the spring of 1936, was the only work that he was to see under this pseudonym. If Caudwell inherited his 'artistic' tendencies from his mother, he most certainly shared on his father's side the Sprigg flair for journalistic writing and the ability to compose rapidly on a wide variety of subjects. The youngest of three children, Christopher was born into a family of journalists that went back at least two generations. His father, William Stanhope Sprigg, helped found the *Windsor Magazine* for Ward, Lock & Co., was a literary editor for the *Daily Express*, represented for a time the *Standard* in New York, and published a pamphlet, 'The British blockade', on the sea blockade during the First World War. His older brother, Theodore Stanhope Sprigg, published some twelve books on aviational matters and it was with him, in the late 1920s and early 1930s, that Christopher embarked on a series of publishing ventures. But it was with his father that the young teenager received his primary education in the world of journalism.

Educated at a Roman Catholic preparatory school at Bognor Regis in Sussex — his father had been a convert and his sister Paula was to enter a convent — Christopher then went to the Benedictine School at Ealing in London. His school leaving certificate shows that among other subjects he passed 'General Science with Distinction'. His brother records that he left school at the age of 15 because his father 'could not, at that time, afford to continue paying the school fees'. But apparently Christopher had been pressing even before this time to leave school and to help with the family finances, and when his father was appointed literary editor of the provincial *Yorkshire Observer* Christopher 'jumped at the opportunity' to join him in Bradford as a trainee reporter. Memories of this period of his life find imaginative outlet in some of the 'serious' short stories he was to write over ten years later. And his novel *This my hand* is set in the fictional Tinford which has many of the qualities that Bradford must have impressed upon him. It was also during this time (1923–6) that he wrote his first poems, probably the 'juvenilia' of the published work, and may have begun the constantly revised poem 'The art of dying'.

After a few years on this paper, for which he eventually did some novel reviewing, he returned to London and gained editorial experience on the trade journal *British Malaya* before joining his brother in a series of publishing ventures. A family legacy helped them expand their journalistic business and the two brothers formed an aeronautical press agency, Airways Publications Ltd, with T. Stanhope Sprigg as Vice-Chairman and Christopher

Sprigg as Joint Managing Director. Among the Papers are share certificates in Christopher St John Sprigg's name for, British Industrial Press Ltd (100 shares), Airways Publications (190 shares) and Aeromarine Advertising Ltd (50 shares). Theodore Stanhope Sprigg, in his 'biographical sketch', writes of his brother at this time (1926–30):

> As a director of the publishing company and as editor of one of its later journals, Christopher Sprigg now began to show that extraordinary capacity for sustained work, rapid writing and inexhaustible fertility of ideas that was so marked a feature of his later work as a novelist. Actively engaged in the conduct of a publishing company, a press bureau and an advertising agency he yet managed to find time to write his first two books, one an exhaustive and still classic treatise on Airships and the other a popular handbook on elementary flying, to obtain the material for which he took a full course of flying instruction at Brooklands Aero Club.

These books were not 'Christopher Sprigg's' first publications. In 1927 and 1929 he saw in print two examples of an abiding interest (science and poetry), an interest that was eventually to culminate in a relational study of these two facets of experience in *Illusion and reality*. It was in 1927 that he saw his first poem, 'Once I did think', in print and two years later his 'Notes for automatic gears' was published in the *Automobile Engineer* and apparently drew much attention.[3] Sprigg's opening observations on procedure foreshadow (albeit in a pragmatic way) Caudwell's later emphasis on the unity of theory and practice.

> Essentially, however, mathematics is an instrument for particularised as opposed to general analysis, and often no one can be more dangerous from the point of view of the practical engineer than the mathematician who does not always bear carefully in mind the fundamental physical laws of which his symbols are a more wieldy translation. In brief, the *a priori* theorizer should shun mathematics and the mathematician *a priori* theorising.

The 'first two books' that Theodore Stanhope Sprigg refers to in his biographical fragment were *The airship: its design, history, operation and future*, published in 1931 and *Fly with me* (1932), written in collaboration with Henry Duncan Davis. *The airship*, especially the second chapter dealing with 'First principles', demonstrates the young Sprigg's knowledge of physics and Newtonian mechanics, and it marks the beginning of a series of books on aviational matters, the last of which, *Let's learn to fly*, was published posthumously in 1937 and was claimed by reviewers (rather than for example *Illusion and reality*) as Christopher Sprigg's 'last book'. In 1934 he published *British airways* and in the same year one of his detective novels, *Death of an airman*, relied heavily on his knowledge of aircraft and flying skills.

The great appeal of the airman and powered flight was that it represented the future and the flyer as a kind of hero-leader. It is no great coincidence that Christopher Sprigg in his *Great flights* (1935) chose to record the bravery of those aviators who took part in the air-race from England to Australia and that Day Lewis should mythologise the same two participants in his 'A time to dance' (1934). Sprigg ends his account of the great flights of recent years the way he began it, by applauding the 'spirit of progress'.

> Thus the airways come, following on the paths laid down by pioneer airmen. But although there may be no more great flights to be made, their spirit remains — a spirit that refuses to accept any standard as final. This spirit is never contented with its achievement, but regards each success as pointing the way to yet a further advance. It is, in fact, the very spirit of progress, which the world can never do without.[4]

Christopher Sprigg was never moved — either in prose or verse — to translate his fascination with aviation into a symbol of 'political' progress, as did many of his contemporaries, despite the fact that his first and last books were devoted to this interest. By the beginning of the decade Sprigg had apprenticed himself in many of the disciplines — poetry, science, popular journalism — that were to engage him until his death early in 1937. He had written a good deal and published at least one of his poems; he had managed to keep up his school science to such an extent that he could write an extensive treatise on the physics of the airship, and he had published his article on the variable gear which had elicited 'much attention'.

There is little or nothing in his writings or letters of these years that would suggest the emergence of a political attitude despite the worsening social situation. However, there are signs at the beginning of the decade that Christopher Sprigg, entrepreneur, was beginning to tire of the business world and that his persona of poet was beginning to assert itself. It was at this time (1930 or 1931) that he got in touch again with his old school chum, Paul Beard, himself a part-time literary man. Sprigg had sent him some poems which call into question the role of religion in both their lives (there are several poems which deal, sometimes satirically, with religious matters), because on 9 May 1932 Caudwell had to write a reassuring reply to Beard's query concerning morality in a world without faith. He concludes his letter thus:

> I have written somewhat at length because — although my way of living has been extremely empirical hitherto — I have been led into a certain amount of speculation about these things by reading 'The Fountain' by Charles Morgan. Have you read it?

Given Sprigg's occupation as journalist, publisher and poet, not to mention his philosophic predilections which were eventually to lead him to adopt Marxism as an all-embracing 'philosophical' world-view — given these various interests, it is understandable why he found in *The fountain*[5] an echo of his own search. The hero of Morgan's book, Lewis Alison, is an amateur philosopher (amateur because his full-time occupation is in publishing with Alison and Ford), his quest to ask 'whether there was not a perceptible unity of all the higher endeavours of the human mind'. This would be a unity that would unite Plato with Vaughan and Newton; that is, philosophy with poetry and science. It was of course such a unity that Caudwell was to seek and felt he had found, eventually, in the Marxian analysis of society and its many products. Writing three years later (27 November 1935), having recently completed the first draft of *Illusion and reality*, Caudwell put it this way:

> Seriously, I think my weakness has been the lack of an integrated Weltanschauung, I mean one that includes my emotional, scientific, and artistic needs. They have been more than usually disintegrated in me, I think, a

characteristic failure of my generation ... The remedy is nothing so simple as a working-over and polishing-up of prose, but to come to terms both with myself and my environment. This I think during the last year or two I have begun to do.

Just as the year 1933 was an important turning point in the decade, so it was too for the young businessman, Christopher Sprigg. It was during this year that the two Sprigg brothers saw their business crash. Ironically enough (considering the economic situation), it was because of rapid expansion and the needs for various loans, most particularly one from an upper-crust individual who then succeeded in engineering their downfall, that they lost their company. George Moberg suggests in his biography that Christopher Sprigg's reaction to the business collapse (what in fact amounted to a 'double-cross') was one of bitterness, a reaction that would lead him to consider more closely the role of politics and economics in the affairs of men.

Regardless of his 'feelings', the young poet-journalist had to make a living, and it was to this end that he saw the publication of his first two detective novels, *Crime in Kensington* and *Fatality in Fleet Street*,[6] a publishing venture that was the first step away from the daily grind of journalistic pressures and which was to lead eventually to an independence from what he called 'office work'. Christopher Caudwell was to attack both the thriller and popular journalism in *Illusion and reality* as being 'full of the easy gratifications of instincts starved by modern capitalism', even though, at the time of writing such criticism (1935–6), Christopher Sprigg was preparing his last thriller for publication. Yet Caudwell as he was in so many of his cultural observations, remains a shrewd analyst. Branson and Heinemann, in their survey of the social background to this period, tell us that it 'never had been so easy for the factory or office worker to live a complete fantasy life in substitution or compensation for the hardships of the real world'. They continue:

The most popular and effective form of escapist reading was the detective story and crime thriller. The number of new mystery-detective stories reviewed increased from a dozen in 1914 and a hundred or so in 1925 to over 200 in 1939; and the technical quality steadily rose. More and more serious writers turned to the thriller form; not only to make money, but also as a way of holding a middle class reader's attention through an exciting novel which might incidentally include comedy of manners, literary criticism or political analysis. Very few were at all like real-life crime as reported in the *News of the World*.[7]

His journalism together with his new venture into light fiction would not make a fortune for Christopher Sprigg, but the detective novels which he could complete, if need be in a matter of weeks, marked the beginning of a new 'literary' independence from the daily grind of Fleet Street. Although, as we shall see shortly, he never escaped entirely from the financial necessity of his hack-work, the 'experiment of giving [him]self more time' resulted in his first efforts at serious prose composition. His new situation also allowed him more time to spend in the London libraries which he loved so much, expanding his reading to include the recent innovations in the 'new' anthropology and the ever-increasing publications in psychology; all these activities culminating, toward the end of 1934, in a new sense of self, in a very real sense the emergence of Christopher Caudwell from within the new and changing activities of Christopher St John Sprigg.

Writing to Paul Beard in December 1934, Christopher Sprigg testifies to his prolific creativeness since he saw his friend last and is buoyant that he is 'beginning to write out of [him]self'. He has been 'through a period of poetic creativeness' but has 'altogether ceased to write verse again', though his recent readings in 'psycho-analytic theories of the unconscious (particularly Baudouin)' have assured him of the 'inspirational' cycles of poetic creativity and he is sure he will write verse again. But most importantly,

The experiment of giving myself more time has been a great success....

I am now writing short stories, some in a vein inspired by Kafka, which I am finding peculiarly congenial, the remainder with a realistic structure (Chekovian realism, not French) about which it is too early to say anything yet, but they may go well.

Also during the last 3 months I have written the following tripe: 1 detective novel. 1 Aviation textbook. 30 aviation articles. 6 detective short stories. Heaven knows how many news paragraphs. Done 4 half-days a week office work.[8]

This letter chronicling a young man's regard for himself as a serious prose writer also marks the first mention of his interest in psychology, especially psychoanalytical theories as shedding light on the genesis and theory of poetry: interests that were to merge with his reading of Marx and help him formulate his theory of poetry in *Illusion and reality*. He had finished the second draft of his most famous book while sojourning in Cornwall during the autumn of 1935, working at a 'rapid pace'. We can assume that he overlooked his reading of Baudouin since he remains unacknowledged in the bibliography which Caudwell compiled after his return to London. Yet it seems probable that his reading of *Psychoanalysis and aesthetics*, with its discussion of Freud's theory of dream — especially the concepts of 'condensation', 'displacement' and 'over-determination', and the application of such 'laws' to poetic creation — it seems probable that this discussion at least stimulated, if indeed it did not introduce, the young man to contemporary psychoanalytic theories of art.

In what is one of the first full-length psychoanalytic studies of an individual poet (Emile Verhaeren), Baudouin, in his introductory chapter, 'The laws of the imagination and poetic symbols', outlines his theory and acknowledges a debt to Ribot and Rignano, both of whom *are* cited in the bibliography to *Illusion and reality*. There are more than a few ideas (albeit in embryonic form) that we can compare with Caudwell's theory of poetry and these shall be taken up when we discuss *Illusion and reality* specifically. At this juncture it is worth pointing out that Baudouin's claim to unite science and art, as in the following quotation from his conclusion to the 'Introduction', would have especially appealed to a mind like Caudwell's.

> We have here a manifestation of the endeavour towards synthesis to which reference has already been made, the endeavour to achieve a mutual understanding between art and science. There has been too much tendency of late years for art and science to regard one another with sovereign contempt — a somewhat puerile contempt which would have made Goethe or Da Vinci smile.[9]

The young writer's search for a 'synthetic', and 'integrated Weltanschauung' that would unite his 'emotional, scientific, and artistic needs' was beginning to achieve a finer focus in the years 1934–5.

The year 1934, then, was a busy and pivotal one for Christopher Sprigg; although still engaged with his 'pot-boilers' (as he called his detective fiction) and churning out his aviation articles, he was only working '4 half-days a week' in an office and this left him more time for his new interests. This was the year, according to his friend Beard, that 'Marxism first began to absorb him', the year that *Viewpoint* appeared, changing its title after the first number to *Left Review*, stating in its inaugural manifesto that it stood for 'militant communism and against individualism and metaphysics in the arts'. It is symptomatic of the times that this was no extremist journal on the fringe of respectable readership, for by the following year, 1935, it stood second in circulation among all the literary monthlies.[10] But one of the most influential books published in 1934 was John Strachey's *The coming struggle for power*,[11] a book — again typical in its pursuit of synthesis — which Caudwell certainly read, not only because he lists it in his bibliography to *Illusion and reality*, but because its influence is so apparent in *Studies in a dying culture*, for which Strachey wrote the introduction. His section, 'The decay of capitalist culture', must have seemed to offer that synthetic diagnosis that Caudwell desired, especially since it included an analysis of the three great talking points of the period. Religion, science and literature are in the process of decay because they are tied to an economic system, capitalism, which belongs to the past.

> The capitalist system is dying and cannot be revived. That is the conclusion to which any honest investigator of the actual facts and possibilities of the present situation must be driven.[12]

But in the future, 'religion, literature, art, science, the whole of the human heritage of knowledge will be transformed'. What seems certain at present is

> that the whole structure of that civilization, which has been built up upon capitalist production, is crumbling. For that structure — that 'culture' as the Germans would call it — was adapted to an age of individualism and 'freedom' alone. And the age of individualistic freedom is very nearly over.[13]

Such a position can be compared with Caudwell's remarks in his Foreword to *Studies*, the key essay of which is 'Liberty: a study in bourgeois illusion'.

In art, philosophy, physics, psychology, history, sociology, and biology the 'crisis' of bourgeois culture is always due to the same cause. And this is no accident, because that destructive illness was originally the dynamic force of bourgeois civilization; but now its utmost potentialities accomplished, it [the illusion of freedom] is a power for ill ... Bourgeois culture is dying of a myth.

Strachey hit a central nerve of the time when he criticised the scientists for supposing that 'science exists in a sort of vacuum unaffected by the social struggles of the present epoch' and his survey of the cultural scene, which includes brief critiques of such figures as Freud, Wells, D. H. Lawrence and Shaw, among others, are taken up in more detail by Caudwell in his *Studies*.

The year 1934 had been a very productive one, even by Christopher Sprigg's standards: apart from his reading he saw his book *British airways* published and another duo of detective novels, *The perfect alibi* and *Death of an airman*. And there is sufficient evidence to suggest that he had conceived if not already sketched out the plots of his next two thrillers, *The corpse with the sunburnt face* and *Death of a queen*, both of which, published the following year (1935), show signs of his recent reading in anthropology.[14] Despite the incredible pace of 1934, Caudwell managed to beaver away at his 'serious' prose stories and toward the end of that year, or early in 1935, he sent his collection of stories, *The rock* (The 'Chekovian' pieces), to Paul and Elizabeth Beard for comment while, as he put it, he left the Kafka stories 'down in the cellar fermenting before being finally decanted'.

Paul and Elizabeth responded separately with criticisms of these 'realistic' stories in the early summer of 1935, both objecting to what they felt was a lack of character development in the interests of overall design.[15] While understanding how his friends might find the longest story, 'We all try', perhaps 'clumsy', he suggests that the story 'might appeal strongly to some people who have been touched by that particular part of the Zeitgeist'. His conviction of just how representative of the epoch his story really was led him later to dramatise it under the title, *The way the wind blows*, a title which signifies more readily the thematic concerns of the original composition.[16]

This as yet unpublished story is important not so much from any 'literary' point of view, but for at least two other crucial reasons. In Caudwell's terms it 'get[s] down to the emotional pattern' of the 1930s and renders the *Zeitgeist* of the epoch in an almost allegorical way; in terms that resemble the motifs outlined in the introduction to this study. But secondly, and perhaps more importantly, considering the story had to be written late in 1934 or very early in 1935, it takes on a special meaning when we consider Caudwell's own move toward the working-class movement in November 1935. 'We all try', through its first-person narrator, tells a story which is emblematic of at least one version of the times: a young upper-middle-class man's disillusionment with his life, his sense of guilt about the parasitic nature of his existence and the concomitant search for meaning and belief. Narrated in a flat tone which at times borders on the sociological report, 'We all try' is composed of most of those motifs — the waste-land of despair, the guilt of inaction, the desire for loss of self in a new system of belief — that helped form the structure of the decade's reality for many of the literary intelligentsia.

The narrator, Brian Mallock, introduces himself in the first paragraph:

> One morning I lay in bed and, with a dry taste in my mouth, realised that I was 27 and a hopeless failure. That is to say it was ten years since I had been an undergraduate, full of confidence in myself and my future, with all life's enchanting possibilities spread before my feet, and now I was still just Sir Willoughby Mallock's younger son, lying in bed in his house in Grosvenor Square, without a job, fed-up, a nuisance to my friends, in love with a woman I despise, hating my father, envying my elder brother, ashamed of all I have done and, worse still, of what I have not done.

The sin of inaction was very important to Caudwell. He copied a quotation from Wassermann to this effect into his notebook, a quotation we shall have occasion to look at again when we consider his 'serious' novel *This my hand*.

> The guilt that arises from what men do is small and scarcely comparable to the guilt that arises from what men fail to do ... [these men] are, so far as I can see, the true criminals. All evil comes from them.

Brian Mallock, for a time, seeks 'salvation' in some form of 'action', but he realises, as did many of the 'fellow travellers' in the 1930s, that his needs were more metaphysical; his central concern was for the annihilation of a dissatisfied bourgeois self, rather than any conscious recognition of necessity. Thus Caudwell takes his modern pilgrim through various vicissitudes — a bourgeois marriage, a sojourn with the 'dull middle-class', divorce, an inferno of drinking — until Brian, working 'side by side' with a cobbler, achieves an epiphany of mystical anonymity as the story's final paragraphs modulate into the present tense:

> As I work in the shop, the other side of the window, a few inches away, people incessantly pass, people seen only as skirts, trousers and overcoats. In this street there are hundreds of these people, this street in turn is part of a district, and this district is a part of London, itself so crammed full of people that it is impossible to imagine them all spread out round one with their individualities distinct. And London itself is only one city, and I am only working in it in one part of its history. But long before I can think of this clearly, it is as if I am on a mountain, and all these streets and districts and towns and centuries — lying in the clear morning air of time beneath me — have suddenly blurred and started to rotate.

Caudwell's unpublished story is important not only as a contribution to the typology of the epoch, but also as a document in his own spiritual biography. Given his own middle-class catholic upbringing and his intellectual predilections, this story is a testament that its author was at least *conscious* of the motivations that attracted many of the younger malcontents to the Workers' Movement, and this almost a year before Caudwell himself made such a move. The story, which sadly lacks focus, is largely the portrayal of a young man driven by guilt and nihilism, a parable, so typical of these years, of a journey without and within in quest of self-salvation and absolution from guilt — an absolution that was primarily brought about through annihilation of that dissatisfied self by identification with a mass movement. Perhaps the most significant aspect of the story is the fact that Brian Mallock's flirtation with communism arises primarily out of a psychological need. Caudwell was certainly right about his capturing the essence of the *Zeitgeist* of the epoch, but the story shows as well that he was less a victim of the mass psychological need of his age than a conscious participant in what he felt to be historical necessity.

Writing to Elizabeth Beard approximately a year after the composition of the story, when he had moved to working-class Poplar, Caudwell acknowledges that the ambiguity of theme might be his 'fault' and sets out for Mrs Beard his central intention, an intention that summarises the motivations of many of the 'fellow travellers' of his generation.

By the way Betty, I don't think I ever told you, you had got the theme *wrong*. My fault, no doubt. It is not to show the necessity of work, but the failure of idealism, as long as it is really only a selfish longing for self-fulfilment, and has no social roots. Working or idling, Brian is equally a failure because he always sees thing[s] in personal, not social terms.[17]

Some months before the above letter to the Beards, on 24 July 1935, Caudwell had addressed a letter to Elizabeth, who was from this point to become the main auditor of his new intellectual pursuits. It is of course impossible to pinpoint absolutely the exact moment of the journalist/thriller writer Christopher St John Sprigg's metamorphosis into the cultural critic, Christopher Caudwell, but this letter documents a declaration of intent the results of which mark the emergence of Christopher Caudwell as we have come to know him. Having agreed to meet the Beards in London the following week, he goes on:

I have now decided to come to S[outh] Cornwall for a couple of months as soon as I have cleared up work here and by a process of elimination have decided on Porthleven. I can never stay with you again! Our evening discussions spurred my poor brain to such feverish activity that after I left you I got a terrific spate of ideas on the nature of poetry.

They started buzzing in my head like infuriated wasps; all my pressing bread and butter works have been delayed and I am half way through a book called 'Verse and Mathematics' A Study of the Foundation of Poetry. What's more, it's a damn good book. The ideas have [been] pouring out at the rate of 4–5000 words a day![18]

37

Christopher St John Sprigg, since his early apprenticeship in journalism, showed a remarkable energy for rapid and sustained 'literary' output on variegated subject matter and these few months in Cornwall, from late August until October 1935, are marked by a similar drive. While still resident there, within a month or so of the above letter, he had sent to the Beards a finished version of the book he now called *Illusion and reality*, retaining the original subtitle and mentioning the 'very impressive bibliography of the 200 or 300 learned books [he had] drawn on', but which he did not send along with the carbon copy. And it was here too, during these few months that he sketched out his last thriller, *The six queer things*, telling the Beards that he wrote it in a few weeks but had not revised it yet.[19] There is evidence also that Caudwell read a good deal during his stay at 'The Atlantic View', Porthleven, though the 'mythologised' version that it was here that his reading resulted in a change of consciousness is not entirely true. Although it is likely that Caudwell began to 'marxify' the first version of his book in Cornwall — the change of title is indicative of this — there is no doubt that much of his reading, mostly done in the London Library, was well behind him, although he continued to have books mailed to him while resident in the village.[20]

Elizabeth Beard had sent him a long letter with detailed criticisms of *Illusion and reality*, which at least Elizabeth had read since the Beards' receipt of the carbon. Elizabeth Beard, an extremely well-read woman, was able to offer her friend commentary on various novelists' views on women; a list which included Turgenev, Tolstoy, Hardy (encouraging him especially to read Hardy for a sympathetic view of women) and Thackeray. Indeed, it was to a great extent because of her probing commentary on Caudwell's treatment of religion and the aesthetic concept of beauty, not to mention her dissatisfaction with his treatment of D. H. Lawrence, that led to the series of essays that were to become *Studies in a dying culture*.[21] After several lengthy exchanges, in a letter dated 30 November 1935 (scarcely a month after his move to Poplar) Caudwell acknowledges the 'effect' Mrs Beard's critiques have had on his 'bread and butter' work. Thanking her for her last letter, he goes on:

> But I shall have to ask you not to write to me, or discuss these matters with me, because they have a most dangerous effect. As you know, our discussions at Newton [the Beards'

farmhouse] on Poetry and the Unconscious resulted in the writing of 'I & R' — 120,000 words of it. After my answer to you on the subject of Beauty, I felt impelled to put on paper all the things I couldn't find room for in the letter. The result is a 10,000 words study on Beauty and the Beautiful, attacked from the same analytic point of view as was used in 'I. and R.' Reflecting further on the subject of Religion, I was led to that of asceticism, and suddenly saw a most interesting causal connection between the thrift of the Puritan, the asceticism of the Roman Church, of the Roman Republican, of the modern Nazi and Youth movements, of the Communist Party in Russia to-day, and the exoticism of the French and English *fin de siècle* movement. Result, a 15,000 words study. This must now cease! It is interrupting me in my Neccessary [*sic*] work, such as for example, 'Internal Air Mail Contracts of the British Isles'.

A book is taking shape, he tells her, 'which will consist of synthetic studies in particularly interesting aspects of modern culture' and he proposes to call the collection 'Studies in a dying culture', taking as his motto Lenin's remark: 'Communism becomes an empty phrase, a mere facade, and a communist a mere bluffer, if he has not worked over in his consciousness the whole inheritance of human knowledge.'[22]

Apart from his residual commitments to popular journalism ('Internal air mail contracts' for example) during his new life in Poplar, Caudwell had three books to see through publication: *Illusion and reality* was with Allen & Unwin for consideration (though eventually published by Macmillan); *The six queer things* needed revision from the rough draft written when he was in Cornwall; and his last book on flying, *Let's learn to fly*, was put together during this period. He had also contracted with Nelson to select and write the introduction to *Uncanny stories* which came out with *This my hand* in 1936, one published under the pseudonym and with a new publisher (Hamish Hamilton), the other with Nelson's and under the old identity. In the introduction to *Uncanny stories* Christopher St John Sprigg discusses the relevance of the modern ghost story in terms that reflect his own recent interests and describe essentially the thematic strains of the new thriller that he was preparing for publication:

Even so, the ghost story's resources have by no means been exhausted. Modern psychiatry has given scientific recognition to the world of the uncanny by its revelation of a whole universe of the irrational, lairing in the subconscious behind the apparently solid facade of the conscious mind. Obsessions and archaic presences quite as weird and eerie as those of ghost stories are to be found here, if we are to credit Jung and his followers.[23]

*Uncanny stories* is an example of how Christopher Sprigg was always ready to accept 'commissions', to finance his new serious work. As late as October 1936 he arranged with a popular writer, Sydney Horler, to read and technically correct on aviational matters his new play, *Lord of terror*, for 20 guineas.

Living an anonymous and itinerant existence (he used at least three separate addresses while living in Poplar) Caudwell worked swiftly on his new 'studies' and filled a small notebook with Russian exercises so that he might, 'like the three sisters', go to Moscow the next year. That of course was not to be, since for him the issue of Spain was to present in action many of the rhetorical battles that were being fought throughout the 1930s. He did, however, correspond with a Russian 'comrade' who, in one letter, thanks him for his information concerning the vigorous new militancy of the English workers.

If Caudwell was busy enough with his various projects, outlined above — the last three books and journalistic work — all of which he characterised as belonging to his 'sentimental past', his life took on an even more 'active' turn when he decided to join the Party proper before the end of 1935. One of the people he lived with suggested in a letter to his brother after Caudwell's death that 'Spriggy's' activities in Poplar during that year could 'fill several volumes' should he decide to write a book about him. Another married couple with whom he lived and who called him 'John' (as did many of his comrades), considered it a 'personal blow' when they heard of his death. Living in one room or another, Caudwell spent most of the day at his typewriter, and returned to it in the evening after the Branch meeting of the Party. His new programme left little time for literary pursuits or social diversions. As his brother was to put it later: 'his writing, his research and his poetry occupied all the time he could spare from his Party work as Secretary of a small Branch in East London and he had none left for social diversions'.[24]

He did, however, take some time off to attend lectures on 'Marxism and Literature' at Marx House. These were given by Alick West, who, in his autobiography, *One man in his time*, has vague recollections of the serious young man who skirted the periphery of the company at the gatherings in the local pub after the classes.

> Caudwell's *Illusion and Reality* had been republished not long after the war, and I was asked to give the opening address at a conference, with George Thomson in the chair, on the importance of his work. Early in 1936 he had come to the course which Garman and I were taking on Marxism and literature. We knew him then as Christopher Sprigge [*sic*], and he said nothing about his own writing, though he must already almost have completed *Illusion and Reality* for in November [actually December] of that year he went to Spain and joined the International Brigade; but at one of the general discussions on the method of the class he said that he thought we were making a mistake in considering the social character of literature without having first considered language. After the class we used to continue the discussion in a pub on Clerkenwell Green, and I have a memory of him standing close to me and considering me with clear eyes, through which I seemed to look into a lucid mind of resolute intelligence.[25]

Some ten years later, writing an appraisal of Caudwell, Louis Harap supplies a piece of information that seems bent on mythology in its interpretation of the facts.

> At one time he was attending a course in Marxism and Literature at Marx House (the London workers' school) and was extremely interested in it. Suddenly he announced that he would have to give up the course. It was later discovered that the task which drew him away, was selling the *Daily Worker* at the Underground entrance.[26]

Caudwell had, of course, more reasons to cut short his course at Marx House than selling the *Daily Worker*, although this was one of his chores and he recorded the anonymity of the experience in his notebook:

Selling 'Daily Worker' in Chrisp Street Market, how one immediately ceases to exist when one starts to sell. A queer thrill, as if one were blotted out, although one's shouts and the poster ought to attract attention to oneself.[27]

But this was only one of a number of duties (and one of the few notes he took of 'local colour') that he had to perform after his involvement with the local branch. Moreover, he was drafting his own studies of 'Marxism and literature' which took up most of the time left over from Party duties. The Minute Book is peppered with his name, in such entries as: 'Cde. Sprig [*sic*] to make a statement on literature at branch meeting'; 'Cde. Sprig to lead discussion'; 'Cde. Sprig to act as Secretary'. His name is mentioned in most entries of the proceedings until, eventually, the handwriting in the Minute Book becomes his own, when he takes over the post of Secretary. Apart from these secretarial duties, Caudwell was responsible for a series of letters to the *East End News* publicising the Party's line on fascism and the threat of war. He wrote letters to the editor, published in the editions 20 March 1936, 27 March, 3 April and 24 April; and the edition of 3 July 1936 carried a report on 'Poplar's fight against war', announcing that 'making the report of the executive committee of the anti-war exhibition to the Conference [would be] Mr. C. S. Sprigg'.

The ideological warfare between left and right, communist and fascist, took place among the intelligentsia mainly through the medium of type. However, London's East End, with its large number of Jewish immigrants, was a target for demonstration by Mosley's British Union of Fascists and there were frequent confrontations between the two sides. One of Caudwell's letters to the *East End News* was to protest against such a provocative meeting of the fascists just up the road from his neighbourhood at Bow Baths. It was not long before his war of words with the fascists became a physical clash. On Sunday, 7 June 1936, he went to Victoria Park (his local park) to hear Mosley speak at a large rally. A group near him began to sing the 'Red Flag' and the Blackshirts 'sailed into the crowd, hitting out indiscriminately'. At first not in any way part of the fracas, Caudwell was hit in the face by a Blackshirt and non-participation now seemed an impossibility. In a letter to his brother, he was 'glad to say that before [he] took the count [he] got in some good ones!' Apart from 'a black-eye, a large bump on [his] forehead, and various cuts and bruises', his major concern, as he outlined the experience, was his treatment by the police. After being picked up from the field of battle, 'more or less woozy', he was 'beaten up again in the police van, and charged at Old Street [Police Station] with *assaulting the police*' (his emphasis). He describes the court appearance in the following way:

> My witnesses declared on oath that I made no attempt to struggle when picked up by the police. I wasn't in fact in a condition to do so. The witnesses were quite reputable people — one was a doctor — and the police made no attempt to cross-examine them. Nonetheless the magistrate ruled that there was no doubt I had assaulted the constable. Of course they denied beating me up in the van. I asked to call witnesses as to character, but the magistrate told me in a paternal way that this was quite unnecessary, he could see I was a nice young man, and then went on to show that he thought I was a perjurer, by finding me guilty and fining me 2 Pounds. The Council of Civil Liberties are taking the case up with the Home Office through their various M.P.'s and K.C.'s but I expect there will be the usual denials.[28]

It is evident from his report to his brother that what mattered to him more (hurt him more) than the superficial injuries was the fact that the police were 'so openly fascist'. Towards the end of his letter he points to the educative necessity of theory and practice; supposing that everyone would think the account of the meeting exaggerated, he goes on: 'I certainly believed some of the accounts I had read in the past, but only in a theoretical way. It is wonderful how vivid a practical experience is!'

Caudwell's first-hand experience of the unity of theory and practice, his first skirmish with the fascists, and a portent of his next when he would be killed by them in Spain, had his brother worried. Caudwell wrote again a few days later assuring his brother that practice had a direct bearing on his writing now and precluded any neutral standpoint:

> I could of course cease active Party work, and merely write, but how should I know how and what to write if I am not actively in touch with the movement? This is just the difference between being a sympathiser and a communist.

One of the pieces he did write during this period (June 1936) is particularly apposite. His study, 'Pacificism and violence: a study in bourgeois ethics', delineates the historical struggle between economic forces, and begins by asserting that the only sure way to secure peace is by revolutionary change in the social system. Since the 'ruling classes resist revolution violently' they in turn must be overthrown by force. His 'little dust-up' provided enough practical experience to allow him to suggest in 'Pacificism and violence':

> If Fascism develops, he [the bourgeois pacifist] cannot suppress it in the bud before it has built up an army to intimidate the proletariat, for he believes in 'free speech'. He can only watch the workers being bludgeoned and beheaded by the forces he allowed to develop.[29]

Toward the end of the essay he suggests how difficult it is to remain neutral; the refusal not to act, in its negative way, furthers the violence of the *status quo*:

> By abstaining from action the pacifist enrolls himself under this banner, the banner of things as they are and getting worse, the banner of the increasing violence and coercion exerted by the *haves* on the *have-nots*. He calls increasingly into being the violences of poverty, deprivation, artificial slumps, artistic and scientific decay, fascism, and war.[30]

Approximately one month after his 'dust-up' with Mosley's Blackshirts, the possibility of fascism and war had become a reality. In July 1936, General Francisco Franco's rebel forces felt that the time had come to move against the struggling Republican government and the war of ideologies found its battlefield in Spain. Although the official British policy was one of non-intervention, committees were formed almost immediately after the outbreak of hostilities, and by September 1936, volunteers from Britain were leaving for Spain in increasing numbers. Eventually, the British government outlawed the departure of such volunteers and the recruits found their way to the fighting through various ruses, some through the Party's organisation for delivering ambulances and medical supplies. A few found themselves there by chance, like Felicia Browne, a young artist and communist who was visiting Barcelona. She joined the militia and was killed on the Aragon Front in August, the first British casualty of the war. Others made their way there individually, like John Cornford, who returned on a recruiting mission to England in September and formed the nucleus of what was to become the British Battalion of the International Brigade.[31] By the first week of December, Caudwell had managed to arrange for himself to join a group, under the auspices of the Party, that was to drive a fleet of ambulances for delivery to the loyalists. Among his papers there is a photograph of him along with five of his co-drivers just before they set out to drive through France. Caudwell is wearing a long leather coat and has in his hand the cloth cap which he had referred to as a symbol of the 'proletarian stage in [his] life'.

His twelve months or so in Poplar had been as productive as the previous years when he had held down an office job and produced his thrillers, sometimes at the rate of two per year. Apart from the daily routine of Party work he had managed to revise and submit hs latest 'pot-boiler' to Nelson's, make the selection and write the introduction to *Uncanny stories*, and write and arrange publication of *Let's learn to fly*. During this period he had the satisfaction of seeing *This my hand* appear in the spring of 1936 under the new pseudonym of 'Caudwell'. Most importantly, he had revised and had had accepted for publication with Macmillan the book for which he was to become known internationally: *Illusion and reality* has been translated into many languages including Turkish, Russian, Spanish, German and French.

Despite this frantic pace, Caudwell had found time to begin his comprehensive critique of contemporary culture. In November 1935, when he could scarcely have settled into Poplar, he wrote to Elizabeth Beard telling her that 'a book [was] taking shape' which he had decided to call *Studies in a dying culture*. This was the task that took up most of the energy left over from Party work during 1936. As early as 23 April 1936, he promised Elizabeth Beard that she would 'be seeing the first parts of [it] soon' since he had completed the writing and was due to start revision. Some of the 'studies' occupied him immediately prior to his departure for Spain. He was still working, for example, on 'one sketch (Physics) [which had] already been expanded to 80,000 words', and which was published as *The crisis in physics* in 1939. Another study of over 30,000 words, *Romance and realism* was also published independently in 1970.[32] In the same letter that he set out his

45

literary remains — the letter dated 9 December 1936, written two days before his departure for Spain and quoted at the beginning of this chapter — Caudwell spoke of the need to revise the 'crude outline of "Studies" ' with the promise to Paul and Elizabeth Beard that 'After that: poetry and the story; on a new plane!'

When he had arrived in Spain, apart from the 'chatty' letters to Theo, most of his free time (sometimes just prior to going on guard-duty) was taken up 'reporting' the situation in Spain for his Poplar 'comrades'. He signed all these letters 'John', the name by which he was known to most of them. An early letter, dated 21 December shortly after his arrival in Barcelona, sets out to describe the emotionally charged atmosphere of that city in those early days of republican hope.

> Barcelona is a wonderful sight. The main hotels and offices have been requisitioned by the workers' organizations and are ablaze with banners. Almost every car seems to carry a party banner or placard. The trams, buses and taxis are painted red and black (the anarchist colours). And on almost every building there are party posters: posters against Facism [*sic*], posters about the defence of Madrid, posters appealing for recruits to the militia, posters advertising 'gran mitings' and even posters for the emancipation of women and against prostitution and venereal disease. These posters are artistically of a high quality and are all prepared by the Trade Union of Professional Artists.

Although there is a natural excitement about being in Spain and at times a frustration with 'training' and a desire for action Caudwell was always aware of the theoretical side of the struggle. Almost all the letters to Poplar urge his friends to maintain the political struggle and to 'keep plugging away to get the Arms ban lifted!' As he put it in one letter, dated 24 January 1937 (a few weeks before his death):

> I thought when I came out here that I should throw off the responsibility of party member and writer too ... But as usual the party never sleeps. I'm a group political delegate ... instructor to the Labour Party fraction ... and joint-editor of the Wall newspaper. Actually, the party organisation played an important part in a crucial moment in stiffening the Battalion.

Caudwell had to write to King Street for precise instructions with regard to whether or not he should remain in Spain, but it is probable that he died before receiving any confirmation concerning his orders. He had written a last letter to his brother (7 February 1937) 'in haste' because, as he put it in an earlier letter to a comrade, 'things look like moving for the Battalion in three or four days'. The 'training' was over at last (Caudwell had actually become an instructor on the machine gun) and so too was all the rhetoric. It was time for action. In the early part of the spring of 1937 there were three notable battles in the war: at Malaga; in the environs of the River Jarama near Madrid; and just outside the city of Guadalajara.[33] Franco's victory in the 'skirmish' at Malaga encouraged a concerted surprise attack in the valley of the Jarama, just southeast of Madrid, which began on the 6 February, just the day before that last letter Caudwell wrote 'in haste' to his brother. After several days of deadlock, the Nationalists succeeded in forcing the Jarama River on the night of 11 February, mainly due to the stealth of their Moroccan scouts who succeeded in knifing 'the sentries of the French André Marty Battalion ... one by one, while standing at their posts'.[34] By the next day, the 12th, they had begun storming the heights of Pingarron, the strategically important hills on the other side of the river.

It was a fierce confrontation with heavy losses sustained by both sides and, finally, no absolute victory for either. The fighting must have been particularly awesome for the 15th International Brigade and its 1st Battalion, the Saklatvala or British Battalion, because this was their first fight. Many had never seen a gun before their arrival in Spain, and their training had been short. It was to them that fell the task of defending what became known as 'Suicide Hill' against artillery and machine gun fire, and at the end of the day only 225 of the original 600 remained alive.[35]

One of the combatants, John Lepper, whose poem, 'Battle of Jarama 1937' was published in *Poems for Spain*, captures succinctly, as do so many war poems, the incongruity of a natural setting torn by war. The first two stanzas are sufficient to give an idea of the tone:

> The sun warmed the valley
> But no birds sang
> The sky was rent with shrapnel
> And metallic clang

Death stalked the olive trees
Picking his men
His leaden finger beckoned
Again and again.[36]

It was here, near the Morata/San Martin road, that Caudwell fell sometime during the afternoon on 12 February 1937. It is not possible to be absolutely certain of the actual circumstances of his death, but it seems that Caudwell and Clem Beckett, a dirt-track rider from Manchester and Caudwell's co-gunner, returned to remove the lock from their gun, thus rendering it inoperable, but were killed by a grenade on reaching the position. He had written his own obituary:

Unhappy men, who roam, on hope deferred
Relying, thinking not of painful death!
Here was Seleucos, great in mind and word,
Who his young prime enjoyed but for a breath.
In world-edge Spain, so far from Lesbian lands
He lies, a stranger on uncharted strands.[37]

As Christopher St John Sprigg he had been journalist, entrepreneur and writer of formulistic thrillers. As 'John Sprigge' he shared for just over a year an existence with the working class. He had fulfilled two-thirds of Lenin's prerequisite for the revolutionary, by working anonymously and at times acting 'illegally'. He was now, after his death, to become known as Christopher Caudwell, the name and identity he had chosen to distinguish his work of the last few years of his life from that of his 'sentimental past'.

## Notes

1. My biographical information is composed of data gathered from the letters, a 'biographical sketch' written by Caudwell's brother and the introduction to the *Poems* written by Paul Beard, all housed in the Humanities Research Center, University of Texas, Austin. I am grateful to Dr George Moberg for allowing me to read his unpublished biography of Caudwell. The few occasions that I have drawn upon it for information are noted in the text.

2. The reputation has come under attack several times, most comprehensively in the *Modern Quarterly* debate, and these criticisms along with others are discussed later.

3. 'Once I did think', *The Dial* (vol. LXXXII, March 1927), p. 187. Sprigg was published in very good company: William Carlos Williams had published 'Paterson' in the previous issue and contributed three poems to the same issue as the young Sprigg. But most significantly, and to my knowledge never commented on, is the fact that in the same issue as Sprigg's poem, T. S. Eliot reviews I. A. Richards's *Science and poetry*, a book which (along with *The meaning of meaning* and the *Principles of literary criticism*) helps shed much light on *Illusion and reality*.

4. *Great flights ... illustrated from photographs.* See C. Day Lewis, *A time to dance: with an essay, Revolution in Writing* (New York, Random House, 1936), p. 32f.

5. Charles Morgan, *The fountain* (New York, Alfred A. Knopf, 1932). Christopher Sprigg was to memorialise the author who had made such an impression on him: one of his detective novels features an Inspector Charles Morgan.

6. Although not political in any real sense (except for perhaps its mild satire under the guise of 'comedy of manners'), *Fatality in Fleet Street*, apart from drawing on his journalistic experience, does have as its mainspring of action a crisis between England and the Soviet Union.

7. Noreen Branson and M. Heinemann, *Britain in the 1930's* (New York, Praeger, 1971), p. 256. This easy form of gratification and escape from the 'real world' was indicative of a cultural malaise which initiated much of the momentum behind *Scrutiny*. See Francis Mulhern, *The moment of 'Scrutiny'* (London, Verso Editions, 1981), especially p. 36 and *passim*.

8. Letter to Paul Beard, 21 December 1934. The Kafka stories he refers to are a series of 'parables' collectively called *The island*. A few of these appear in *Scenes and actions*. Kafka had been enjoying increasing success since the publication of the Muirs' translation. Edward Upward, whom some hoped would be the English Kafka, published, coincidentally enough, one of his Kafkaesque parables, 'The island', in *Left Review*, vol. I (January 1935).

9. Charles Baudouin, *Psychoanalysis and aesthetics* (London, Allen & Unwin, 1924), p. 34.

10. See Neal Wood, *Communism and British intellectuals* (New York, Columbia University Press, 1959), pp. 58–9, for a discussion of publications at this time. Stuart Samuels' unpublished dissertation 'Marx, Freud and English intellectuals: a study of the dissemination and reconciliation of ideas' (Stanford University, 1971) also has a comprehensive discussion of such publications.

11. John Strachey, *The coming struggle for power*, (London, Gollancz, 1934). Both Branson and Heinemann, *Britain in the 1930's*, and Wood, *Communism and British intellectuals*, document the important effect of this book among 'younger intellectuals' and Symons, who discusses the book in some detail, remarks that it 'helped to create a whole climate of opinion'. See J. Symons, *The thirties: a dream revolved* (London, Cresset Press, 1960), pp. 43–7.

12. Strachey, *The coming struggle for power*, p. 155.

13. Ibid., p. 156.

14. *The perfect alibi* features another figure prominent in the 1930s mythology, the armaments manufacturer, and it alludes to the 'cases'

explored in the two books published the following year; one of them, *The corpse*, is set partly in West Africa and the other, *Death of a queen*, deals with the intricacies of matrilineal succession.

15. Some of these stories draw on the young Christopher's experiences while living in Yorkshire some ten years previously, as does the setting for his serious novel, *This my hand*, the composition of which he mentions in his reply to the Beards's criticism. A few stories from *The Rock* are in the recent collection of previously unpublished prose, *Scenes and actions*.

16. He submitted this play, unsuccessfully, for consideration by the Westminster Theatre.

17. Letter to Paul and Elizabeth Beard, 21 November 1935. Original italics.

18. Scott Buchanan had published in 1929 a book called *Poetry and mathematics* (New York, The John Day Co., 1929). The relevance of Caudwell's working title for *Illusion and reality* and possible influences are taken up later in my discussion of that book.

19. Undated letter from Porthleven to Paul and Elizabeth Beard, most likely written toward the end of September 1935.

20. It is probable that *Illusion and reality* went through three versions and shifted in primary focus from a psychological/anthropological base to that of a Marxist perspective. The final version (and especially the doctrinaire final chapter, 'The future of poetry') was almost certainly written during his membership of the Party and residence in Poplar throughout 1936. Some of these ramifications are discussed when I deal with *Illusion and reality* and in the Appendix.

21. Many of the subjects of the studies were of course *causes célèbres* during these years; many of these debates – for example on T. E. Lawrence and heroism, Freud, H. G. Wells, etc. – found their way into the pages of *Left Review*, as did Caudwell's own comments on pacificism after his death. This was a section from his reply to Aldous Huxley's 'What are you going to do about it?'. Caudwell's manuscript, 'The people's front', published in part by *Left Review*, is among his papers. There is some discussion of this in Chapter 5.

22. Actually he chose some remarks by Max Planck to point up the decay of modern civilisation.

23. Christopher St John Sprigg (ed.), *Uncanny stories* (London, Nelson, 1936).

24. A note by Theodore Stanhope Sprigg among the Caudwell papers.

25. Alick West, *One man in his time: an autobiography* (London, Allen & Unwin, 1969), pp. 181–2.

26. Louis Harap, 'Christopher Caudwell, Marxist critic, poet and soldier', *Worker*, 24 November 1946.

27. Notebook (unpaginated), Humanities Research Center, University of Texas, Austin.

28. Letter to his brother dated 9 June 1936. See Robert Graves and Alan Hodge, *The long week-end: a social history of Great Britain 1918–1939* (New York, W. W. Norton, 1963), pp. 312–13, on the fears of a possible 'reactionary Fascist state', and p. 439 for their comments on the East End. Julian Symons describes in some detail a demonstration very similar to the one Caudwell reports to his brother, and he quotes the Liberal

MP Sir Percy Harris as stating that 'there is a feeling going right through the East End that somehow or other the police are acting in collusion with the Fascists' (Symons, *The thirties*, pp. 52–3). This was certainly Caudwell's opinion.

29. *Studies*, p. 115.

30. Ibid., p. 126. Like all of Caudwell's writings this study is understood better in the context of the time. Pacifism and the threat of war is a key debate in the rhetoric of the 1930s. This is discussed in Chapter 5.

31. See Peter Stansky and William Abrahams, *Journey to the frontier: Julian Bell and John Cornford: their lives and the 1930's* (London, Constable, 1966), p. 360f. for an account of Cornford's activities during this time. Caudwell was to join the British Battalion in training at Albacete and it is one of those ironies of war that he and Cornford did not meet. Still suffering from a head wound sustained at the Battle of Boadilla, Cornford was asked to remain in Madrigueras (near Albacete) to help train the new English recruits, Caudwell among them. Cornford declined, however, and left on Christmas Eve, 1936, to fight at the battle of Lopera where he was killed on 28 December, the anniversary of his birth.

32. Although not published until 1949, in the volume *Further studies in a dying culture*, it is almost certain that he wrote the essays on 'Beauty' and 'Religion' first. The order of composition is discussed more fully in Chapter 5.

33. Hugh Thomas, *The Spanish civil war* (Harmondsworth, Penguin Books, 1977), pp. 582–96.

34. Ibid., p. 592.

35. Figures vary slightly, but Thomas's, ibid., p. 592, seem most reliable.

36. Stephen Spender and John Lehmann (eds), *Poems for Spain* (London, Hogarth Press, 1939), p. 33.

37. The poem is one of young Sprigg's translations from the Latin.

# 3

## The Poet and Novelist

*Is the proletariat made conscious of its goal by rhymed economics?*
*No, verse is not, and never was, the instrument of propaganda in this*
*sense.*

Caudwell

The first work Caudwell allowed publicity under this new identity
was his psycho-social study of murder *This my hand*, which, like
some of the later poetry bears the scars of Caudwell's effort to
align his creative work with that of his new-found *Weltsanchauung*.
There is no space here to deal with either the poetry or the
detective fiction, except to offer the conviction that had Caudwell
survived Spain we would not have seen published many of the
*Poems*[1] compiled by his friend and literary executor, Paul Beard.
Indeed, we might not have seen *any* of these poems published
under the 'Caudwell' pseudonym: it was Beard's idea to use the
name that Sprigg/Caudwell reserved for his serious work, a
pseudonym and persona that the author may have been reluctant
to utilise for a body of poems that epitomise in many ways those
'bourgeois' idiosyncracies that he took careful pains to criticise
in the work of others. His criticism of Eliot in particular[2] (that
his world view was literary) takes on a special irony when we
consider that a great deal of his own poetry owes a debt to Eliot's
method and, one imagines, to the latter's popularisation of the
metaphysical poets.

Many of the *Poems* combine a 'metaphysical' sensibility with a
phrasing and diction that recalls the verse form of the Augustans;
as if Donne's colloquial tone and syntax were transferred through
Marvell to Pope:

Ah, when I'm bald, and love becomes disgust
(your love will last up to that date I trust
But cannot know) you cannot imp on me
The years or hairs you now give easily.
No, for my girl at that not-distant date
You will unwillingly render to Fate
Each gift he asks back: hair, smooth skin, bright eyes,
The brave spring of your bosom, your curved thighs.

This poem, 'The hair', owes a great deal to Donne's 'The relique' and Caudwell's concluding couplet — 'Not even then, for round your ribs will be/The bare arms of my own anatomy' — where the speaker refuses to be separated from his mistress even in death, is of course a variation on Marvell's 'The Grave's a fine and private place/But none, I think, do there embrace.' This poem and 'Donne's reverie', where the poet, near death ('lean-shanked, all hair and bone') meditates on his past life, are the most overtly literary of this selection of verse, but in general the poems are marked by a 'study vocabulary' and a range of experience that 'smells of the library', those very elements that Caudwell noted as characterising Donne and the other meta-physicals.[3] Indeed *Poems* shares with Donne a fascination with eros and death, and with Donne and Eliot that private drama of the self in its struggle to reconcile sexual love with the demands of the spirit.

It is difficult to say how Caudwell would have developed as a poet. One thing certain is that he would have had to face his own criticism of writers such as Auden, Day Lewis and Spender, and confront also the problematic that punctuates the debates of this era: how can a socially committed poet, whose background and literary sensibility belong to a bourgeois world, write the sort of verse appropriate for a society that has not yet come into being? There is evidence in some of the *Poems* that Caudwell was attempting to drag his poetic persona into his 'new world', but the attempt, in such poems as 'The coal' and some of the 'Twenty sonnets of Wm. Smith' results only in a demonstration of all the seven types of ambiguity — a complexity that invites an anarchic diversity of response. Indeed, Caudwell was writing exactly the kind of poem that he as critic would have attacked, and one wonders whether Caudwell could ever have integrated the poet with the philosopher. There is evidence in a few of the published poems that Caudwell was moving away from literary self-indulgence and that his hope was to become 'a poet of the future'; but on the samples that we have it seems probable that he would have had a long struggle to bring his poetic self into the 'new world' as he envisaged it.

Another, older, poet of the 1930s, W. B. Yeats, had said, 'We make out of the quarrel with others, rhetoric, but out of the quarrel with ourselves, poetry.' Caudwell, it seems, had decided, if only temporarily, to take the fight outside the bounds of self.

## The novelist

Christopher St John Sprigg had little regard for his 'pot-boilers'. In a letter dated December 1934, just about the time he had embarked upon the 'serious' work, he classified such writing, along with the other journalistic pieces he was still turning out at this time, as 'tripe' which had become 'a sensori-motor habit, quite independent of the cerebrum'. Writing as 'Caudwell' approximately a year later, he was even more caustic concerning such work:

> The modern thriller, love story, cowboy romance, cheap film, jazz music or yellow Sunday paper form the real proletarian literature of today ... This art, universal, constant, fabulous, full of the easy gratifications of instincts starved by modern capitalism, peopled by passionate lovers and heroic cowboys and amazing detectives, is the religion of today, as characteristic an expression of proletarian exploitation as Catholicism is of feudal exploitation.[4]

Such sentiments did not preclude Sprigg from turning out at least one more 'amazing detective' novel and editing with an introduction the *Uncanny stories*. All these books — with the exception of *The six queer things* which is more sombre in tone — are 'orthodox' examples of the classical detective story or 'whodunit' which flourished during the 1920s and 1930s and are typical in their lack of any contemporary social commentary. Julian Symons in his history of the genre is representative in his commentary on Sprigg's work, both in the erroneous number of books he ascribes and in the juxtaposition of the slight work with the 'philosophy'.

Christopher St John Sprigg (1907–1937) reversed the usual pseudonymous course by producing under the name of Christopher Caudwell the poems, essays on politics and culture, and the philosophical work *Illusion and reality* by which he is remembered as the most interesting English Marxist theorist of his generation. His detective stories were written without a protective mask. He produced eight of these lively but orthodox (and unpolitical) books between 1933 and 1937, when he was killed fighting on the Republican side in the Spanish Civil War.[5]

When Symons specifies 'eight' books it must be surmised that he had in mind (along with the seven detective novels) the collection *Uncanny stories* which Sprigg edited, since it is inconceivable that he could have classified *This my hand* (if he had read it) as 'lively but orthodox'. Roy Fuller, a friend of Symons and one-time Professor of Poetry at Oxford, offers a modification of Symons' assessment:

Is there any vivacious criminal louse on the locks of literature not already combed out by Julian Symons in his critical books and lists? Certainly all my favourites appear to be there, justly evaluated ... Though I have not read all of them, the detective stories of C. St. John Sprigg seem accurately described as 'lively but orthodox'. But his one 'straight' novel, *This my hand* (1936) written under the pseudonym he used for his poetry and Marxist works, Christopher Caudwell, I think would now be categorized as a 'crime novel' in the Patricia Highsmith genre. It is full of interest on its own account as well as presenting yet another facet of its still youthful author's remarkable talent (he was killed in the Spanish Civil War the year after its publication at the age of 29).[6]

*This my hand* is an extremely interesting work 'on its own account' and Caudwell thought highly enough of it to allow it to be the first book to appear under the name reserved for the philosophical work. It is less a 'thriller' or 'mystery' novel than a naturalistic account of crime and punishment and the psychological effects of guilt. For these reasons, among others, it deserves separate treatment as a peculiar and important element within the total *œuvre*. The book[7] is a novel of crime and detection only in the sense that *Caleb Williams, Crime and punishment* and *L'Etranger* are crime novels. The act of homicide is present not as the mainspring of a mystery, but as a vehicle for the exploration of guilt both within the individual conscience and, less cohesively, the extent to which society shares responsibility. Sprigg's 'whodunits' are enjoyable as representative and unpretentious examples of the form: Caudwell's novel, although still concerned with murder, is a 'mystery' in another meaning of the word. It is terribly flawed and formless and the author's intention — whatever that was — remains an enigma. Caudwell, immersed in the writings of Marx at this time, may have been stimulated by the latter's discussion of crime and punishment. Marx considers at length the ethics of punishment and the associated responsibility of society in his discussion of Eugene Sue's *Mysteries of Paris.* These views are summarised in the following quotation from an article that Marx published in the *New York Times* in 1853 and could well serve as an epigraph to Caudwell's philosophical thriller.

> Punishment, at bottom, is nothing but society's defense of itself against all violations of its conditions of existence. How unhappy is a society that has no other means of defending itself except the executioner.[8]

There is a theory that the psychological function of the 'whodunit' offers a cathartic release from guilt through a ritualistic and symbolic sacrifice of a permanent scapegoat, and Caudwell has one of his characters approach such a theory within the sociological plane of his novel. Salmon, a salesman with a philosophical bent, acts as a kind of 'chorus' in this modern tragedy:

> The murderer must be left to his own conscience. None of us has the right to punish another. All of us have been guilty at some time of a wish which, if our wishes were gratified, would result in a death. We are all the innocent-guilty. Our very interest in a murder is due to our feeling that the murderer is bound to us in this way. He is atoning for our wicked thoughts.[9]

And a little later in the novel (p. 188) Salmon talks of the murderer in society as a 'sacrifice, like a scapegoat, that one hardly dares touch'. If Christopher St John Sprigg's 'whodunits' offered an unconscious expiation of guilt for the reader, Caudwell's serious novel brings to consciousness society's complicity in what Auden called 'the dialectic of innocence and guilt'.[10]

As in most of Caudwell's work, the presence that hovers over *This my hand* is that of Freud. As we shall see in the next chapter, not only Freud's theory of dream influenced the writer of *Illusion and reality*, but the later sociological work, *The future of an illusion* (1927) is of crucial importance to any understanding of that book. The text that most informs *This my hand* is the other late sociological work, *Civilization and its discontents* (1930), the intention of which was, in Freud's words, 'to represent the sense of guilt as the most important problem in the evolution of culture, and to convey that the price of progress in civilization is paid by forfeiting happiness through the heightening of the sense of guilt'. Just as the advent of 'the Great War for Civilisation' had a marked effect on Freud's thinking, it had also a profound effect on Caudwell's generation. As a teenager he had written a series of poems on the war entitled *The requiem*. In this novel he presents a post-war waste-land world where emotions run high and happiness seems chronically elusive. Ian Venning, estranged from his demented wife, Celia, remarks to his lover, Barbara, on the difficulties of their particular situation, while at the same time voicing one of the larger issues of the book, the seeming hopelessness of the human plight.

> They discussed the War. It seemed as remote and unaccountable as a nightmare long after one has awakened.
>
> 'Why do we torment ourselves,' he asked irritably. 'I mean nobody wants these things and yet they happen. It's a kind of obstinacy I suppose. And yet it's more than that. It's just as if we deliberately spoilt our own chances of happiness as soon as we got hold of them.' (pp. 94–5)

The 'nightmare' of the First World War haunts the novel as recurrent motif and it is the war acting as catalytic agent that is responsible for bringing the three main characters together — three human beings who, in the name of love, destroy one another. This is not a conscious wish on the part of Ian Venning, Celia Harrison or Barbara Mitton, but rather they seem the victims of some force beyond their wills. The outcome, after all three are dead, is perhaps best described in Barbara's words when, earlier in the novel, she pronounces the suicide of a young girl in the book as 'a crude tragedy'.

In the same letter that he announced the near completion of his new book, Caudwell also mentions that the idea he had had for writing a novel on the Macbeth theme now seemed 'impossible'. Yet, as any reader of *This my hand* will discover, there are numerous allusions to Shakespeare's play, such as the 'spot of blood' on Ian's hand after he kills his wife and his description of her death as being 'like a candle that goes out'. The title itself comes from Act 2, Scene 2 of *Macbeth*, when the protagonist, shortly after Duncan's murder, contemplates the magnitude of his crime and the impossibility of absolution:

> Will all great Neptune's ocean wash this blood
> Clean from my hand? No, this my hand will rather
> The multitudinous seas incarnadine,
> Making the green one red.

What must have originally interested Caudwell in the tragedy of Macbeth — and the concern is central to the novel he did eventually write — was no doubt the psychological effects of a shared guilt leading to inevitable catastrophe. It is no mere coincidence that he was drawn to the constituent teleology of the detective novel and attracted to the rigorous necessity of tragedy; that he attempted to amalgamate in his creative as well as his theoretical work the two great exponents of determinism in the modern age. Just as in *Orestes*, composed around the same time (1934/5), this novel explores the idea of psychology as fate. *This my hand* (in a way similar to the verse-play) attempts to dramatise a determinism that wrests power from supernatural agencies and places destiny within the psyche — what human beings are driven to do as if against their own volition. In the year or so before his death, Caudwell was making a sustained attempt to give a coherence to his many intellectual pursuits by imposing the structure — the 'necessity' — of dialectical materialism, but there is no doubt that his art (the few serious examples that we have) remained under the influence of the psychic determinism of Freud.

That *This my hand* is not a good novel stems to a great extent from the fact that Caudwell had yet to incorporate successfully his new-found *Weltanschauung* into the world of his art. The novel lacks, in every sense of the term, a point of view. We are left in the hands of an omniscient narrator without, as it were, any personality, any prejudices. It is my opinion that the unsatisfactory nature of the book reflects a tension within the author during the time of its composition. It was during this period (1935–6) that he was in the process of 'marxifying' his debt to Freud with regard to his theoretical work and unsure how to achieve the synthesis in the realm of his art (*Orestes* suffers from a similar problem). And so Caudwell opted, perhaps not consciously, to remain outside his work, not so much 'paring his fingernails' as wringing his hands in despair of a method. Once again, as in the poetry, he is his own shrewd critic. Writing to the Beards after the book's publication (in April 1936), Caudwell agrees with their criticism of the novel and remarks that his method 'was an attempt to gain an impartiality which, in the nature of things, I now see is not possible. People seen only externally still remain people "seen by someone", and the problem of the observer remains the central problem of the novel.' Caudwell the critic had learned from his first attempt at a serious narrative; his words to the Beards are a virtual paraphrase of his remarks on the novel in his 'study' which was to be published as *Romance and realism* and which he was writing at this time (1936).

> The lack of a common world-view, therefore, comes in the novel as the problem of the observer, of the seeing eye ... The novel's problem is epistemological, the problem of knowing, of the spectacles through which one sees...[11]

The highly objective — one is tempted to say 'clinical' — narration of *This my hand* gives us a truncated psycho-biography of Celia, Ian and Barbara before they become enmeshed in one another's lives just after the war. It is during the last months of the war that Celia meets Ian Venning while both are guests of the Firth family who amount to 'local aristocracy' in the environs of Tinford, Yorkshire, a city that is no doubt modelled on the Bradford of Caudwell's youth. Unlike Celia, Ian 'did not possess any intense inner life, but lived simply in his environment ... But this environment had been stirred by the War as one stirs a puddle with a stick.' The very fact that Ian, who had befriended young Charles Firth in the war, is a guest of the Firths at all is evidence of this social flux. The son of a shopkeeper, he had worked for a firm of builders before the war and helped himself to one thousand pounds of the company's money. 'He had no guilt as regards the transaction itself, but a natural fear of being found out.' Venning seems a straightforward sort of fellow and the new 'luxurious surroundings of Charles Firth's home', not to mention the attention of Celia begin to bewilder him, so that he spends a good deal of his time 'adapting himself to existence at the Firths'. Celia is attracted to Venning, most especially by a certain coarseness in his nature that she feels is exemplified by his hands. Eventually, the hand that attracted Celia kills her almost by design, illustrating a central ironic motif of the book: that Venning's hands, metonymically representing both his coarse attractiveness and his desire for contact with fellow humanity, bring about his own and others' destruction.

After Ian's marriage to Celia they at first seem to muddle through — Ian is given a position of responsibility in the Firth family firm — but Celia's old neurotic personality begins to manifest itself in various ways, making Ian's life a misery. Yet despite the pain she causes him, he is aware that on some inexplicable level, she loves him, just as she had loved the little dog she tortured as a child. A doctor attempts to explain to a perplexed Ian the nature of Celia's psychosomatic illnesses, in terms that Caudwell was to use as a central focus in his study on the origin and function of poetry, that is the relationship between illusion and reality.

> The illness isn't deliberate. She's suffering physically and mentally. She's suffering from what we all suffer from more or less — the difficulties of adjustment to life, of squaring our dreams with reality ... she never means to hurt you. Remember that, my boy. It's like a puppy who bites when he feels himself falling. (pp. 61–2)

But Ian, convinced that Celia is 'possessed by some evil spirit of the perverse', is driven into the arms of Barbara Mitton with whom there seems a possibility of salvation through genuine love.

We are then given, in a way similar to Celia's background, a short biography of Barbara Mitton from her childhood until the time she meets Venning. Brought up by her mother to whom she felt superior, Barbara, 'ever since she could remember ... longed to sacrifice herself — as a doctor, as a Florence Nightingale, as a Joan of Arc'.

> Then the War came and with it the opportunity to work. She had already started to study medicine, but she threw it up and became a nurse. She worked like a slave, and the

maimed bodies of thousands of young men passed through her hands, but she realised one day that they might have been so many pieces of broken china. (p. 180)

Barbara begins to question her lack of 'charity' and after her return to Tinford she asks herself, as should all these characters, 'Am I incapable of love?' At the same time that Barbara falls in love with Venning, she is troubled, as are all in this novel, by 'strange' presageful dreams.

> She dreamed she was in hospital and they were putting the screens round a man who had died. Presently they put him on a trolley and wheeled him away. As the trolley passed, she saw that the man was alive, and in horror she pointed this out to the nurse. The nurse answered curtly: 'But of course we always bury them alive', and suddenly it seemed to her that she had gone through life forgetting this elementary fact, but now she perfectly knew the truth of it; 'All of them would be buried alive; all of them', and thinking of the horror of her own fate, that perhaps she would not even get out of the hospital but would be buried there, it seemed as if all the sorrows of all the partings that had ever been weighed on her. (p. 92)

Puzzled at first, Barbara begins to understand the symbolism of her dream when, her 'fate' inextricably bound to that of Ian and Celia, she leads an existence best described as death within life.

Ian, driven to distraction by Celia's unpredictable behaviour and her threat to inform the police about his earlier theft, strikes her dead in a fit of anger. The only person he can turn to is Barbara and her calm efficiency (somewhat like Lady Macbeth's) helps him to cover up the murder, making it look like a robbery. But now Ian feels that Barbara has a hold over him just as Celia had had with the knowledge of his theft, and this shared knowledge begins to drive a wedge between their love for each other. Their life together, both before and after their marriage, revolves around this repressed guilt, each afraid that the other will be tempted to utter 'the forbidden thing'.

In what Ian believes to be a 'surreptitious atonement', Barbara gives herself over to social work and we get a flavour of the exigencies of working-class life:

She loathed the bed-bugs that swarmed out of the cracks in the walls and left round the beds, mattresses or heaps of rags used for sleeping, a collection of squashy blood-stains. It did not occur to her that, seen through the eyes of the men and women who lived there, these were perhaps the least discomfort. The dirt in which one is brought up is never uncomfortable. Smells are a matter of habit. Overcrowding is better than loneliness. And even bugs are things to which one can be accustomed. But one can never become accustomed to the anxiety of losing a job, the boredom of unemployment, the overpowering pressure of the daily task, or the menace, like a secret cancer, of the end of one's days, without savings, with only the workhouse. These things are the nightmares and tortures of those who live in the dark depths of poverty. (p. 174)

But Barbara's attempt at an expiatory altruism brings only further misery when a young girl she has befriended kills herself after being 'outraged' by her working-class father. 'It was as if life said: "There is nothing you can do, nothing at all." ' This realisation and the fact of her ever-increasing awareness that her love for Ian 'ceased to be of any use' leads her to put her head in the gas-oven and kill herself.

It seemed now, after Barbara's death, that Ian would be able to return to the state of 'innocence and forgetfulness' that had been his life before he met Celia.

It was just because Barbara knew everything, that he could never shut Celia out of his mind ... It seemed to him — not perhaps consciously, but nevertheless all happened as if it were so — that she was in fact his guilt, that she was the guilty one, the only thing that stood in the way of innocence and forgetfulness. (p. 190)

Such a state of guiltless bliss is not attainable for Ian Venning, however, because he is driven by an inner compulsion, continual 'gestures [to] his other self', that make it seem more and more evident that some part of him desires apprehension and punishment. There is, for example, his friendship with the detective, Holroyd, who investigates Celia's murder. Ian suffers from 'a kind of phobia as long as the policeman [is] out of his sight' and, like Raskolnikov, he is under a compulsion to bring up the subject

of the crime when in his presence. Also, to escape the intensity
of his relationship with Barbara, he has taken up with a young
prostitute, Mary Britain, in order to satisfy a yearning for a
relationship that would not 'finger his soul'. But Ian Venning is
condemned to repeat himself. Just as he had slept with Barbara
on the night of Celia's death, so he now sleeps with Mary on the
same night that Barbara kills herself. He finds it difficult to
understand why, as 'a desperate gesture to his other self', he
half-jokingly tells Mary that he is a murderer, that he has killed
his first wife and was responsible that very day for the death of
his second, Barbara Mitton. It is, ultimately, Mary Britain's death
that brings Venning to the scaffold. This brief scenario epitomises
in small compass the Freudian paradigm of compulsion, repeti-
tion, and an unconscious death-wish, which characterise much
of Venning's psycho-biography.

Venning had been tied to Celia through her knowledge of his
'theft', then to Barbara because of her conspiracy in Celia's
murder; now he is reluctant to let Holroyd out of his sight and
he is locked to Mary because of his half-serious 'confession'. To
add to this web of entanglement there is also Salmon, the
salesman-cum-philosopher who Ian is certain knows some secret
about how to lead a life free from anxiety; he is convinced, too,
that Salmon is privy to his recent calamities. Ian is so intrigued
by Salmon that he eventually moves to live in the same boarding
house. He is, at the same time, repulsed and strangely attracted
to this man in whom there seemed 'no flaw'. But in this novel no
one is innocent and it turns out that Salmon was at one time one
of Mary's frequent customers and had a predilection for the
'pawing of young girls'.

Yet Salmon has achieved a kind of hypocritical peace with
himself through the belief that the body must be allowed to 'gratify
its appetites' in order that the soul may remain free. Otherwise
the resultant struggle only ends in guilt. When he expounds his
personal philosophy to Ian he demonstrates that he has read and
digested his Freud:

'Guilt, guilt, nothing but guilt!' said Salmon more cheerfully.
'That, in my opinion, is the modern disease. Indeed there
is a system of psychology which assumes that practically all
mental phenomena are based on it. For all I know it may
be true of the modern soul. The War was perhaps only a

large-scale voluntary expiation. Hence the eagerness with which we all rushed into it.' (p. 237)

At one stage, infuriated by Salmon's divination of the truth of his past, Ian almost kills him, but seems reassured that the 'mystic' has only a philosophical interest in his plight and the guilt that attaches to it and thus offers no threat.

It had begun now, if not before, to seem to Venning that 'everything was hostile, everything was incompatible, except Mary — her body, comforting, friendly, his'. But this temporary optimism is short-lived, because within a few pages of the narrative he learns of Mary's infidelity, another instance in the novel of his 'hopeless battle against the world'.

> Life had always been the same! Time after time. The least love, the least regret, had put him at the mercy of others — Celia, Barbara, Mary, they were like a mistake endlessly repeated, a narcotic habit. (p. 279)

Angered and frustrated by this reversal of fortune, Ian confronts Mary with the charge and learns not only that she has all the time hated him, but for some time has suspected him of being a murderer. In 'a sudden gust of rage', just as he had killed Celia, Ian grasps Mary by the throat and throttles her, fulfilling (it seems) a psychic determinism:

> He did not feel frightened or horrified. He felt as if a great mechanical arm which had been waiting to work had come round and hit him ... He had done what he was bound to do. (p. 282)

This time he makes no attempt to escape and is arrested next day by his policeman friend, Holroyd, the man who had investigated Celia's death. The wheel has turned full circle.

The last chapter, by far the best of the book, is set within the prison, where Venning's presence and imminent execution is 'like a repressed madness ... in the heart of [the] isolated community'. This last section has a quality reminiscent of Camus' *L'Etranger* — which Caudwell's novel predates by six years — in its portrayal of the hypocrisy of the judicial system and the bewildering (to Venning) interpretation of the facts. This last chapter could almost stand on its own as a moving appeal against capital punishment, regardless of the overwhelming evidence of the murderer's guilt. Compared with Venning's 'involuntary', impassioned slaying of Celia and Mary, the message here is that society's slow, clinical revenge is inhuman. And although Ian Venning is at last found 'guilty', so too, by implication, is society. The last sentence of the book describes the departure of the hangman just after the execution: 'It looked almost as if there had been a substitution and the real murderer was escaping.'

It is difficult for any reader of this unusual and dark novel to know where to apportion sympathy or blame; it is (as Ian puts it toward the end of the narrative) 'just as if things went wrong and no one could do anything'. It seems, despite the lack of any point of view, that we are to afford some sympathy to Ian Venning; that in the words of the London *Times* review of March 1936: 'Ian Venning is not so much a "natural-born criminal" as an unhappy wretch who is not big enough to battle successfully with his environment.' And we should remember too those words that Caudwell copied so carefully in his notebook from Wassermann:

> The guilt that arises from what men do is small & scarcely comparable to the guilt that arises from what men fail to do. For what kinds of men are these, after all, who become guilty through their deeds? Poor, wretched, driven, desperate creatures, who lift themselves up & bite the foot that treads them under. Yet they are made responsible & held guilty & punished with endless torments.

These sentiments may have seemed appropriate to Caudwell as far as Venning's case is concerned, a man who is, as it were, bludgeoned to death by life itself: but what of Celia and Barbara and Mary who are equally 'driven'?

It is possible that Caudwell was trying to work out some kind of tragedy of 'the modern soul' afflicted by collective guilt in the aftermath of war, a war where 'murder' took place on such a grand scale. This seems to have been the point of view of Salmon who is the only character in the novel who affords the reader any sort of perspective.

> 'Not until the modern soul does penance, in a kind of general confession of its sins — not even then,' said Salmon, twirling his watch still more rapidly, 'not until it has also received an absolution in which it believes (though God knows where

that will come from) — not until then will it be at peace.'
His voice became soft, persuasive: 'You too, young man,
can hardly have escaped the disease. You were in the War.
Answer for your generation.' (p. 237)

Such an allegory of guilt and responsibility may have been
Caudwell's intention, but what comes through most forcibly after
a reading of this novel — and this may not be altogether divorced
from such an intention — is the realisation of the failure of love
to alleviate lives of pain and decay. Early in the novel an
exasperated Ian asks Celia what she wants and she replies: 'I
want to be loved.' To love one another or die seems to have been
the categorical choice confronting these characters. The denoue-
ment offers little hope. A few other words from *Macbeth* are
appropriate as a description of the central vision: in the final
analysis, the lives of Celia, Barbara, Ian Venning, and the young
prostitute Mary Britain, are 'full of sound and fury/Signifying
nothing'.

Caudwell's attempt at a social and psychological synthesis in
his creative work, most notably the verse-drama *Orestes* and *This
my hand*, were not successful. However, at the time of writing these
texts, he was formulating one of the most crucial innovations in
critical theory produced in the mid-1930s, his synthesis of Freud
and Marx. More specifically, his adaptation of Marx's Eleventh
Thesis on Feuerbach — 'The philosphers have only *interpreted* the
world, in various ways; the point, however, is to *change* it' — and
Freud's theory of the distortion of reality through dream. Men,
the Caudwell of *Illusion and reality* believed, by dreaming socially,
that is through poetry (or imaginative fiction generally), could
change each other and the world. It is to this vast project that
we must now turn our attention.

## Notes

1. Christopher Caudwell, *Poems* (London, Lawrence & Wishart,
1965). First published, with a 'Biographical note', by John Lane, 1939.
These are now included in the *Collected poems*. One wonders how many
commentators bothered to read *Poems* when they were available in the
earlier editions. In an otherwise helpful bibliography to Frederick Benson,
*Writers in arms: the literary impact of the Spanish Civil War* (New York, New
York University Press, 1967), p. 326, the *Poems* are listed in a section
devoted to 'poetry ... concerned with the Spanish Civil War'. The desire
to make him a 'war poet' is evident also in Stanley Weintraub, *The last*

*great cause: the intellectuals and the Spanish Civil War* (New York, Weybright & Talley, 1968), p. 41, where we read of Caudwell that 'before he had gone to Spain he had written a poem he had titled "The Art of Dying" .' Weintraub omits to tell us that he had worked on this poem for nearly ten years.

2. See, for example, Caudwell's *Romance and realism*, pp. 127–9.

3. See his comments on Donne in *Illusion and reality*.

4. *Illusion and reality*, p. 107. See Francis Mulhern, *The moment of 'Scrutiny'* (London, Verso Editions, 1981) for a similar, if not so Marxist, concern with English civilisation at this time. All references to *Illusion and reality* are to the 1955 edition.

5. Julian Symons, *Mortal consequences* (New York, Harper & Row, 1972), p. 227.

6. *The Times Literary Supplement*, 5 June 1981, p. 633. Fuller's remarks were in response to a request for relatively unknown and underrated crime novelists.

7. *This my hand* (London, Hamish Hamilton, 1936). This is a very difficult book to get hold of (there are only two copies listed as being extant in the United States), and for this reason I shall give a more than usual account of the narrative in attempting to situate the novel in the context of Caudwell's other work.

8. Quoted in H. B. Acton, *The illusion of the epoch: Marxism-Leninism as a philosophical creed* (London, Cohen & West, 1955), p. 211.

9. *This my hand*, p. 155. Henceforth all references to the novel will be cited within the body of the text.

10. W. H. Auden, 'The guilty vicarage', in Leslie Fiedler (ed.), *The art of the essay* (New York, Thomas Y. Crowell, 1969), pp. 234–44. First published in *Harpers Magazine* (May 1948), pp. 406–11.

11. *Romance and realism*, pp. 126–7. It is a nice touch of irony that Caudwell, never one to waste paper, used a page of typescript of *This my hand* in order to compose his 'study'. The typescript for pp. 224–5 of the published version of the novel has on the verso the holograph for p. 78 of *Romance and realism*.

# 4

# The Socialisation of Dream: *Illusion and reality*

*A spider conducts operations that resemble those of a weaver, and a bee puts to shame many an architect in a construction of her cells. But what distinguishes the worst architect from the best of bees is this, that the architect raises his structure in imagination before he erects it in reality.*

Marx

*In the fashioning of consciousness the great instrument is language. It is language which makes us consciously see the sun, the stars, the rain and the sea — objects which merely elicit* responses *from animals.*

*Illusion and reality*

*Reality, however complete, has to be altered by being turned into art, so that it can be seen to be alterable and be treated as such.*

Brecht

*What is characteristic of illusions is that they are derived from human wishes.*

Freud

## Introduction

*Illusion and reality* is an extremely complex book, a complexity that is the result of at least two interrelated causes. Firstly, it is due to the hurried nature of the book's composition and the hastily added emendations as Caudwell read and thought more about Marxist theory. Secondly, the very scope of the work, with its enlistment of numerous disciplines, makes it a challenge for even the most erudite of commentators.

It is not Caudwell's most lucid production, but it represents a fertility of thought across a formidable range of disciplines, that is remarkable for so young a thinker. *Illusion and reality* is the most enigmatic of his books, and it is for this reason that I have opted to give it more attention than some commentators think it deserves.[1] Most importantly, from the point of view of the impetus of this whole study, this book reflects the metamorphosis of Christopher Sprigg, poet, into Christopher Caudwell, cultural anatomist. In this sense it records a young man's intellectual growth, the urgent and enthusiastic desire to record on paper the results of a wide and hurried reading. This chapter sets out to document that growth, to help explain the appearance of a book that not only surprised and perplexed Caudwell's contemporaries, but continues to surprise and perplex even today.

When Caudwell's book appeared in the spring of 1937 he was already dead and this no doubt added a note of poignancy to its reception. But, regardless of this fact, the work elicited a response based on its intrinsic merit: nothing quite like it had appeared in English critical theory before. In the realm of 'socialist' criticism there had been the work done by William Morris in the 1880s; and Shaw, whom Lenin had described as 'a good man fallen among Fabians', provided economic insights in some of his 'Prefaces'. Oscar Wilde, who had written *The soul of man under socialism* (1891), was loth to make any firm links between 'art' and the social system from which it arose.[2]

Raymond Williams has remarked that 'the political writing of the 1930s was primarily a response to actual conditions in England and Europe, rather than a conscious development of Marxist studies'.[3] This is of course true, but it is not surprising; indeed in a Marxist context it is inevitable that historical conditions, no matter how mediated, should determine the mode of discourse of a given epoch. As has been noted in earlier chapters of this study, just as the political tide of events worsened, as unemployment rose, as fascism and war became imminent, so too did the desire to make 'letters', both creative and critical, take on a political stance. Christopher St John Sprigg's fellow detective novelist, G. D. H. Cole (who was to go on to write many volumes of Marxist commentary) brought out his *Politics and literature* in 1929; this was not in any way a Marxist treatise, but was emblematic of the growing desire to unite these two areas of enquiry. The most influential work done in the field of Marxist critical exegesis before the advent of *Left Review* in 1934 (after which there was a series of books and essays), was that of John Strachey in his *The coming struggle for power* (1932) and *Literature and dialectical materialism* (1934). The former book, with its section on 'The decay of capitalist culture', had, as we noted in Chapter 2, a profound influence on the younger intellectuals. However, the pages devoted to literature concentrate on contemporary figures such as Wells, Shaw, Lawrence and Huxley — figures that Caudwell was to take up in his 'Studies'. There is no broad historical sweep, nor any attempt at a 'philosophical' explanation of literature's role within society.

There was, then, a burgeoning of 'Marxist' writings between 1934 and 1936. Not only within the theory of literature, but in fine art (Herbert Read and Anthony Blunt), in science (J. D. Bernal), and imaginative literature, as exemplified by *New country* (1933), discussed earlier. Nevertheless, despite the variegated 'response to actual conditions' (Williams) — in this sense *Illusion and reality* was determined, *overdetermined*, by the events and texts of the period — when Caudwell's book appeared it was both a revelation and, for many, the culmination of nearly a decade of quest. Auden spoke for his 'generation':

> We have waited a long time for a Marxist book on the aesthetics of poetry ... Now at last Mr. Caudwell has given us such a book.
>
> *Illusion and reality* is a long essay on the evolution of freedom in Man's struggle with nature ... and of the essentially social nature of words, art and science, an approach which enables Mr. Caudwell to make the clearest and most cogent criticism of Freud and Jung, while using their discoveries which I have ever read ... This is the most important book on poetry since the books of Dr. Richards, and, in my opinion provides a more satisfactory answer to the many problems which poetry raises.[4]

What must have impressed Auden and his contemporaries more than anything else was that this unknown young man had made a valiant attempt to unite the findings of the two great modern interpreters of human society. Marx and Freud, as Louis MacNeice put it, were 'The figure-heads of [his generation's] transition.' Moreover, the book seemed to supply an answer to that recrudescent question of the decade: how can art, or poetry, have any effect on the desire for change? At the heart of Caudwell's thesis lay the notion that the preparation for action, and thus all change, lay within the imagination, that the consciousness of men, so dependent on the symbolic, could then be changed by the symbolic, most particularly through the language of poetry.

> Language, and the phantasy which has generated it, and the conscious psyche which is their offspring, and ... man whose struggle with Nature in association has created all three, are bound together with a relation which Marx was the first to express in those hastily-scribbled eleven *Theses on Feuerbach* that marked the beginning of a new era in human thought: 'The philosophers have only *interpreted* the world in various ways; the point, however, is to *change* it.'[5]

As remarked upon earlier, the Eleventh Thesis which Caudwell quotes here was, of all the writings of Marx, the sentence that struck the deepest emotional chord in the heart of the 1930s. On a less emotional level (although he does not quote it directly) another of the Theses resides at the centre of his belief in the power of the 'subject' to effect change. In the First Thesis Marx condemns 'all hitherto existing materialism' because it considers 'the thing, reality, sensuousness ... only in the form of the object or of *contemplation*, but not as *human sensuous activity*, *practice*, not subjectively'.[6] This implies, as Caudwell was to stress elsewhere, that the 'thing-in-itself' becomes a 'thing-for-us', and that if human beings have a hand in constructing their 'reality' it is also possible for them to change it. Such an 'interactionist' epistemology (rather than a monistic determinism) is bound to have, as we shall see later, a bearing on how we view the Marxist theory of the base–superstructure relationship. However, this stress on the subject was also to lead eventually to Caudwell's Marxism being branded as heretical.

Whatever the book's position within the Marxist canon, there are between its covers, sometimes in scattered and embryonic form, areas of crucial interest to contemporary thought about man, his art, and his place in the universe. One has only to glance through the 500 or so books listed in the bibliography to get an idea of just how diligently this young man tried to keep abreast of contemporary scholarship. Many of the works cited were published only the year before he left for Spain. His was a mind that was alert for any new contribution that would enlarge, and become integrated with, his grand synthesis that set out to explain the origins and function of poetry.

Writing in defence of Caudwell, E. P. Thompson has generously provided us with a summary of the enormous scope of Caudwell's endeavour as represented by the bibliography:

> A rough-and-ready breakdown into categories gives: Linguistics, 14; Mathematics, 14; Philosophy, 33; General Science (including genetics, physics), 37; Ancient Civilizations (Egypt, Greece, Rome), 39; Marxism, 39; History, economics, general politics, 64; Literary criticism and the arts, 75; Psychology and neurology, 78; Anthropology and archaeology, 122. A few titles evade even these classifications. And there are two or three volumes of poetry.[7]

Of course, as Thompson implies, it depends on how one categorises many of these books and it is not intended as a quibble if I accentuate the two dozen or so works dealing with mathematics and the history and theory of symbolic systems.[8] I emphasise the inordinate amount of such books in a treatise on 'aesthetics' because such a realisation may help us to arrive at the core of Caudwell's original intention, before he went to Cornwall and 'steeped himself' in the Marxist classics. If we add to the category of the books just mentioned those works on language and anthropology, especially the 'linguistic' anthropology of Sapir — an anthropology that accentuates man as a creature of his language, or, more broadly, of symbolic systems which help to define his place in the world — then I believe we arrive at the genesis of a book that had as its first title, 'Verse and mathematics'. At the centre of *Illusion and reality* is a concern with the symbolic function in human evolution.

It was, in part, just within this very context that Freud, whose influence, even while being negated, is a major force in the book, held an attraction for the 'pre-Marxist' Caudwell. In his study of Freud he wrote that, despite his 'mythological' system, 'we owe much to Freud for his symbolic presentation of the discord between the deep and recent layers of men's minds'.[9] Caudwell's interest in Freud and in psychology in general — in 'the deep and recent layers of men's minds' — was a part of his erudite interest (as again the bibliography testifies) in the evolutionary process in all its manifold aspects. Taking the above predilections into consideration it is perhaps possible to envisage Caudwell's original project, a project that adopted eventually a particular, all-embracing point of view with regard to evolution in human affairs, that of historical materialism.

Paul Beard approaches a crucial truth about the making of *Illusion and reality* when, in his brief review of the book, he outlines his friend's intellectual quest over the previous years. The work, Beard tells us, 'represents three different strands which had become united in [Caudwell's] personality'. The first of these was an abiding interest in poetry, with science running a close second. So that *Illusion and reality*, Beard feels, is an attempt at 'resolving a question that had long puzzled him', that of bringing together the seemingly distinct worlds of science and art. He goes on:

> The third strand, the last woven into his character, is that of the Marxist who believed he had at last discovered a world-view to which both of the former [science and art] had to be adjusted to become fully intelligible and purposeful ... Fundamentally every way of understanding the world is shown to be a form either of art or science. Illusion and reality are the names he gives to these two fields of feeling and knowing, subject and object, which together — polarized yet interpenetrating — symbolize the complete universe.[10]

The significance of Beard's remarks is not merely the stress on his friend's need to blend his dual interests into one grand symbolic plan, but also his emphasis on the chronology of the new-found 'world-view' to which these interests had to be 'adjusted'. It was in this context, let us remember, that Caudwell had written to Beard in November 1935, shortly after the first draft of *Illusion and reality*, remarking that his 'weakness [had] been the lack of an integrated *Weltanschauung*', one that would unite his 'emotional, scientific, and artistic needs'.

The imposition of his 'world-view' on the two realities of science and art led him, I would suggest, to a revision of his project which

73

is exemplified by the ambiguity of the revised title. The 'illusion' is now not merely the symbolic projections of the heart and the head that enable humankind to make sense of their world, but has become also the 'bourgeois illusion', the ignorance of necessity that obstructs the path to 'social freedom'. *Illusion and reality* becomes now a book very much about the evolution toward such 'freedom' as the epigraph from Engels clearly emphasises. Only through the 'recognition of necessity', both with regard to the outer environment (science) and man's inner self — how his psyche adapts to the environment with the help of art — can humankind ever hope to evolve to 'real' freedom. With its epistemological base of evolutionary change toward liberty, *Illusion and reality* is very much a text of its epoch.

Writing somewhat later, one of Caudwell's contemporaries, Alick West (he had given those lectures on Marxism and literature that Caudwell attended), summed up the book's visionary impact and stressed its ideological importance:

> The condition of Caudwell's new understanding of poetry is his vision of change, of the advance to Communism. That vision enables him to see poetry as a means to winning the freedom, as being itself a form of the freedom, which Communism will enlarge and extend ... The consciousness and conviction of this advance is the basis of *Illusion and reality*; the main lesson to be learned from it is to gain the same quality of vision. Caudwell's ideas about poetry concern every comrade because the lifeblood of those ideas is that the history of man is the advance to freedom.[11]

*Illusion and reality* not only dealt with aesthetic matters, but also projected in teleological fashion, especially in its final chapter, a Marxist vision of the future.

Yet despite the enthusiasm of his comrades and the optimistic spirit in which the book was received, it was only a matter of time before the 'vision' that had satisfied West and the men of his generation was subjected to a more rigorous critique.[12] As the spirit of the 1930s steadily evaporated, Caudwell's fellow Marxists were to debate among themselves as to just to what extent Caudwell was heretical in the marshalling of his various interests under the rubric of historical materialism. It was a hurried, and as we shall see, not a fully realised organisation of his previous reading that led, not only to his questionable applications of Marxist theory to literature, but also to distortions in the book's organic structure. I indicate some of these distortions in the Appendix to this volume and suggest that Caudwell's revision of *Illusion and reality* took place while he was drafting his 'Studies' and that material from the latter project influenced that revision. This might help explain some of the comments on the poor structure of the book. Hence, Maynard Solomon remarks, after explicating the text as far as the end of Chapter 3: 'Following this exposition, the argument of *Illusion and reality* is interrupted (and contradicted) by a long excursus (Chaps. 4–6) on the history and development of British poetry.'[13] And David Margolies divines what I feel to be a truth about the book's composition when he remarks that 'Caudwell's fullest idea of function was probably evolved only while he was actually writing *Illusion and reality* [because] it is never fully explained at any one time.'[14]

Whatever the faults in the book's structure and what seems to be the 'layered' nature of its composition, the contemporary breed of English Marxist (as opposed to, let us say, George Thomson, Alick West or E. P. Thompson) are adamant that there is nothing to be learned from Caudwell. Terry Eagleton is representative of the school that regards Caudwell almost as an embarrassment within any attempt to forge a materialist aesthetic. Speaking of the 1930s, Eagleton remarks:

> That so much of this writing is now of merely historical interest is one aspect of our present dilemma, even though one name at least survives from that era. Who is the major Marxist critic? Christopher Caudwell, *hélas*. It is in such pat question and answer that the problem of a Marxist criticism in contemporary Britain is most deftly posed. For though Caudwell is the major forebear — 'major', at least, in the sheer undauntedness of his project — it is equally true that there is little, except negatively, to be learnt from him ... Insulated from much of Europe, intellectually isolated even within his own society, permeated by Stalinism and idealism, bereft of a 'theory of superstructures', Caudwell nevertheless persevered in the historically hopeless task of producing from these unpropitious conditions a fully-fledged Marxist aesthetic. His work bears all the scars of that self-contradictory enterprise: speculative and erratic, studded with random insights, punctuated by hectic forays into and out of alien territories and strewn with hair-raising theoretical vulgarities.[15]

There is a good deal to answer here if one were to rehabilitate Caudwell within the Marxist fold, and although this is not the object of my discussion of *Illusion and reality* some consideration of these matters will be addressed later. Suffice it to point out here, however, that if he was 'bereft of a "theory of superstructures" ' (Eagleton no doubt has in mind the work of Gramsci, Althusser and Macherey, among others), Caudwell made a brave attempt to construct his own theory directly from his reading of Marx and Engels. And, ironically enough, it was what was thought to be the lack of a Stalinist perspective (Caudwell's emphasis on the role of the subject in the materialist epistemology) that led to the orthodox Stalinist attack on his work between the covers of *Modern Quarterly*, of which there is some mention below.

Nevertheless, although this book makes a real contribution to a Marxist theory of art — especially its economic origins and developing function — Eagleton is justified in many of his criticisms. To generalise all poetry after the rise of capitalism as 'bourgeois' or 'capitalist' is to say everything and nothing. Perhaps the most 'vulgar' aspect of Caudwell's Marxism is his 'economism', a mode of explication based on an unmediated relation between literature and the economic infrastructure pertaining at the time.[16] As Raymond Williams has pointed out (and such a view finds its authority in, among other texts, Engels's letter to Joseph Bloch), 'even if the economic element is determining, it determines a whole way of life, and it is to this, rather than to the economic system alone, that the literature has to be related'.[17] It is unfortunate that Caudwell, who I believe had something to contribute to the *theory* of superstructure (his insistence on language and literature's ideological role, its reaction on the base) should have taken such a simplistic view of its historical manifestations. It is likewise regrettable that — as his Russian translator has pointed out — he is 'extremely schematic' in tracing the decline of capitalist art and projecting the socialist art of the new world, as if ideology was always *simply* an equivalent to what takes place in the economic sphere. That there are problems with Caudwell's 'Marxism', then, there seems little doubt, but in this context we should bear in mind that Marx — who at one time described himself as not being a 'Marxist' — left no detailed nor definitive theory of the superstructure or the role of art within it. Orthodoxy, especially in a system that stresses an historical base, cannot be eternal.

Such a spirit of enquiry — stressing the relativity of 'orthodox' ideas — informs the essay by E. P. Thompson already cited. What is most significant in Thompson's appraisal is the fact that it is based on his decentralisation of *Illusion and reality* within the total *œuvre*. Thompson argues that the book was written at a time when Caudwell was undergoing a 'conversion' and had not fully integrated his recent reading of the Marxist classics, that the 'Studies' were written later and that these present a more mature Marxist position. This is, I feel, essentially true. What Thompson does not suggest — what in fact may have flawed the book that he feels 'beyond repair of close criticism' — is the fact that the very drafting of those 'Studies' might have had a detrimental effect on the final revision of *Illusion and reality*. (Such a possibility is explored in the Appendix to this book.)

At the heart of *Illusion and reality*, constituting its epicentre and, I believe, the mainspring of its inception, is a concern with the function of poetry in relation to the other great symbolic systems of religion, science and the other arts; a concern with mankind's psychical development within the wider spectrum of human evolution. It is within this context that Caudwell offers valuable and thought-provoking insights into the role of language and literature, insights which are not specifically Marxist in their importance.

It is my belief that the chief claim to interest of *Illustion and reality* must rest on the following premiss: a book which discourses about the origins, functions and evolution of society's reliance on symbolic representation and incorporates this with psychoanalytic interpretations of such artifacts, a treatise which, ultimately, bases its theory of communication on an intersubjectivity dependent on the symbolic — such a book as this must have more than mere historical importance. A thinker who resembles Caudwell more than any other I can think of, has, coincidentally enough, summarised the heart of Caudwell's intention in *Illusion and reality*. Jacob Bronowski, himself a poet, mathematician and scientist, whose central interest was an exploration of art and science as expressions of the human imagination, made the following statement shortly before his death:

> What makes the biological machinery of man so powerful is that it modifies his actions through his *imagination*. It makes him able to symbolise, to project himself into the consequences of his acts, to conceptualise his plans, and to weigh them, one against another, as a system of values. We as men are unique. We are the social solitaries. We are the

creatures who have to create values in order to elucidate our own conduct, so that we learn from it and can direct it into the future.[18]

In the spirit of the above remarks — that is, as regards Caudwell's contribution to the study of the imagination's role in human progress — I wish now to remind the reader of some main points in the book's argument. In so doing I will not consider here Caudwell's long critique of the historical development of British poetry, what Solomon calls 'a long excursus', but will concentrate on what I feel to be the book's strengths and its indisputable modernity.[19]

Caudwell begins his discussion of how 'illusion grows out of reality' by drawing on the work done by the anthropologists. In the tribe, 'the instincts must be harnessed to the needs of the harvest by a social mechanism'. After the 'phantastic' representation of the harvest in the group festival ('the matrix of poetry'), the ungrown harvest takes on a 'greater reality', spurring the participants 'on to the labours necessary for its accomplishment'.

> Thus poetry, combined with dance, ritual and music, becomes the great switchboard of the instinctive energy of the tribe, directing it into trains of collective actions whose immediate causes or gratifications are not in the visual field and which are not automatically decided by instinct.[20]

George Thomson, the classical scholar who wrote the introduction to the 1946 edition of *Illusion and reality* and who came to Caudwell's defence during the *Modern Quarterly* debate, was greatly influenced by the anthropological aspects of Caudwell's theory even to the extent of nomenclature. In *The prehistoric Aegean*, Thomson remarks:

> Why do poets crave for the impossible? Because that is the essential function of poetry, which is inherited from magic. In the wild transport of the mimetic dance the hungry, frightened savages express their weakness in the face of nature by a hysterical act of extreme mental and physical intensity .... By a supreme effort of will they strive to impose illusion on reality. In this they fail, but the effort is not wasted. Thereby the psychical conflict between them and

their environment is resolved. Equilibrium is restored. And so, when they return to reality, they are actually more fit to grapple with it than they were before.[21]

These emotions associated with the collective are still present in solitude, because the method of communication — the symbolic world — is social. Not only do natural phenomena, 'spring, a sunset, the song of the nightingale', become social signs encrusted with meaning through a common 'social ego', but such signs in poetry are further enriched by intertextuality: 'To the monkey ... the rose would be something perhaps edible, a bright colour ... to the poet it is the rose of Keats, of Anacreon, of Hafiz, of Ovid and Jules Laforgue'. (p. 29)

The rituals associated with mythology and the performance of art have similar functions: 'the adaption of man's emotions to the necessities of social cooperation'. Whereas mythology is self-regulating (the 'illusions', like poetry, are modified to suit the needs of society), the birth of 'true religion' arrests the development of this regulating system; it no longer adjusts itself to the organic needs of the tribe. The 'death of mythology' as a developing phenomenon heralds the birth of class religion, a system that has no future as an illusion.

After the lengthy discussion of the 'development of modern poetry', and the analysis of the work of various figures from Shakespeare to some of his contemporaries, Caudwell returns to poetry's essential characteristics. And it was no doubt such 'characteristics' which prompted Auden to call Caudwell's treatise 'the most important book on poetry since the books of Dr. Richards'. The 'affective' and 'cognitive' qualities of the word are important to Caudwell's theory and stand within a hierarchy of other binary oppositions, or (as Caudwell would insist) dialectical complexities: instinct/environment, emotion/rationality, poetry/science, illusion/reality, and music/mathematics. When, for example, mathematics — the symbolism of referentiality — is taken to its extreme, it cuts loose from reality and becomes the consistent sign-system of logic; music, in which the purely emotive side is taken to its extreme, also loses touch with referentiality and becomes the internationally translatable (as in logic) system of musical notation. Thus the two extremes of the emotive and referential meet in a completed circle. Poetry, in Caudwell's system, stands between these extremes:

What does poetry become if all external reference is eliminated, in the way that all value-judgments are eliminated from a scientific argument to make it become logistic? Poetry becomes 'meaningless' sound, but sound full of emotional reference — in other words, *music*; and music, like logistic, is translatable and universal. Thus we see that the mingling of reference and emotion, which is characteristic of poetry, is not an adulteration, but expresses a dialectic relation between the opposite poles of instinct and environment, a relation which is rooted in real concrete social life — English, French or Athenian. (p. 130)

There is always a dialectical relation between the object and the attitude struck towards it: 'language is stamped everywhere with humanity as well as with man's environment. Just as science is near the environmental pole, so poetry is near the instinctive ... Science yearns always towards mathematics, poetry towards music' (p. 134). The fact that words have an affective and a cognitive value arises from the dynamic process of their very invention. Humanity, the subject, which helps formulate reality, the object, cannot help but strike an attitude towards it: Just as the primitive cry has 'a "feeling-tone" ', so too it has 'an objective side, a *reference* to something perceivable in reality' (p. 139). The cry, for Caudwell, evolves into the word.

This duality, or dialectical, nature of language — the subjective/objective element — is exploited by the two great symbolic systems of art and science, each for its own purposes, the latter (as much as possible) to 'eliminate' the subject, the former 'to build it up', although they are interdependent and inextricably linked by a dialectical relation. 'Science and art are like the two halves produced by cutting the original human hermaphrodite in half, according to the story of Aristophanes in Plato's *Symposium*, so that each half evermore seeks its counterpart' (p. 154). Illusion, which the Greeks had discovered as important to literary art, is also the linchpin of humanity's other system of belief, as Caudwell's comments on the illusory observer in science and the social ego in art help to show:

The scientist has tended to regard this understood observer as just a piece of scaffolding, and to assume that, if it were necessary, the scaffolding could easily be knocked away ... This queer, universal 'Mock Ego' of science is illusory and yet necessary: all the reality which science's language symbolises is attached to 'him' ...

Now in precisely the same way when poetry — or literary art generally — wishes to 'symbolise' the social ego ... it is still compelled to make some statement about reality. The emotions are only found in real life adhering to bits of reality; therefore bits of reality — and moreover *organised* bits — must always be presented to achieve the emotional attitude. But the statement about reality selected for the underlying emotional attitude is not supposed to be about *material* reality, any more than science's Mock Ego is supposed to be a real man. It is a mock world; it is an illusion, accepted as such. So, by a long road, we have arrived back at the illusion, the *mimesis*, which is the essence and puzzle and method of literary art. (pp. 153–4)

So, just as science posits a 'Mock Ego' to observe 'non-qualitative' reality, poetry conceives of a mock reality, an illusion, as the vehicle for the qualitative emotional attitude. The conscious illusion, the 'as if' of the poem, is there in order to re-present reality, to afford a human perspective, an emotional stance. This is why poetry cannot be all 'latent' content, because although it goes 'beyond mimesis' it comes full circle to the world again, a world changed by that human perspective. And here we can have 'truth', as Keats suggested, because truth resides not *in* reality ('What reality is stares man in the face') but in man's relation to reality.

However, the 'conscious illusion' of poetry should not be confused with the delusion of dream or 'true' religion, because, as Sidney maintained some time ago, poetry 'nothing affirmeth'. In the dawn of civilisation, religion, like poetry and science, was still part of an undifferentiated mythology, a 'collective dream'. But when this system of interdependent symbolic truth separates out into science and art, religion attempts to confirm aspects of both: religious illusion 'mixes' the subjective wish with the objective fact:

But religion still mixes the subjective with the objective. It announces as truths what man hopes to be true ... It takes poetic illusions, valued and considered true for their subjective content, and demands that men give them the status of statements symbolic of external reality. (p. 192)

The 'illusions' of poetry, unlike religion, have a beneficial psychological and biological function in helping to experiment with 'the eternal adaptation of the genotype to its eternally changing environment'. Caudwell continues:

> If poetry becomes religion, if the non-symbolic [the pseudo-statement] is taken to be symbolic, the emotional attitude becomes frozen like the neurotic attitude. Thus the value of poetry's illusions in securing catharsis, as compared to religion's, is that they are known for illusion, and as compared to dream, that they are social.
>
> If poetry's emotional attitudes pass, what is their value? It is this; experience leaves behind it a trace in memory. It is stored by the organism and modifies its action. (pp. 266–7)

Since language, for Caudwell (after Marx), is the 'great instrument' in the fashioning of human consciousness it constitutes a kind of metasymbolic system in the affairs of human beings and requires careful consideration. If language (along with other symbolic processes) helps constitute consciousness and 'reality', it is then possible to modify consciousness and reality through language. Wittgenstein, in the *Tractatus*, is in error when he suggests that language is a 'passive photograph of the universe' (Caudwell). He makes the same mistake as

> philistines who imagine that a painting must be exactly like the scene it portrays. They do not see ... that the relation of language and thought to reality is not a passive reflection but an active and tendentious reaction ... The mirror reflects accurately: it does not know. (p. 195)

Wittgenstein was partly right in assuming a projective correspondence between a statement and what it refers to, but he neglected to recognise, Caudwell believes, a correspondence between 'the symbols and inner reality'.

In an intelligent modification of Wittgenstein's famous observation on language's correspondence to facts ('Whereof we cannot speak, we must pass over in silence'), Caudwell suggests that the philosopher limits the function of language in an area crucial to verbal art. Art speaks in the affective manifold what 'man nicht sprechen kann' in the logical manifold: or, to put it another way, in a poetic text there may be an 'irrational', an 'ungrammatical', aspect to the mimetically oriented structure, but this only serves to express what we *can* say in the underlying, affectively organised structure.[22] It is 'part of the technique of poetry [that it] treats words antigrammatically to realise their immediate and even contradictory affective tones'. But the poem cannot be all 'affective structures' because in its essence and origin 'language was created to signify otherness'.

Caudwell recognises the crucial work done by Freud, both with regard to the large social issue of the 'conflict between man's instincts and environmental reality' and also the work done in dream analysis and the bearing this has on 'poetry's dream work'. We might point out here that one of the earliest uses of Freud's dream theory in an attempt to explain the poetic process, was that by F. C. Prescott[23] who concentrates more on poetry as 'wish-fulfilment' than on the 'dream work' of the poem, but the grand design bears comparison with Caudwell. Prescott maintains that:

> The desires of mankind furnish the energy which moves the world and makes for progress.... It is these desires, as has been said, which inspire dreams by night and day, including the dreams of the poet. Not finding outlet in activity and denied actual gratification they provide for themselves a fictional gratification, creating through the imagination what is wanting in reality. (p. 56)

Caudwell maintains that there is a fundamental relationship between the linguistics of the poem and that of the dream. However, although there are many enlightening comparisons — displacement, condensation, over-determination and latent and manifest content — the signs of dream are explicable absolutely only in terms of personal biography. The poem, on the other hand, wrought out of a consciousness that is aware both of an inner desire and the outer environment, is *expressed* (turned out) in signs that belong to a community. Just as the referential element of such signs belong to a 'common perceptual world', so too does the affective nature of words belong to the 'social ego'. This latter concept is transmuted by Caudwell from 'the "god" of early Greek tribunal', the idea of a common 'feeling-tone of reality', to that of an intersubjective sign-system in which the social basis of consciousness mints transindividual emotional utterances as social coin.

Poetry is, then, in these terms 'inverted dream': the 'I' of the dream, being unconscious and therefore 'unfree', attempts to adapt reality to the instincts, whereas the poet adapts his instinctual desires to reality. In poetry emotion is 'socialised', there is poetic dream *work* and the artist becomes a producer within poetry's function in the ongoing evolutionary process of psychic adaptation to the environment. The illusion of dream has a 'biological value' in its attempt to modify reality, but the social basis of consciousness requires that poetry, to be communicable, must be in some way 'the socialisation of dream'.

Caudwell's poetic theory sets out to demonstate a fundamental wish of his generation, that poetry 'like the poetry of the harvest festival', and just as importantly as science, could be 'a guide and spur to action'. In his final chapter, 'The future of poetry', he moves from a study of art's characteristics and its historical role 'as an organic part of society' to the more urgent, contemporary, problem of its role in an age of transition. Here the voice changes to that of the communist expressing his hope for poetry in the imminent classless society, where 'the movement forward from bourgeois culture to communism is also a movement back to the social solidarity of primitive communism'. Unlike 'an ideal wish-fulfilment world like that of religion, jazz, or the detective novel', there will be 'a great expansion in the poet's public'.

> As freedom and consciousness become the right of all and not the prerogative of a class, the poet's public must become gradually coincident with society, and poetry once more fulfil a function similar to that of poetry in the primitive tribe, but with this difference — that the tremendous growth of the productive forces has differentiated poetry from the other arts, the arts from the sciences, and changed poetry itself from the poetry of a tribe to the poetry of individual men. (pp. 293–4)

The future of poetry is, in Caudwell's system, a matter of great ontological importance: just as primitive man achieved a richer state of being through undifferentiated ritual, so too can modern man fulfil his innate potential. 'Thus Art', Caudwell tells us in the last sentence of the book, 'is one of the conditions of man's realisation of himself, and in its turn is one of the realities of man'.

Such were the central ideas of the book that appeared in the spring of 1937, but the eventual form that *Illusion and reality* took was the result of a process that we must now examine.

## The making of *Illusion and reality*: Caudwell's reading

On 24 July 1935 Caudwell wrote to Elizabeth Beard telling her that he had decided to go to south Cornwall for 'a couple of months' and that he was at that time 'half way through a book called "Verse and mathematics" ', a project that their 'evening discussions' had for the most part precipitated. Later, in September, writing from Porthleven, Cornwall, he described the new book to his brother. Having remarked that the project has been 'progressing at a dizzy pace', he goes on:

> It incorporates all the biological, psychological, etc., etc., theories I have been forming in the course of my reading during the last few years ... I shall publish it (if any feeble-minded publishers can be found) under a pen-name. The author of such a volume could not, of course, bear the same name as a writer of low-brow detective tales.

In fact some of the reading that went into the 'serious' book had found its way into the work of the writer of 'low-brow detective tales'. His reading in anthropology is evident in *Death of a queen* and *The corpse with the sunburnt face*, both of which were published in 1935, and the machinations of a diabolical psychoanalyst are the focal element for the plot of *The six queer things* (1937), the thriller Caudwell had sketched out while in Cornwall.

When Caudwell wrote to the Beards again (in an undated letter, but probably September 1935) he was now calling his book 'Illusion and reality', and was careful to defuse any charges of plagiarism should they have arose.

> You may notice a similarity in many parts between my views and those of Ogden and Richards (Meaning of Meaning), even to the terminology: e.g. use of word 'symbolic'. This is I believe a complete co-incidence, as I have only just read their book. I think in the book as published I shall have to make some extended reference to 'Meaning of Meaning', otherwise it might be thought I had cribbed their ideas without acknowledgement.
>
> The biological and sociological bits, and also the general analysis of the arts, are, however, so far as I know not to be met with anywhere else.

There are a few references to the work of Ogden and Richards in Caudwell's book, the most 'extensive' appearing as a footnote on page 150. Here the work by the authors of *The meaning of meaning* is acknowledged, but Caudwell places it within a large historical context as if to testify to the diversity of his sources:

> The distinction between the affective and rational significance of words is of course an old one. Hindoo philosophy recognised the 'dhvana' or hidden meaning of words as characteristic of poetry. Dante distinguished between *signium rational* and *signium sensuale* which in turn was based on a division recognised by William of Occam. Milton's well-known definition of poetry as simple, *sensuous*, and passionate was no doubt influenced by this conception. Ogden and Richards' analysis of meaning is based on a distinction between the symbolic and emotive meaning of words.

The scope of Caudwell's reading and Richards's influence is taken up in more detail later in this discussion. I wish to explore at this point the broad philosophical co-ordinates within which his enterprise was carried out, and especially those 'biological bits' which are fundamental to Caudwell's thesis. As suggested in the introductory section of this chapter, the central concern of *Illusion and reality* is one of humanity's evolution toward freedom, toward a realisation of our full potential as social beings. Poetry is, in Caudwell's system, a crucial agent in the 'non-biological and specifically human adaptation to existence'. Just as men in association group together to change nature (science), to prepare for the future, so men in association, through their great symbolic system, language, attempt to change their fellows' emotional vision, their 'social ego'; this so that they may grapple all the better with their environment and participate in changing it. The book traces the vicissitudes of the poetic function from the primitive culture where it was born to the 'dying culture' of the 1930s. And the book speculates beyond its own era, to 'the future of poetry' in the new classless society.

As the above skeletal outline suggests, the movement of human history was, ultimately, explained for Caudwell by the scientific socialism of Marx, but, as we shall see, his search for a comprehensive (and biological) explanation of human endeavours owes a great deal to Darwinian biology and evolutionary anthropology, as do the two major influences of his system — Marx and Freud. Caudwell learned from his reading in anthropology how primitive man's ritualised illusions, at first an undifferentiated 'magic', evolved into the triform symbolic projections of art, religion and science. In the writings of the psychologists he read just how closely related modern man was to his primitive ancestor in regard to his instinctual desires, and how such desires manifested themselves in more 'sublimated' symbolic acts. For Caudwell this reliance of humanity on this symbolic function takes place within, and is a crucial contributor to, the human species' adaption to its environment.

Stanley Edgar Hyman has recorded the chronology and the interrelationship of the nineteenth-century trend to which the twentieth century and Caudwell were heir.

When Darwin concluded *The Origin of Species* (1859) with a call for evolutionary treatment in the sciences of man, he opened the door to a variety of genetic studies of culture, and when he showed in *The Descent of Man* (1871) that human evolution was insignificant organically although vastly speeded up, culturally (we might not be so quick to say 'ethically' as he was), he made cultural studies the legitimate heirs of evolutionary biology. The same year as *The Descent* in response to *The Origin* E. B. Tylor's *Primitive Culture* appeared, drawing an immediate fan letter from Darwin. It staked off quite a broad claim to cultural studies in its subtitle 'Researches into the Development of Mythology, Philosophy, Religion, Language, Art and Custom'.[24]

Such were the beginnings of evolutionary anthropology, a movement that blossomed in the late nineteenth and early twentieth centuries. The theoretical work of Frazer, Jane Harrison and the ethnographer Malinowski, the great fieldwork done by the linguist Sapir and the researches by Lewis Morgan among the American Indians — all these contributed to the making of *Illusion and reality.* As we shall see, the path from such anthropological findings, with their accent on the social and, with few exceptions, *economic* sources[25] of humanity's 'illusions', to the adoption of Marxian analysis as an overall system was not an inconsistent or strenuous one for Caudwell to take. Marx himself had planned to write a book on Morgan's *Ancient society* (1877), to show how anthropologists, quite independently, had confirmed 'the materialist conception of history'. The copious notes that he made for the uncompleted project were used eventually by Engels for his *Origin of the family* (1884). Caudwell's other major mentor, Freud, also drew on anthropology, most notably in *Totem and taboo* (Vienna, 1913), for confirmation of the 'historical' origins of his theories.

These, then, are the broad philosophical parameters of Caudwell's book. He found in his reading of anthropology a link between the psycho-genesis of humankind's symbolic projections (their 'illusions') as well as a discussion of the evolution of their social function. Such a nexus allowed him to synthesise, eventually, his interests in science (biology and psychology) with his other great love, poetry, in a project that saw the latter as a vital factor in humanity's full realisation of itself. His is a teleological universe that seeks to demonstrate a dialectical unity between man's social and biological realities. The contradiction between individual instinctive man (what Caudwell designates as the 'genotype') and associated social man is what makes art and literature a *necessary* aspect of human evolution.

The 'biological bits' that he refers to in the letter to Beard quoted above are less manifest in the published version than in an earlier untitled typescript which I believe represents the project he called 'Verse and mathematics', a manuscript which, I suggest, he rewrote both in Porthleven and, more radically, on his return to London. However, although rarely discussed, the biological foundation of Caudwell's thesis is present in *Illusion and reality* and in fact serves as a frame for the whole discussion of poetry's function within society.

> This differentiation and specialisation of language with increasing civilisation is of course characteristic of all civilised functions. The development of civilisation consists of a continually differentiating division of labour, which is not opposed to but is the cause of a continually integrating web of social economy. Just as the human body, because of the specialisation of its parts, is more highly integrated by an elaborate nervous system than a jelly-fish, from which parts can be severed which will continue to live, so the productive basis of society grows in elaborateness and differentiation at the same time as it becomes more and more unified. (p. 15)

Towards the end of the central discussion, before Caudwell looks into 'the future of poetry', we are given a more literal summary of art's participation in human evolution.

> If we are asked the purpose of art, we can make an answer — the precise nature of it depending on what we mean by *purpose*. Art has 'survived'; cultures containing art have outlived and replaced those that have not, because art adapts the psyche to the environment, and is therefore one of the conditions of the development of society ... It remoulds external reality nearer to the likeness of the genotype's instincts, but since the instinctive genotype is nothing but an unconscious and dynamic desire it remoulds external reality nearer to the heart's desire. Art becomes more socially and biologically valuable and the greater the art the more that remoulding is comprehensive and true to the nature of reality ... [both the pleasure and the pain of 'reality', because] ... An organism which thinks life is all 'for the best in the best possible of worlds' will have little survival value. (p. 261)

The sociobiological stance here is clear enough and is representative of many such scattered statements throughout the book — such as, for example, when Caudwell proposes that poetry may well be a 'vestigial organ' within capitalist economy (p. 31) — but the earlier version demonstrates a more sustained interconnection between biology, psychology and Marxism and provides an opportunity for us to see Caudwell's project in the process of its own evolution.

Although there are many ideas that one can recognise as coming to fruition in the published work, there is not (to the best of my knowledge) one paragraph of this manuscript that survives verbatim in *Illusion and reality* which suggests that Caudwell comprehensively re-thought and re-wrote his original project. I explore some of the reasons for this in my Appendix; sufficient to point out here that Caudwell's 'marxism' in this early version is not as comprehensive — does not *permeate* his discourse in the same way as in the published version. The 'bourgeois' are there, but the underlying theme of 'the bourgeois illusion' that underscores *Illusion and reality* has not made its appearance yet. And, allied to this, neither does the emphasis on the bourgeois separation of subject and object, so prevalent in *Studies* and in evidence periodically throughout *Illusion and reality*. As a consequence there is in 'Verse and mathematics' no investigation of the evolution of 'English poetry' as it represents the various stages in 'the bourgeois illusion', from the years of 'Primitive accumulation' (Shakespeare) to 'The final capitalistic crisis' (Lewis, Auden, Spender). This survey, along with what E. P. Thompson calls 'a notorious "table"', comprise Chapters 4, 5 and 6, and along with the previous chapter 'The development of modern poetry', forms a wedge between Caudwell's discussion of mimesis at the end of Chapter 2 and his continuance of this discussion in Chapter 7. It is such additions (along with others I explore in the Appendix) that make the book, in Thompson's words 'ill-organized, involuted and repetitive'. A great deal of the sustained and explicatory analogical analysis of biological and social evolution that gives the original conception its cohesiveness was jettisoned in the interests of what Caudwell must have felt was a more pervasive Marxist analysis. The reader might well turn to the Appendix now in order to get a representative sample of this earlier version, as well as textual evidence of the disruptive influence of the *Studies* on *Illusion and reality* as we now have it.

Caudwell must have read even faster than he wrote. The sources for *Illusion and reality* are, as we have seen in E. P. Thompson's breakdown of disciplines, wide and numerous. Even if a competent enough commentator could be found, it would require a large volume to cover comprehensively the ground that went into Caudwell's search for a composite picture of the interdependence of art and science within the human imagination. Apart from Marx and Freud, whose dual influence affords the structuring principle of *Illusion and reality* (a structure with which I want to deal separately in the next section), Caudwell drew upon a host of modern thinkers. These include the philosophers Bergson, Spengler, Whitehead, Russell and Wittgenstein; the anthropologists of the Cambridge School; the psycholinguistic ethnographers such as Sapir and Malinowski; the various other schools of psychology (Adler, Jung, Rivers); and of course every book he could lay his hands on with regard to evolution. It was in the last context that he discovered a precedent, if not a model, in A. C. Haddon's *Evolution in art*. Although there is little in common between the two books, Haddon was a biologist who purported to study 'the artistic results of a people's relation to their environment'.[26]

90

There is, then (when one considers the sheer coverage of his project), a fundamental difficulty of knowing where to begin amidst all this erudition; but if we remember Paul Beard's remark — that Caudwell sought to unite the 'strands' of science and art — then this affords an overall structure to our investigation. It is with such a quest in mind that I wish to begin by discussing two books which are *not* in Caudwell's bibliography, but which, I feel, may have greatly impressed the young Caudwell (or, if you like, the young poet Sprigg) and in which we may detect the germ of his future project.

I recorded earlier in this study the fact that Caudwell had written to Beard on 21 December 1934 telling him of his reading of 'psycho-analytic theories of the unconscious (particularly Baudouin)' and a brief survey of this book will indicate why the young poet/scientist was impressed. Baudouin, remarking that the 'new psychology would almost seem to have been especially designed to explain the poet', sets out to provide a *scientific* approach to poetic symbolism. His first chapter, 'The laws of the imagination', discusses extensively the symbolic 'laws' of dream and those of poetry, and acknowledges 'Freud's supreme service'. It was here that Caudwell must have been introduced to Ribot and Rignano, whose work Baudouin cites in his search for 'a mutual understanding between art and science'. In his third chapter he discusses the sublimation of instincts as revealed in poetic imagery and places this within the wider realm of human evolution.

> Even the skeleton of a Plato retains a vestige of the ancestral tail. This is the sign of evolution, and the evolution of lower instincts into higher mental manifestations need not disturb our self-esteem any more than it is disturbed by the biological evolution from lower animals to man. Who ever accepts the fact of bodily evolution, must accept mental evolution as well. Such writers as Nietzsche and Freud, who have endeavoured to sketch 'the genealogy of morals' and of mental life, setting out from the primitive instincts, have merely drawn the psychological inferences of the theory of evolution — though they have often done so in a paradoxical and aggressive fashion.[27]

The 'psychological inferences of the theory of evolution' became, particularly in the first version of his book, of prime importance to Caudwell. It was from Baudouin's book too, I believe, that Caudwell got the idea for writing his verse-drama *Orestes*. In the course of his discussion of Verhaeren's psychological dramas, which are modern lyrical renderings of Oedipal themes, Baudouin advises that the poet need only be 'sincere in his lyricism, in order to imbue with life those 'monsters' which modern psychology has shown to be slumbering in the depths of our subconscious'. Caudwell paid close attention to Baudouin's discussion and took the trouble to follow up the latter's references to the work of Paulhan.

Although, again, not listed in his bibliography to *Illusion and reality* it is hard to believe that Caudwell did not look at I. A. Richards's *Science and poetry* (1926). This was reviewed by T. S. Eliot in the same issue of *The Dial* as the young Sprigg saw in print his one and only published poem.[28] Considering his scientific interests at this time (1927), he must have been attracted by the title alone. Richards's book (published in the popular 'Psyche' series, some titles of which appear in Caudwell's bibliography) discusses the function and future of poetry in a world of failing belief brought about mainly through scientific advance. *Science and poetry* utilised and abridged many of the ideas from Richards's earlier works, *The meaning of meaning* (1923) and *Principles of literary criticism* (1924) and there are considerable similarities of interest between Richards's Arnoldian vision and Caudwell's underlying premisses.

A possible threat to poetry, its possible extinction, may have come about, Richards feels, because of the change in man's 'world-picture', a transference from 'the Magical View of the world ... the beliefs underlying ritual' to the scientific. The magical viewpoint developed inside the social group had given life 'a shape, a sharpness and a coherence that no other means could easily secure'. And what has modern man evolved to replace this 'magical' world-view that helped primitive man to tame and come to terms with his environment by making it signify? Modern man has science, but science cannot fulfil the emotional need of man's nature; 'it cannot tell us what we are or what this world is' mainly because many of these questions are not really questions at all. They are, in Wittgensteinian terms, 'pseudo-questions', and in Piaget's terminology, appeals for assurance rather than demands for scientific exactitude. If science cannot answer these questions, neither can philosophy or religion in the modern world. The result of this fractured belief-system will be a 'biological crisis' unless poetry can fulfil the function of giving 'order and coherence, and so freedom, to a body of experience'.

Poetry *can* do this and yet not conflict with scientific truth, because 'it is not the poet's business to make true statements ... which is why some mathematicians cannot read it'. Just as Caudwell points up religion's pretence to 'symbolic' (i.e. referential) truth, so Richards insists that we must 'cut our pseudo-statements free from belief, and yet retain them, in this released state, as the main instruments by which we order our attitudes to one another and to the world'. In this modern defence of poetry, Richards emphasises humanity's psychological need for both intellectual knowledge (science) and emotional attitude (poetry) in a way similar to Caudwell's epistemological halves that together signify's man's universe.

The better known *Principles* which Caudwell does cite in his bibliography dealt with many of the concerns that *Science and poetry* presented in abridged form. It is important to remind ourselves here that Richards, in the *Principles*, set out to rescue aesthetics from post-Kantian idealism and establish a materialist, a *scientific* foundation for the discussions of any work of art. It may not be altogether clear, hidden behind the paraphernalia of diagrams and discussion of nerve-systems, but Richards's book concerns itself in a fundamental way with poetry's function within human evolution. Put crudely (and the author is guilty of doing such himself), the poem presents a stimulus to which there is a complex response by the human organism. In the chapter 'Art, play, and civilization,' we can hear echoes of the theme of 'biological crisis' that was noted above in *Science and poetry*:

> Nor is Art, as by way of corollary is sometimes maintained, a thing which had its function in the youth of the world, but with the development of Science becomes obsolete. It may very possibly decline and even disappear, but if it does a biological calamity of the first order will have occurred. Nor again is it something which may be postponed while premillennial man grapples with more immediate problems. The raising of the standard of response is as immediate a problem as any, and the arts are the chief instrument by which it may be raised *or lowered*.[29]

The 'response' required by an imaginative work of art, a poem in this instance, is one, not of intellectual satisfaction, but of 'emotional accommodation and adjustment'. The attitudinal response to a poem in Richards's system, emotional resolution without overt action, owes something, as we shall see shortly, to anthropological discussions of ancient ritual, a source that Caudwell was to use also. And, like Caudwell after him, Richards insists that the reading of imaginative literature is no mere 'phantom aesthetic state'; that, in Caudwell's terms, although we should not confuse the 'mock world' of the poem with reality, it will have a bearing on any future dealings with reality. It will have, as Arnold maintained, a bearing on life, and will be in this sense an agent for change. Here is Richards on this aspect of the function of art:

> It is not the intensity of the conscious experience, its thrill, its pleasure or its poignancy which gives its value, but the organization of its impulses for freedom and fullness of life ... The after-effects, the permanent modifications in the structure of the mind, which works of art can produce, have been overlooked. No one is ever quite the same again after any experience; his possibilities have altered in some degree. And among all the agents by which 'the widening of the sphere of human sensibility' may be brought about, the arts are the most powerful, since it is through them that men may most co-operate and in these experiences that the mind most easily and with least interference organizes itself.[30]

An important aspect of Richards's book was what Baudouin called the 'psychological inferences of the theory of evolution'. Caudwell was to move to a position in which economic relations dictate the way that 'men most co-operate', but he nevertheless maintained that the arts are the 'most powerful' agency in the search for 'freedom and fullness of life'.

That there are points of similarity between Caudwell's system and Richards's theoretical premises seems self-evident, but the question of direct influence is more problematic. It was noted above that Caudwell had written to his friend Beard that although there was 'a similarity in many parts' between his 'views' and those of Ogden and Richards, he had 'only just read their book'. As we have already seen from the short discussion of the manuscript of 'Verse and mathematics', Caudwell was working out his own theory of the symbolic function within biological and social evolution and had already been introduced to many of the thinkers

— Wittgenstein, Rignano, Ribot, Bergson — that Ogden and Richards were to cite in support of their hypotheses. It is not so much (as one commentator has suggested), that 'Caudwell's theory is a faithful reproduction of Richards' views', as that Caudwell found in Richards a confirmation of some of the 'principles' he himself was forming out of his reading.. It was in this sense, I think, that *The meaning of meaning* which he had 'only just read' introduced him to many other theorists whose work he could call upon for the re-writing of his book.[31]

That Caudwell extended his bibliography by reading *The meaning of meaning* there seems little doubt. As suggested above, he came across some of the thinkers Ogden and Richards cite before reading their book, but it was from their book that he followed up references to Frege's book on mathematics, Vendrye's book, *Language*, Wundt's *Volkerpsychologie* and R. M. Eaton's *Symbolism and truth*, to name but a few. It may well have been this book, too, that introduced Caudwell to the work of Sapir and the psycholinguistic researches of Malinowski. Whatever new material Caudwell gathered from *The meaning of meaning* he must have been taken aback by the 'coincidence' (as he put it to Beard) of a great deal of his own theory and the more systematised approach of Ogden and Richards. He would have discovered, at the beginning of their chapter on 'The canons of symbolism', a discussion of the symbolic nature of mathematics that was close to his own ideas as conceived in 'Verse and mathematics'.. Scott Buchanan, who dedicated his book *Symbolic distance* (1932) to 'the authors of *The meaning of meaning*', had obviously given thought to Ogden and Richards's distinctions. His book, *Poetry and mathematics*, considered science, mathematics and poetry as analogical systems for an understanding of the universe. If Caudwell read this book he never mentioned it in letters, nor in his bibliography. The following will give an idea of Buchanan's position, a position which, in its formal outlines, bears comparison with Caudwell:

A purely formal and therefore literal statement is never possible. Pure poetry and pure mathematics, like pure music, are never expressed. The extreme case would be symbols expressing themselves, but even there the distinction would have to be made between symbols as things and symbols as ideas. Discourse is allegorical or nonsensical.

For the poet facts, like words, are symbols, and knowledge

consists in the insight into the symbolic relation. For him the world is a poem to be read. Its laws are the laws that govern his words. For the mathematician and scientist facts are to be referred to principles and causes. The allegorical correspondence of his ideas with the facts is the truth. The world is a network of relations which his formulae reflect.[32]

In *The meaning of meaning* Caudwell would have found a discussion of the importance of the 'sign-situation' in biological and psychological adaptation, and may very well have followed up Ogden and Richards's citation of Lloyd Morgan's *Habit and instinct* (Caudwell read it in the 1896 edition), which they offered as proof of the importance of the sign in the organism's adaptation to its environment (see p. 52ff.). Their discussion of the work of the linguist Vendryes, especially his chapter on 'Affective language', could well have supplied Caudwell with his notion and nomenclature for the 'antigrammatical' structure of a poetic text with regard to its reference. Vendryes maintains that 'it is by the action of affectivity that the instability of grammars is to a great extent to be explained'. Communicative utterances, he assures us, are not 'algebraic formulae' and in the poetic utterance, *par excellence*, 'affectivity always envelops and colours the logical expression of the thought'. If he had not discovered the work of Sapir by the time he read *The meaning of meaning* (the autumn of 1935), Caudwell would have found a good introduction to his work in Ogden and Richards's book. Most importantly, their discussion of Sapir's remarks on translation must have helped him formulate his own theory. In his book *Language* (Caudwell read it in the 1921 edition), Sapir maintains that in scientific discourse its essence is 'untinctured by the linguistic medium in which it finds itself', whereas 'Literature moves in language as a medium, but that medium comprises two layers, the latent content of language [and] ... the specific how of our record of experience.'[33]

Apart from the bibliographical aid and the introduction to numerous figures who were relevant to his own project, Caudwell would have been greatly impressed by the sheer coverage of this book that stressed the importance of symbolisation in human development. It proclaimed itself to be (in its subtitle) a 'Science' and attempted to trace humanity's communicative efforts from the emotional primitive cry to the signs of 'physics, the furthest interpretive effort of sign-situations'. It was this scientific methodology on which Richards purported to base his theoretical edifice that appealed to Caudwell primarily, rather than, as some commentators have pointed out, the particular influence of such notions as the affective and cognitive aspects of language. This latter aspect of the nature of language was very much a product of the work of the ethnographers and anthropologists, as we shall see in a moment. In any case, any debt which Caudwell owed Richards in this province would have been supplanted by his reading of N. B. Bukharin's essay, 'Poetry, poetics and the problems of poetry in the USSR'.[34] Bukharin developed a dialectical theory of the 'intellectual' and 'emotional' poles of language and, macrocosmically, applied this dialectic to the worlds of science and art. Caudwell may very well have been introduced to the *distinction* by Richards, but it was from Bukharin's *dialectic* relation that he built his argument of language as 'a dynamic social act'. There is always the dialectical relation between 'reality, the objective sector of the conscious field on the one hand, and on the other hand the subjective attitude towards it' (*Illusion and reality*, p. 159ff.).

Many of the 'dialectical' theories on culture and language, such as those constructed by Plekhanov and Bukharin, had their concrete foundation in the work of the field anthropologists. Ogden and Richards, particularly in their chapter 'The power of words', draw on such anthropological research as well, and in 'Supplement I' to their book, Bronislaw Malinowski provides a practical account of Ogden and Richards's theories based on his ethnographical researches in the Trobriand Islands. Caudwell was to find in Malinowski a powerful ally in his criticism of Freud's ethnocentricity, but the former's remarks on the nature and function of language were of prime importance to Caudwell's argument in *Illusion and reality*.

Malinowski insists that in any exploration of 'meaning' we must move from 'mere linguistics into the study of culture and social psychology'. Language, 'essentially rooted in the reality of [any given] culture', is not only a means of referential and emotive communication, but also 'a biological arrangement of enormous importance ... rooted deeply in the instinctive and physiological arrangement of the human organism'. In the following quotation we can detect a version of Caudwell's belief (in contradistinction to the early Wittgenstein) in the 'reality-producing' aspects of language:

Thus the consideration of linguistic uses associated with any practical pursuit, leads us to the conclusion that language in its primitive forms ought to be regarded and studied against the background of human behaviour in practical matters. We have to realize that language originally, among primitive, non-civilized peoples was never used as a mere mirror of reflected thought ... In its primitive uses, language functions as a link in concerted human activity, as a piece of human behaviour. It is a mode of action and not an instrument of reflection.[35]

Such a position is very close to Marx's viewpoint of language as practical consciousness and it is not surprising that he believed he had found in the work of the anthropologists a verification of many of his theoretical premises. Caudwell had read extensively in this field and it would not have been a gigantic, or a contradictory, step for him to accept Marxism as the ultimate explanation of the evolution of human affairs. He was familiar with a great many works on anthropology and the related descriptions of cultural sociology and linguistics. To mention Bucher, Cornforth, Durkheim, Frazer, Van Gennep, Levy-Bruhl, Malinowski, Mead, Morgan, Westermarck and Weston, would be to list the better-known figures recorded in his bibliography. But of all this extensive reading, it would be difficult to find a single book in this field which influenced his central concerns more than Jane Harrison's *Ancient art and ritual* (1913). The central concerns of Harrison's book could just as easily have prefaced *Illusion and reality*: 'The object of this book ... is to try and throw some light on the function of art, that is on what it has done, and still does to-day, for life'.

Indeed, this volume (without misrepresenting its content) could have been subtitled, 'A study in the social function of illusion'. Harrison united the social, psychological and even biological importance of symbolic projection in ancient art forms. Beginning with the fundamental assumption that 'art is in its very origin social ... human and collective', Harrison (although dealing primarily with 'primitive' art) stresses also the contemporary importance of her study. Since 'our own behaviour is based on instincts kindred to his [the primitive's]', by understanding the psychology underlying his 'illusions' we might come to understand all the better our own art which is after all only 'a later and more sublimated form, more detached form of ritual'. Her intelligent discussion of the psycho-social origin and function of 'mimesis' in primitive society is very similar to Caudwell's understanding of the concept of 'illusion'. Indeed, without having to go to Marx, Caudwell would have found a materialist basis for primitive psychology in Harrison's discussion of how primitive man attempted to symbolise his world within the realms of art, magic and religion. She quotes her colleague Frazer in support of the economic genesis of primitive ritual:

> The two great interests of primitive man are food and children. As Dr. Frazer has well said, if man the individual is to live he must have food; if his race is to persist he must have children. 'To live and to cause to live, to eat food and to beget children, these were the primary wants of man in the past, and they will be the primary wants of men in the future so long as the world lasts.'[36]

Her discussion of mimesis must have had a crucial influence on how Caudwell arrived at his notion of the 'mock-world of art'. Harrison insists that a representation is different from a copy. As Caudwell pointed out and Harrison asks rhetorically, 'why should anyone desire to make a copy of natural fact?' Rather, ritual and its off-shoot, art, are based on the desire to 'recreate an emotion'; as in Caudwell's analysis of the ancient harvest festival, although a 'stereotyped action', ritual is 'not wholly cut loose from practice'. Art, as Richards was to point out and Caudwell was to emphasise, is no mere transient aesthetic state but, as Harrison maintains, it 'is of real value to life in a perfectly clear biological sense; it invigorates, enhances, promotes actual, spiritual, and through it physical life'. She continues with a view of art that resembles closely the matrix of Caudwell's book — the belief in art's function as a prelude to action and thus change:

> Life is enhanced, only it is a different kind of life, it is the life of the image-world, of the imaginative ... It is a life we all, as human beings, possess in some, but very varying, degrees; and the natural man will always view the spiritual man askance, because he is not 'practical'. But the life of imagination, cut off from practical reaction as it is, becomes in turn a motor-force causing new emotions, and so pervading the general life, and thus ultimately becoming practical.[37]

And there are similarities of treatment, not only in the broad aspect of art's function within society, but also in *how* art functions.

An essential facet of poetic mimesis (as Richards and Caudwell were to remark) is that in order to present the emotion, to give it utterance, we must re-present it and that is why art contains '*an element of imitation*' (Harrison's emphasis). The referential aspect (in Richards's terms) is there so that (in Caudwell's terminology) reality may be 'stamped' with human emotion. But these poetic representations are not in any way to be mistaken for scientific fact, for 'reality', as the illusions of religion would like to be taken. The 'emotional power' of religion and art, their symbolic representations, are similar, but they also differ in a fundamental way:

> Primitive religion asserts her imaginations have objective existence; art more happily makes no such claim ... Religion has this in common with art, that it discredits the actual practical world; but only because it creates a new world and insists on its actuality and objectivity.[38]

Jane Harrison concludes her book with a vision of the future when, she believes, art will once more attain its social and collective purpose; that 'even today, when individualism is rampant' there remains positive hope for the future. 'Science', she tells us, 'has given us back something strangely like a World-Soul, and art is beginning to feel she must utter our emotion towards it'. Such a vision of the interdependence of science and art in a united *Weltanschauung* was Christopher Caudwell's personal goal as an artist and one of the structural principles of *Illusion and reality*. It is no wonder, then, that this little book, perhaps more than any other single volume, afforded Caudwell many of the constituent elements from which to build his own theoretical world, the hemispheres of which are symbolised by art and science.[39]

It is impossible to give with any accuracy the actual chronology of Caudwell's reading but, as the following extracts demonstrate, his eventual study of Marxism would have made it seem as if all the previous reading had been a preparation. The following, then, are meant simply as intellectual co-ordinates rather than a chronological survey.

In Baudouin he would have seen united his interest in science (particularly psychology) and art, and been introduced to a methodology:

They [psychoanalytic interpretations] show that we have laid the foundations of the psychology of art, of a science of aesthetics which shall be genuinely scientific ... a mutual understanding between art and science.[40]

The 'pre-Marxist' Caudwell would have found in Bergson — whose particular brand of 'finalism' sought to explain not only the arts, but physics, biology and modern developments in science — a teleology that was, in places, not far from the 'philosophy' he was finally to embrace:

> The history of the evolution of life ... shows us in the faculty of understanding an appendage of the faculty of acting, a more and more precise, more and more complex and supple adaptation of the consciousness of living beings to the conditions of existence that are made for them.[41]

In Ogden and Richards he would have found a comprehensive treatment of the area within which he himself was working in 'Verse and mathematics': that any epistemology must be based on a symbolic system, either the referential sign-systems of science and mathematics, or the emotive structure of a poetic sign. In this book, too, he would have found united the researches of the anthropologists and the findings of the psychologists, confirming what he called the 'genotypical' similarities of human beings that allow them to communicate emotionally. Here is Ogden and Richards's variation on this theme:

> The surface of society, like that of the sea, may, the anthropologist admits, be in perpetual motion, but its depths, like the depths of the ocean, remain almost unmoved. Only by plunging daily into those depths can we come in contact with our fellow-man; only — in the particular case of language — by foregoing the advantages of this or that special scientific symbol system, by drinking of the same unpurified stream, can we share in the life of the community ...
>
> We may smile at the linguistic illusions of primitive man, but may we forget that the verbal machinery on which we so readily rely ... was set up by him, and may be responsible for other illusions hardly less gross and not more easily irradicable?[42]

The anthropological linguistics of Sapir would have confirmed the contemporary relevance of such 'linguistic illusions', most especially language's social nature and its crucial role in perception and the structuration of the psyche:

> Human beings do not live in the objective world alone, nor alone in the world of social activity as ordinarily understood, but are very much at the mercy of the particular language which has become the medium of expression for their society. It is quite an illusion to imagine that one adjusts to reality essentially without the use of language and that language is merely an incidental means of solving special problems of communication or reflection. The fact of the matter is that the 'real world' is to a large extent unconsciously built up on the language habits of the group ...
>
> The understanding of a simple poem, for instance, involves not merely an understanding of the single words in their average significance, but a full comprehension of the whole life of the community as it is mirrored in the words, or as it is suggested by their overtones.[43]

Bronislow Malinowski moved even closer to a materialist view with regard to the structure of language when his researches led him to remark:

> The grammatical categories with all their peculiarities, exceptions, and refractory insubordination to rule, are the reflection of the makeshift, unsystematic, practical outlook imposed by man's struggle for existence in the widest sense of this word.[44]

And, finally, Jane Harrison discusses the subject-object relation, in terms that sum up the *raison d'être* of *Illusion and reality*. Striking an emotional attitude to the object, stamping reality with human emotion, leads to a desire for action, for change.

> The outside world, the other half, the object if we like, so to call it, acts upon us ... to put it roughly, we perceive something, and as we perceive it, so, instantly, we feel about it, towards it, we have emotion ... we *re*-act towards the object that got at us, we want to alter it or our relation to it.[45]

It is no great remove from the standpoints oulined above to a Marxist analysis of cultural artifacts as defined thus:

> Aesthetic phenomena are studied in a context of socio-historical processes, and in this way are regarded as part of a broad, 'civilizational' activity by which the species *homo sapiens* advances slowly to realize an innate potential.[46]

Such a definition would not please all Marxists, but it is, I believe, particularly apposite to Caudwell's central vision. It is now time to consider how he attempted to amalgamate the ideas of two seemingly antagonistic thinkers, Marx and Freud.

## Freud and Marx

Freud and Marx dealt essentially with the determining factors of human illusion. They purported to offer a science of humanity, a *Weltanschauung* that would explain human behaviour. At a time when other belief-systems were breaking down, 'Freudism' and 'Marxism' offered what seemed to many intellectuals to be integrated explanations of the machine of society. They each offered a different (some thought complementary) form of philosophical anthropology, delineating not only humanity's 'species essence' — teleological beings who help create their world through the mediation of symbolic structures — but also humanity's *potentiality*. Freud, the more pessimistic of the two thinkers — the 'species' defined, more or less, through its 'capacity for neurosis' — was optimistic enough to keep as a reminder, if not a motto, the belief that 'Where Id is there shall Ego be.' Both thinkers were fundamentally concerned with the investigation and recognition of necessary laws that would enhance human freedom.

Just as in Caudwell's reading we saw a progressive, almost inevitable, move toward a social, if not Marxist, explanation of human affairs, so too there seems an inner necessity, a logical progression, in his movement from biology, through psychology, to a consideration of human interaction and co-operation. The important link for Caudwell between 'man's' biological and sociological realities, is the unique formation of the human psyche and its manifold productions. In a word, Caudwell was interested in 'ideology' in all senses of that word, ranging from the formation of ideas given by sense-perception (what he called 'phantasy') to the sort of 'false consciousness' that he was eventually to scrutinise in his series of studies.[47]

If the unpublished manuscript that is discussed in the Appendix to this book tends to emphasise the former meaning of ideology, the peculiar human attribute of 'imagination' in evolution, and the *Studies* tend to accentuate the latter (the sociological emphasis rather than the biological), then *Illusion and reality* can be seen as an interim project. Broadly speaking, it is concerned with how human beings experiment and imaginatively project their desires on reality, and how such art-forms can become an ideological force. In any move from biology to sociology one must confront the majestic figure of Freud, whose theories stand at the gateway leading from biological being to social man. For Caudwell such a synthesis was not consciously sought after, but was, rather, an adaptation of a thinker who had fascinated him long before his reading of Marx.

Like others of his generation, Caudwell could not have escaped the attraction that Freud held, and it was a question of amalgamation and modification (sometimes only a difference in nomenclature) rather than any total rejection of the analyst's views. There is evidence to suggest that Caudwell, as is the case with most introspective young men, came to psychology and particularly psychoanalysis through an analysis of self. In some important respects his renunciation, or attempted modification, of the 'bourgeois individual psychology' of Freud, and the search for a social psychology that would support his new *Weltanschauung*, is a reflection of his own private drama. It parallels his metamorphosis from a 'bourgeois' poet concerned with Eros and Thanatos to communist spokesman on ideological matters.

As we have seen already, he had in his creative work, most particularly in *Orestes* and *This my hand*, made an attempt to mix the social sphere with that of the psychological and shared such a creative synthesis with many contemporaries, most notably Auden and Upward. But, as they always do, these artistic syntheses reflected (and gave rise to) more purely social or ideological concerns. Auden put his finger on many of these important aspects:

> Both Marx and Freud start from the failures of civilization, one from the poor, one from the ill. Both see human behaviour determined, not consciously, but by instinctive needs, hunger and love. Both desire a world where rational

choice and self-determination are possible ... Marx sees the
direction of the relations between outer and inner world
from without inwards, Freud vice versa. Both are therefore
suspicious of each other. The socialist accuses the psychologist of caving in to the status quo, trying to adapt the
neurotic to the system, thus depriving him of a potential
revolutionary: the psychologist retorts that the socialist is
trying to lift himself by his own boot tags, that he fails to
understand himself, or the fact that the lust for money is
only one form of the lust for power; and so that after he has
won his power by revolution he will recreate the same conditions. Both are right. As long as civilization remains as it
is, the number of patients the psychologist can cure are very
few, and as soon as socialism attains power, it must learn
to direct its own interior energy and will need the psychologist.[48]

It was, as we shall see, Caudwell's use of such concepts as
'instinctive needs' and 'interior energy' that led to his brand of
Marxism being judged heretical.

Auden was not the only intellectual to apply the ideas of Marx
and Freud to the welfare of society. Alasdair Browne, a psychologist who wrote articles for *Left Review*, is typical in his belief in
communism as a form of salvation from neurosis.[49] Alluding to
Marx's Eleventh Thesis that it is *the world* that needs to change,
and noting that a professor at the Moscow Institute of Mental
Hygiene 'could not find a case of manic-depressive insanity to
show his students after three months search', Browne remarks:

There can be little doubt that the direct revolutionary
approach has already proved itself in the one country where
the experiment has been tried ... The rate of incidence of
neurosis, psychosis, and feeble-mindedness is rising in
Europe and America, and has risen every year since statistics
were kept. In the Soviet Union it seems to be falling.[50]

There was widespread faith in the great 'experiment' (notice
that Auden does not say 'if' but '*as soon as* socialism attains power'),
a belief that the new society would assure freedom from neurosis.
Freud, although contributing greatly to knowledge of the 'inner
world', the subject, was thought to have neglected the object, the
environment. This was essentially Caudwell's position, and

despite his debt to Freud he felt he had to break with him when it came to the concept that informs most, if not all, of his work — the idea of 'freedom'. Society, 'civilisation', does not cripple the 'free' instincts but, rather, is the very medium whereby man realises true freedom as a social being. There is not enough space here to discuss or elaborate on how Caudwell 'read' Freud, but as the discussion immediately following will demonstrate, there are many instances where his own theory of conflict as creative principle varies very little from that of the psychoanalyst.

We will remember that a key function of art in *Illusion and reality* was that of helping adapt man's instinctual desires to the necessity of the environment. Caudwell's theory belongs, as do those of Darwinian species antagonism, Marxian dialectics and Freud's inner antagonism, to a contradictory principle that creates a dynamics of progress. He opens his 'The psyche and phantasy' chapter by remarking that the 'contradiction' which generates poetry is part of the broader contradiction which drives on society, 'the contradiction between man's desires and Nature's necessity'. A little later he attempts to distinguish his sense of 'conflict' from that of Freud's:

> The neurotic conflict is a real thing and Jung and Freud are right when they see the germs of it in all civilised beings. But they are wrong in supposing it to be a pathological product of civilisation which would be removed if only we could do away with civilisation. The conflict between man's instincts and environmental reality is precisely what life is, and all the products of society — hats, art, science, houses, sports, ethics and political organisation — are adaptations evolved to moderate and cure that conflict. Since the successful issue of this conflict is freedom, it is nonsense to talk of these adaptations as crippling freedom *qua* adaptations ... It is therefore pointless to ask oneself, as Freud does, whether civilisation is worth the price one pays for it in the frustration and crippling of the instincts, for it was precisely to moderate and lessen the frustration and crippling of the instincts by the *environment* that civilisation was evolved.[51]

Caudwell continues: '[the] elaborate superstructure of society' was constructed by man 'to *sublimate*, in Freudian nomenclature, to *resolve*, in ours, the contradiction between his environment and his instincts'.

This passage seems typical enough, when we remember the progression of Caudwell's reading and thought, in seeing the 'splendid edifice' of the superstructure in terms of evolution, or of a specifically human adaptation to the environment. And the fundamental question for Caudwell here is whether we see such cultural projections as sublimations that result from the un-freedom of repression, or, as he would have it, as resolutions in the ongoing evolutionary process toward freedom. In his study called 'Love', based on biological/sociological distinctions — 'love is man's name for the emotional element in social relations' — we hear, stated unequivocally, Caudwell's fundamental dis-agreement with Freud: that his ideological stance 'inverts the process of evolution'. In 'Love', and again in his essay 'Freud', Caudwell considers what he calls Freud's various 'mind deities' ('eternal Eros', the Id, and so on) in terms of other symbolisations of the bourgeois conception of liberty, such as Rousseau's 'natural man', for example.[52]

In his attempt to symbolise 'the inner structure of ... neuro-logical behaviour', Caudwell believes that Freud set up a system based on an 'eternal dualism' which *'cannot* be resolved' (Caudwell's emphasis). Such a dualism is, Caudwell believes, just an ideological variation on previous human projections; it can be traced in aspects of barbarianism, through Zoroastrianism, to elements in Christianity. Psychology, says Caudwell, 'must be extracted from sociology' because the social relations that came about through the changing modes of production are prior to the 'organism' and 'determine its consciousness and will'. Most importantly (and here his remarks reflect the transitions of his own intellectual interests), in any investigation of human development one must distinguish between biological matters and those of psychology and sociology:

The innate responses of an organism, the so-called instincts, as such are unconscious, mechanical, and unaffected by experience. Psychology therefore is not concerned with them, for they are the material of physiology. Psychology, in its study of consciousness or unconsciousness, can only have for its material all those psychic contents that results from the *modification* of responses by experience. It is this material that changes, that develops, that is distinctively human, that is of importance, and psychology should and in practice does ignore the *unchanging* instinctual basis as a cause.[53]

These remarks, recalling Caudwell's emphasis in the earlier version of his book, that what is 'distinctively human is the nature of man's adaptation, ideologically and socially mediated, instead of genetically implanted', help clarify a central question concerning the nature of his Marxism which shall be taken up presently. But before examining the problematic of Caudwell's modification of Freud into his 'new world-view', we might do well to examine briefly a Freudian text which helps, paradigmatically, to represent Caudwell's transformation of his earlier debt to Freudian ideas on culture.

It was noted above (in the quotation from the study 'Love'), that despite Freud's valuable contribution to the study of human behaviour, Caudwell believed that he had inverted the process of evolution. In *The future of an illusion* (Vienna 1927), where Freud had 'returned to the cultural problems which had fascinated [him] long before', he contemplates the nature of human illusion as an aspect of man's feeling of helplessness in regard to his environment. Freud remarks that 'what is characteristic of illusions is that they are derived from human wishes' and he continues:

> Thus we call a belief an illusion when a wish-fulfillment is a prominent factor in its motivation, and in doing so we disregard its relations to reality, just as the illusion itself sets no store by verification.[54]

Now aspects of this statement are close to Caudwell's (and Richards's and the anthropologists's) notions that in verbal art the referential illusion of the poem 'sets no store by verification'; but having taken this into account, Caudwell would object that 'we can disregard its relations to reality'. Although agreeing with Freud about the illusory nature of religion,[55] Caudwell, as evident from the nature of his whole enterprise, regarded illusion through imaginative experiments as being a key factor in human *evolution*. Freud put great store on 'scientific work' as 'the only road which can lead us to a knowledge of reality outside ourselves', for having achieved such knowledge 'we can increase our power and arrange our life'.[56] Caudwell believed that 'scientific work' was only half of the human endeavour; that there is a place for imaginative experiment, or illusion, in humanity's dealings with reality. The transitory illusion of art (not the 'delusion' of religion), by projecting 'human wishes' on reality, helps modify man's response to it and can inspire the desire for changing it. In the words of Brecht: 'Reality, however complete, has to be altered by being turned into art, so that it can be seen to be alterable and be treated as such.'

Although distinguishing the illusions of art from the 'obsessional neurosis' of religion, Freud nevertheless sees its role as compensatory rather than an element in the evolutionary process that makes (for Caudwell) the biological species 'distinctively human':

> As we discovered long since, art offers substitutive satisfactions for the oldest and still most deeply felt cultural renunciations, and for that reason it serves as nothing else does to reconcile a man to the sacrifices he has made on behalf of civilisation.[57]

But for Caudwell it is not a question of 'renunciation' or 'sacrifice' in the face of 'truly' free instincts; art is part of the ideological process that helps the genotype *become* human, become free, by helping modify the 'so-called instincts' in terms of the necessity of the environment. It is not a question of repressed, or sublimated freedom, but its very realisation. Marx had said that Hegel's system was 'turned on its head' and that he had only turned it 'right side up'. This is what Caudwell felt he was doing to 'the great investigator', Freud; this inversion is perhaps encapsulated in Caudwell's belief that artistic artifacts could, in a very important sense, be 'an illusion of the future'.

A great many Freudians would argue that Caudwell's understanding of Freud was not comprehensive enough,[58] just as many Marxists believe that his understanding of Marx was insufficient. Whatever our opinion is of this indictment (whether or not he fell 'between two stools'), it is certain that his attempted amalgamation of the two thinkers in *Illusion and reality* was one of the first such comprehensive treatments. And in his emphasis on the role of the subject to effect change, to reshape reality through an 'inner desire', he opened up a debate within Marxism that still has contemporary relevance.

We must now turn to his later, but more crucial reading of the other 'great investigator', Marx. A fundamental problem in discussing his use of Marx is the question as to how he got hold of some of the texts which seem to have influenced him, yet were not readily available until after his death. Consider, for example, Caudwell's belief that aesthetic objects are so only due to the intermediacy of social signs, that it is 'language which makes us consciously see the sun, the stars, the rain and the sea', that a 'sun-set is a social event'. Compare this with Marx's remarks in the *Economic and philosophical manuscripts* of 1844 — not easily available until comparatively late — that 'the senses of the social man are other senses than those of the non-social man'. One assumes that Caudwell read sections from Marx's early work in various periodicals and was introduced to selections from the complete canon by reading Emile Burns's *A handbook of Marxism* (1935), which contained extracts 'selected so as to give the reader the most comprehensive account of Marxism possible within the limits of a single volume'. And he would have supplemented such reading with books such as Plekhanov's *Fundamental problems of Marxism* (cited in his bibliography), where he would have read in the chapter on 'Base and culture' the following remarks so important to his own theory:

> In the sphere of the ideology of primitive society, art has been studied better than any other branch ... testifying in the most unambiguous and convincing manner to the soundness ... of the materialist explanation of history.[59]

Plekhanov surveys such a study of primitive art — taking in, for example, Bucher's theory that 'the origin of poetry is to be sought in work' — in terms that are readily recognisable in the early parts of *Illusion and reality*. It is more than likely that it was in this book, too, that Caudwell was introduced, and fastened on to, the theory of 'the illusion of the epoch'. In comparing Marx's system to that of Hegel's (in his chapter entitled 'The psychology of the epoch'), Plekhanov notes that the 'inversion' of Hegelianism 'did not prevent Marx from recognising the action, in history, of the "spirit" as a force whose direction is determined at any given time and in the final analysis by the course of economic development'. He continues: 'That all ideologies have one common root — the psychology of the epoch in question — is not hard to understand; anyone who makes even the slightest study of the facts will realize that.'[60] The 'one common root' that Caudwell chose to concentrate on (some would say, became obsessed by) was that of the illusion of freedom. But a 'common root' does not deny complexity and of course it is not a question of any one single illusion, since bourgeois ideology manifests itself in multiple ways; and, besides, although elements of the ideology of a particular era *may* be detectable in the verse of that era, the relation is never as direct and schematic as Caudwell's 'notorious table' (see pp. 117–22) represents it. Bemused, one feels, by his own ingenuity ('Bourgeois poetry is individualistic because it expresses the collective emotion of its era'), it is not so much that what Caudwell says is *wrong*, but rather that his discussion is too general to be considered as literary criticism. For example, in 'The period of primitive accumulation',[61] in discussing 'the depth with which Shakespeare moved in the bourgeois illusion' at this stage — a period of 'unbounded self-realisation' — we get some shrewd insights. Thus, even that scoundrel Parolles fits the ideological mould: 'Simply the thing I am/Shall make me live.' Similarly, when Caudwell sees the 'lawlessness'[62] of this period of expansion reflected in the 'absolute individual will' attempting to override all other wills which, playing against necessity, must ultimately end in tragedy, he may offer a methodological framework for Elizabethan tragedy but he is far from explaining the *familial* battle of wills in *King Lear*. However, to be fair to Caudwell (and here I agree with E. P. Thompson) to regard him as a literary critic is to look for his weaknesses rather than his strengths. I suggested earlier in this study that these chapters (Chapters 4–6 of *Illusion and reality*), represent an incursion into Caudwell's discussion of poetry's function within the realm of ideology, and it is on this latter aspect which I want to concentrate.

Caudwell's reading of Marx supplied him not only with an integrated *Weltanschauung* but a rhetorical voice. Throughout *Illusion and reality* we hear echoes of Engels and Marx, as when Caudwell applies their analysis to a different sphere of the ideological superstructure. Thus where Marx comments on the nature of religion in the 'Contribution to the critique': 'Religious suffering is at the same time an *expression* of real suffering and a *protest* against real suffering ... It is the opium of the people.' In Caudwell's text this becomes:

> The modern thriller, love story, cowboy romance ... form the real *proletarian* literature of today ... It [this literature] is at once an expression of real misery and a protest against that real misery ... It is the opium of the people.[63]

This is only one of countless examples that could be cited to show how Marx's ideas and rhetoric permeate Caudwell's discourse as the young man hurried to marxify his earlier version. One of Caudwell's early commentators[64] suggested that Marxism had furnished Caudwell with a new language in which to think he was speaking figuratively, but any reader of *Illusion and reality* may discern for himself just how literally such a statement might be taken.

Over and above this attraction to the rhetorical flourishes of Marx and Engels, Caudwell discovered a comprehensive theoretical language that afforded him a structure in which he could situate his various interests. A key text for this structuring principle, and one which forms the foundation of any discussion of Marxism, is Marx's Preface to 'A contribution to the *Critique of political economy*'. Since it is germane to the rest of our discussion it is worth quoting a good portion of it here. Marx reflects on his earlier findings:

The general result at which I arrived and which, once won, served as a guiding thread for my studies, can be briefly formulated as follows: In the social production of their life, men enter into definite relations that are indispensable and independent of their will, relations of production which correspond to a definite stage of development of their material productive forces. The sum total of these relations of production constitutes the economic structure of society, the real foundation, on which rises a legal and political superstructure and to which correspond definite forms of social consciousness. The mode of production of material life conditions the social, political and intellectual life process in general. It is not the consciousness of men that determines their being, but, on the contrary, their social being that determines their consciousness ... With the change of the economic foundation the entire immense superstructure is more or less rapidly transformed. In considering such transformations a distinction should always be made between the material transformation of the economic conditions of production, which can be determined with the precision of natural science, and the legal, political, religious, aesthetic or philosophic — in short, ideological forms in which men become conscious of this conflict and fight it out. Just as our opinion of an individual is not based on what he thinks of himself, so can we not judge of a period of transformation by its own consciousness; on the contrary, this consciousness must be explained rather from the contradictions of material life, from the existing conflict between the social productive forces and the relations of production.[65]

This statement, vague as it is, can be considered as the *locus classicus* of the materialist conception of history. The essential elements here — that the consciousness of human beings is a social product corresponding, in however an oblique way, to the productive relations (the 'economic base'), a set of circumstances which in turn give rise to various ideological discourses — are expanded and modified by Marx and Engels throughout their work.

We have already seen how Caudwell was entranced by one aspect of the 'illusion' of ideology as expanded by Marx in *The German ideology* and popularised by Plekhanov in his discussion of the 'psychology of the epoch'. In Marx's text he would also have found a basis for his theory that language is constitutive of consciousness. This is reflected in the important role that Caudwell gives language in the structuration of the psyche, making the psyche, in the final analysis, a 'social product'. In *The German ideology* Marx argues that 'language *is* practical consciousness that exists also for other men ... language, like consciousness, only arises from the need, the necessity, of inter-course with other men'.[66] Such an approach has important ramifications on any search for a social psychology as we shall see later in this discussion.

At the same time he and Engels were collaborating on *The German ideology* (1845), Marx sketched out his *Theses on Feuerbach*, a text which Engels described retrospectively as 'the brilliant germ of the new world outlook'. It has already been remarked upon how many of the radical intellectuals embraced the Eleventh Thesis — that the essential task was to *change* the world — as a motto. And although such a desire lies at the centre of Caudwell's poetics — experimental illusion can lead to a desire for a new reality — Caudwell was careful to consider as well two of the other theses which modify the purely determining factor of the material base and accentuate the role of the subject. In the First Thesis Marx criticised 'all hitherto materialism' because 'reality, sensuousness, is conceived only in the form of the object of *contemplation,* but not as *human sensuous activity, practice,* not subjectively' (Marx's emphases). And, in the Third Thesis, he stated that the materialist doctrine that 'men are products of circumstances and upbringing, and that, therefore, changed men are products of other circumstances and changed upbringing, forgets that it is men who change circumstances and that it is essential to educate the educator himself'. Such changes help modify the seemingly 'one-way' determinism of the base on the ideological superstructure as suggested in the 'Contribution to the *Critique*' quoted above. Here we have the counterbalance of the action of human beings on their environment, an interaction which allows for the subject's role in the making of 'reality'.

Caudwell believed that 'men', especially poets, could 'change circumstances' by altering their fellows' conscious outlook. As Alick West pointed out in his review of *Illusion and reality*, Caudwell's seemingly outrageous statement near the beginning of his book, that 'poetry is something economic', can be understood in the sense that it helps transform instinctive into conscious energy. In Caudwell's system the 'instincts' are transformed into emotions as part of the evolutionary process, bringing them closer to directed thought and the aims of consciousness. This is why poetry for Caudwell is, in a literal sense, part of the process of evolution:

> The tool adapts the hand to a new function, without changing the inherited shape of the hands of humanity. The poem adapts the heart to a new purpose, without changing the eternal desires of men's hearts.[67]

If, in the interaction of the subject and object in the process of evolution, of becoming, Freud 'chooses the subject' (Caudwell) which leads to idealism, then a great many Marxists choose the object which results in an equally unsatisfactory mechanical materialism. Caudwell's epistemology is based on a dialectical interplay of subject and object, of inner desire and outer reality, and this had profound critical consequences for his version of Marxism.

Although Marx's ideas and rhetoric exerted a decisive influence on Caudwell, it is my belief that he may have come to Marxism initially through the work of Engels, who must have held a special attraction for the young Caudwell, especially since both shared similar scientific interests. In *Anti-Duhring* Engels provided the origins and principles of historical materialism with a clarity that made it one of the most popular accounts of 'the new world outlook'. It was Engels who stressed dialectics within the field of materialism and applied it to various scientific fields, including that of evolution. Caudwell would have been drawn to the following passage, for example:

> An exact representation of the universe, of its evolution, of the development of mankind, and of the reflection of the evolution in the minds of men, can therefore only be obtained by the methods of dialectics with its constant regard to the innumerable actions and reactions of life and death, of progressive or retrogressive changes.[68]

Engels was wont to stress the evolutionary, teleological aspect of scientific socialism: After the socialisation of the means of production 'then for the first time man ... is finally marked off from the rest of the animal Kingdom ... It marks the ascent of man from the Kingdom of necessity to the Kingdom of freedom.'[69] The evolution towards freedom seemed almost as dear to Engels as it was to Caudwell, and it was from him (although he could have found the idea in Spinoza or Hegel) that he took the dictum which forms the epigraph to *Illusion and reality*: 'Freedom is the recognition of necessity'.

It was Engels (in his letter to Joseph Bloch) who stressed the interaction between the economic elements and the various ideological forms and who, in his letter to Franz Mehring, offered a definition of ideology that links the concept with psychological processes:

> Ideology is a process accomplished by the so-called thinker consciously, it is true, but with a false consciousness. The real motive forces impelling him remain unknown to him, otherwise it simply would not be an ideological process.[70]

In his study, 'Liberty: a study in bourgeois illusion', Caudwell conjoins Engels's ideas on the recognition of necessity and 'false consciousness' with the 'illusion of the epoch', which (as we have seen above) he took to be the idea of freedom:

> Like the neurotic who refuses to believe that his compulsion is the result of a certain unconscious complex, the bourgeois refuses to believe that his conception of liberty as a mere

deprivation of social restraints arises from bourgeois social relations themselves, and that is just the illusion which is constraining him on every side.[71]

Here we see Caudwell applying that key concept from Marx's 'Contribution to the *Critique*', how in fact a certain kind of being can determine consciousness. But as we have seen already, Caudwell was just as concerned, if not more so, to accentuate the subject's role, the dynamics of inner desire, in social evolution. In Caudwell's scheme art has an ideological role to play as an agency for change by experimenting imaginatively with 'reality'. As Plekhanov had taught him, although social being determines consciousness 'it does not follow that consciousness has no place in the historical progress of mankind'.

Caudwell was not the only intellectual to consider Freud's findings concerning consciousness within the realm of 'historical progress'. One of the most interesting and sustained attempts at a Marx–Freud synthesis in the 1930s and (although unknown to him) one which bears comparison to Caudwell's work, was that by Reuben Osborn.[72] Of particular importance to our discussion was Osborn's emphasis on the subject's interaction with the environment, the dialectic of inner compulsion and outer necessity in the production of ideology. John Strachey, a populariser of Marx's ideas whose brother, James, did a great deal to introduce Freud's theories to the English-speaking world, summarised the essential position in his introduction to Osborn's book:

> The principal conclusion to be derived from the study of psychoanalytic theory is, it seems to me, that the emergence of a particular type of consciousness — a particular set of political, religious, scientific, and miscellaneous opinions, a particular ideology, that is to say — must not be conceived of as the passive reflection of a given social environment. It must be conceived of rather as the interaction of the social environment with certain dynamic, subjective urges within man himself. This view, Mr. Osborn is able to show, is fully consonant with the outlook of Marx and Engels. Indeed, they would probably have severely characterized any other as mechanistic and undialectical.[73]

Osborn's book, unduly neglected as a pioneering work in the history of ideas, considers the 'reality of dream life' as a source of satisfaction denied to human beings in 'reality'. It remarks on the fact that instinctive impulses have a bearing on social designs, and that 'sublimations may be considered, therefore, as the main subjective sources of social progress'. Recognising that 'culture is ideologically slanted to justify class interests', Osborn attempts an equation of Freud's concept of 'rationalisation' with that of Engels's 'false consciousness'. While recognising that social being determines consciousness, he points out that the relationship of the ego to the external world is not merely one of passive reflection:

> The ego, in other words, does not only mirror reality for the id, but strives to reshape reality the better to serve the ends of the id. In this way, Freudian theory enriches the bare Marxist dictum about social reality determining consciousness.[74]

In pointing out the potential dialectical interplay of Freudian and Marxian ideas, Osborn maintained that materialism must 'conquer the realms of subjective life, hitherto left to the abstract mystifications of idealist philosophers'.[75] Although Caudwell would have eschewed what he would have here called the 'mythological' nomenclature, it was his search for a dialectical interplay of inner and outer forces, his attempt to 'conquer the realms of subjective life', which led eventually to the attack on his understanding of Marxism.

Maurice Cornforth, who launched the *Modern Quarterly* 'debate' on Caudwell's work in the early 1950s, while recognising Caudwell's criticism of Freud in the 'study', felt that for Caudwell to reject Freud entirely it would be necessary for him to 'scrap the greater part of *Illusion and reality*'. Cornforth's thorough critique of Caudwell's work — seeing it as essentially a 'biological-psychological account of society' — raises important issues that get to the heart of Caudwell's intention, although, in the final analysis, misunderstanding it. The following, for example, needs careful scrutiny:

> The whole idea of the genotype and the instincts is a piece of made-up idealist metaphysics. For it supposes that something exists within the organism — the genotype and the instincts — which is not susceptible to change; which is not born and modified and developed in the course of the life of the organism, but which precedes it and stamps its own pattern upon it.[76]

Cornforth regards this as 'a singularly reactionary theory [because] it teaches that human nature never changes, but remains "at bottom" always the same'. But Caudwell is *not* saying this: he is not suggesting that there is 'something ... within the organism ... which is not susceptible to change', something that is not 'modified'. It is the interaction with and modification of the common biological, physiological pre-human organism with regard to the environment which produces change, which produces '*human* nature'. Although there is a certain amount of ambiguity concerning his use of such concepts as 'the genotype' and 'the instincts' in *Illusion and reality*, Caudwell attempts to clarify them elsewhere. In 'Beauty', for example, he remarks that: 'Such simple responses to external or internal stimuli *change* from age to age, but, in relation to the rapid tempo of social life, there is a consistency about them which leads us to separate them as *hypothetical* entities' (*Further studies*, p. 90. My emphases). And in his essay, 'Consciousness', he links instinct and genotype together in the following way:

> Living responses or sensibility, including conscious mentation, consists of *potential* instinct, which is the whole sum of inborn responses to somatic stimuli or environmental stimuli. This is a purely *fictive* conception, but methodologically useful, like the 'genotype' in heredity (*Further studies*, p. 196. My emphases).

Although Caudwell is careless in his use of these terms — personifying at times the genotype by talking of its 'secret face' and its 'secret desires' — his intentions are clearer, in general, outside the covers of *Illusion and reality*. Even in the earlier manuscript of 'Verse and mathematics' he is careful to point out that 'the genotype is a pure abstraction ... one of Vaihinger's "as-ifs" ', because it is only due to the interaction with the environment that such potentiality of the organism is able to show itself. The genotype and the instincts are, in Caudwell's system, something like Kant's 'thing-in-itself', unknowable, but a necessary postulation, a necessary thesis in contradistinction to the antithesis of the social environment. E. P. Thompson, I think, has put Caudwell's notion of the genotype quite succinctly when he answered Cornforth's charge that Caudwell's theory is 'singularly reactionary'.

118

But, of course, Caudwell does not 'explain society and its development' in terms of the genotype ... for if he could have explained social development in this way, then no function would have been left for the arts. Nor is it correct that the genotype is synonymous with 'human nature'. The genotype gives us, rather, 'brute nature' — the nature of man as a brute, prior to his or her acquisition, through socialisation and culture, of humanity, or human nature ... [Moreover] it is clear that Caudwell intends the concept (or hypothesis) of the genotype to stand, not for human nature, but for pre-human nature, a common biological and instinctual ground, persisting relatively unchanged through historical time, prior to acculturation. So far from being a 'reactionary' thesis, which seeks to reduce all change to a timeless human nature, it emphasises that *everything* that is 'human' arises within society and culture.[77]

The essence of Cornforth's criticism was that Caudwell had set up a 'metaphysical dualism' which was anti-Marxian. But as we have seen above this was the very basis of Caudwell's critique of Freud — that the latter had postulated a 'dualism which *cannot* be resolved' — and it was Caudwell's project to work what he considered Freud's dualistic universe into a dialectic one. In this task he was greatly aided by K. N. Kornilov's 'Psychology in the light of dialectical materialism', which appeared in *Psychologies of 1930*, a book which is cited in Caudwell's bibliography. Kornilov stresses the second law of dialectics — 'the law of the mutual penetration of opposites' — as the groundwork for any Marxist psychology. The key concept here — one which is uppermost in Caudwell's epistemology and which he had picked up as much from Piaget as from dialectics — was that of interaction between the subject and the environment. Stressing the importance of dialectical theory with regard to 'the idea of evolution', Kornilov argued against those 'who hold the anti-dialectic, the metaphysical point of view', both the subjective psychology of Freudianism *and* the mechanical materialism of the other extreme, the physiologically-based Reflexology.

An important element in Kornilov's theory was his emphasis on the 'adaptive function of consciousness' and the role of imagination in human affairs. The unique position of the human being in the hierarchy of evolution is that he or she can dream of changing reality before the process itself and furthermore, this 'dream', this imaginative experiment, is part of the labour process because it is a guide to action. Kornilov quotes a paragraph from *Capital* to illustrate his point: it is a quotation which is also pertinent to the central aims of *Illusion and reality*.

> The spider performs an operation, akin to weaving, and the bee constructs its waxen cells in a manner which might well put to shame certain people — architects for instance. But the worst architect is distinguished from the finest bee in that, previous to constructing the cells in wax, he has just constructed them in his head. The results of the process of labour were already present before this process began, in the imagination of the worker.[78]

As we have seen already, art for Caudwell is one aspect of this imaginative faculty of humanity (science being its counterpart) which makes illusory experiments with reality that can have a lasting effect. Towards the end of his discussion of art's function (pp. 262–3) he summarises art's significance as being 'like a magic lantern which projects our real selves on the Universe and promises us that we, as we desire, can alter the Universe, alter it to the measure of our needs'.

A useful guideline to the above discussion of Caudwell's position within a Marxian view of culture is afforded by two essays by Raymond Williams in this area. Williams is a helpful commentator, because as a sympathetic 'outsider', his attempt to come to terms with a materialist aesthetic serves as an intelligent guideline to its evolution. In his *Culture and society* (1958) Williams, remarking on the ambiguity of the structure/superstructure relation as outlined by Marx in the text we have already examined, maintains, rightly, that Marx 'outlined, but never fully developed, a cultural theory'. Summarising the various embellishments made to Marx's outline by thinkers such as Engels, Plekhanov and Lenin, Williams concludes that although the economic base seems primary in any Marxist theory of culture, this was still 'an emphasis rather than a substantial theory'. It was on such an insubstantial theory that the Marxists of the twentieth century had to build.

There is also a great deal of truth in Williams's contention that a great many of the English 'Marxists' belonged to a tradition that came down to them from the Romantics (the poet as unacknowledged legislator), where culture is seen as 'ideally embodying the future', rather than being 'passively dependent on social change'. He poses the fundamental choices with regard to the social environment and art's role within it in the following way:

> Either the artists are passively dependent on social reality, a proposition which I take to be that of mechanical materialism, or a vulgar misinterpretation of Marx. Or the arts, as the creators of consciousness, determine social reality, the proposition which the Romantic poets sometimes advanced. Or, finally, the arts, while ultimately dependent with everything else, on the real economic structure, operate in part to reflect that structure and its consequent reality, and in part, by affecting attitudes to reality, to help or *hinder* the constant business of changing it.[79]

Although there is a good deal of the 'Romantic' attitude in Caudwell, it was essentially the third and last role of art in Williams's breakdown which attracted him. 'In part' he attempted to show how the 'bourgeois illusion' as manifested in the history of British poetry reflected 'the real economic structure'; but, more interestingly, he also attempted to demonstrate how art operates in, as Williams puts it, 'affecting attitudes toward reality' (close to Caudwell's very words) so that it may help stimulate the desire to change it. This latter role gives art an ideological role to play in achieving what Gorki called 'the desired, the possible'. Williams notes in his essay that there has been a tendency in English writers to find 'the desired, the possible in terms of the inner energy ... of which Caudwell wrote'. And while this position, Williams tells us, 'may be an improvement of Marx [it] would seem to deny his basic proposition about "existence" and "consciousness" '.

The question is whether such a position, based on the inter-action of subject and object, is a denial of Marx's meaning or a modification of the Marxist position, a modification that is based on other Marxist writings. In the light of the First and Eleventh Theses on Feuerbach (that materialism must take into account the active participation of the subject, and that human beings should strive to change their world rather than contemplating it), how are such primary Marxist goals to be carried through if consciousness, ideology, is irrevocably fixed, like a fly in amber, by the very infrastructure that is wished changed? To posit a form of consciousness that is determined by social being may very well be the primary factor in any Marxist social psychology, but once formed, that consciousness, prone to inner desires and impulses, wants to reshape reality, to change it, in Caudwellian terms, 'closer to its heart's desire'. There is, properly understood, nothing 'idealist' in such a position. To conceive of humanity's relation to the world as a reaction, a response, is not to deny the reality of objective factors. On the contrary, the relational, interactionist, model serves to confirm both the reality of the environment *and* humanity's modification of it.

In *Culture and society,* as we have seen, Williams had found 'Marxist theories of culture confused', but in *Marxism and literature* (1977) he approached the subject again, this time armed with the hopeful sign that 'Marxism ... has experienced at once a significant revival and a related openness and flexibility of theoretical development.' So much so that Williams could now read 'the English Marxists of the thirties differently, and especially Christopher Caudwell'. Yet this mention in a prefatory note is all the attention that Caudwell receives. This is especially disappointing, because the 'flexibility' of approach of which Williams speaks was already present in embryonic form in Caudwell's work, particularly the part played by language in the formation of consciousness, a social psychology based on what Caudwell called (after Marx) 'the great instrument' in human co-operation.

In his discussion of the need for a genuinely objective psychology based on sociological, not physiological or biological principles, Williams praises the work done by V. N. Volosinov, a theorist who disappeared during Stalin's purges and whose interests and methodology bear comparison with the kind of position Caudwell was attempting to establish.[80] Volosinov, too, based his social psychology on language, 'the social nature of the sign', and although he and Caudwell discourse in a different vocabulary — Volosinov using semiotic terminology — there are many similarities of approach to the question of language, consciousness, and their relation to ideology. For example, Volosinov's central premiss that consciousness is an entity where inner and outer signs meet and dialectically interpret and modify one another is a conception which is implicit throughout *Illusion and reality* and bears comparison with Caudwell's eccentric notion of 'the social ego'. Even in the unpublished manuscript that is examined in the

Appendix to this volume, Caudwell, with his strange nomenclature, was attempting to work out a theory of what Volosinov
would call the semiotically derived ideological content of
consciousness:

> Therefore the study of ideology is the study of private and
> public phantasy. Its private forms are accessible individually
> by introspection or interrogation. In its public form ... it is
> everything contained in a nation's language, its recorded or
> spoken science, religion, speculation and literature ... For
> general convenience we may call private phantasy, simply
> phantasy, and public phantasy, simply ideology. Naturally
> public phantasy is that part of private phantasy capable of
> projection, but the relation is a dialectic one. Ideology
> moulds phantasy and vice-versa.[81]

If we translate Caudwell's terminology and realise that what he
intended by 'phantasy' was the human imaginative faculty of
encoding what he called 'the photography of conscious percep-
ion', then we arrive at a position not far from Volosinov's.
Caudwell, too, saw that consciousness was not directly derived
from nature, but realises itself through communicable symbols
attained socially, the intermediacy of social signs. He never lost
sight of Marx's dictum in *The German ideology* that 'language *is*
practical consciousness', that language allows human beings,
unlike other species, to be 'practically' conscious.

Although Williams does not mention Volosinov's other main
work, *Freudianism: a Marxist critique*, it too has obvious relevance
to Caudwell's position in the context of Marxian exegesis. Indeed,
at the close of his first chapter Volosinov provides a summary of
modern ideological motifs — those of Bergson, Driesch and
Weissman, among others — that provides a useful framework for
Caudwell's own intellectual evolution and affords a focus on the
essential problematic of his amalgamation of Marx and Freud.
This was a movement of interest — as I hope this chapter has
demonstrated — away from the biological organism to human
specificity which is, in the final analysis, dependent on the
socialising of the psyche. Volosinov puts his position like this:

> The abstract biological person, biological individual — that
> which has become the alpha and omega of modern ideology
> — does not exist at all. It is an improper abstraction. Outside

society and, consequently, outside objective socioeconomic conditions, there is no such thing as a human being ... In order to enter into history it is not enough to be born physically. Animals are physically born but they do not enter into history. What is needed is, as it were, a second birth, a *social* birth. A human being is not born as an abstract biological organism but as a landowner or a peasant, as a bourgeois or a proletarian, and so on — that is the main thing. Furthermore, he is born a Russian or a Frenchman, and he is born in 1800 or 1900, and so on ... Not a single action taken by a whole person, not a single concrete ideological formation (a thought, an artistic image, even the content of dreams) can be explained and understood without reference to socioeconomic factors. What is more, even the technical problems of biology can never find [a] thoroughgoing solution unless biology takes comprehensive account of the social position of the human organism it studies.[82]

There is much here with which Caudwell agreed and tried to express. But rather than an 'improper abstraction', Caudwell believed that it was useful to postulate as a necessary fiction, a 'hypothetical entity', the concept of the 'biological person', which is of course, as Volosinov implies, a contradiction in terms. Obsessed by the concept of freedom in man's evolution, it must have seemed *necessary* for him to posit the concept of a 'thing' which, if 'left to itself', would be a slave both to its environment and to inner compulsion. However ambiguously he put it, there is no doubt that Caudwell believed with the Marx of the Sixth Thesis that *human* organisms are made by social relations, that 'the essence of man is not an abstraction in each separate individual [but is] rather the aggregate of social relations'. In the final analysis Caudwell's position is not all that far from that taken by Volosinov in the extract just quoted. Caudwell puts it like this:

When we speak of 'man' we mean the genotype or individual, the instinctive man as he is born, who if 'left to himself' might grow up into something like a dumb brute, but instead of this he grows up in a certain kind of society as a certain kind of man — Athenian, Aztec or Londoner ... Man cannot choose between being an artist or a scientist in a society which has neither art nor science; nor between biology and psychology where science is still no more than vague astrological superstition.

The genotype is never found 'in the raw'. Always it is found as a man of definite concrete civilisation with definite opinions, material surroundings, and education — a man with a consciousness conditioned by the relations he has entered into with other men and which he did not choose but was born into.[83]

Fortunately for us, Caudwell was 'born into' a society that allowed him to reflect on art and science, allowed him to 'choose ... between biology and psychology'. *Illusion and reality*, for all its flaws, is an index of an ingenious and prolific mind.

## Notes

1. See p. 75, for E. P. Thompson's remark about 'down-grading' *Illusion and reality*.

2. For a brief synopsis of 'Marxist' criticism in England before the 1930s, see Maynard Solomon (ed.), *Marxism and art: essays classical and contemporary* (New York, Alfred A. Knopf, 1973), p. 306. Solomon has also some shrewd remarks to make on Caudwell.

3. Raymond Williams, *Culture and society 1780–1950* (Harmondsworth, Penguin Books/Chatto & Windus, 1976), p. 262.

4. W. H. Auden, Review of *Illusion and reality*, *New Verse*, vol. XXV (May 1937), pp. 20–2. Auden had just recently returned from Spain, and had retired to the Lake District where he read Caudwell's book for review while working on his new poem, *Spain*. One of Auden's biographers feels that 'Caudwell's view of history and its relation to the action of individual men' had some influence on Auden's poem. See Humphrey Carpenter, *W. H. Auden: a biography* (London, Allen & Unwin, 1981), p. 217.

5. *Illusion and reality*, p. 197.

6. Marx's emphases. The subject-object relation informs a great deal of Caudwell's writing, most especially the *Studies*. See, for example, 'Reality', in *Further studies in a dying culture*, pp. 218–19, where the First and Eleventh Theses are conjoined in a definition of reality.

7. E. P. Thompson, 'Caudwell', in *The socialist register* (London, Merlin Press, 1977), p. 273.

8. This is no mere parochial interest. To give a representative selection, we have: Ogden and Richards, *The meaning of meaning*; Markey's *The symbolic process*; D'Alviella's *La Migration des symboles*; Brodetsky's *The meaning of mathematics*; Frege's *Grundgesetze der Arithmetik*; Russell and Whitehead's *Principia mathematica*; C. I. Lewis's *A survey of symbolic logic*; and Wittgenstein's *Tractatus logico-philosophicus*.

9. *Studies in a dying culture*, p. 192.

10. Paul Beard, 'Views and reviews: *Illusion and reality*', *The New English Weekly*, 30 September 1937, p. 411.

11. Alick West, 'On "Illusion and reality" ', *Communist Review* (7–13 January 1948), p. 6.

12. It would be misleading to suggest, however, that the book was received with universal sympathetic acclaim. An extremely negative review appeared, predictably enough, in *Scrutiny* where H. A. Mason called it 'tedious and unconvincing ... [that] for all the apparatus ... the book does not get anywhere' ('The illusion of cogency', *Scrutiny*, vol. VI, no. 4 (March 1938), pp. 429–33). See Francis Mulhern, *The moment of 'Scrutiny'* (London, Verso Editions, 1981) for a good appraisal of *Scrutiny* and its relation to Marxist exegesis.

13. Solomon (ed.), *Marxism and art*, p. 306.

14. David N. Margolies, *The function of literature: a study of Christopher Caudwell's aesthetics* (New York, International Publishers, 1969), p. 29.

15. Terry Eagleton, *Criticism and ideology: a study in Marxist literary theory* (London, Verso Editions, 1978), p. 21.

16. Thus: 'Pope perfectly expresses the ideals of the bourgeois class in alliance with a bourgeoisified aristocracy in the epoch of manufacture.' However, Caudwell's remarks on the *form* of the heroic couplet and its relation to the social structure of the time are far from being 'vulgar' Marxism.

17. Williams, *Culture and society*, p. 272.

18. J. Bronowski, *The visionary eye: essays in the arts, literature, and science* (Cambridge, Mass., MIT Press, 1978), p. vii. Ernst Cassirer's work is also of relevance here.

19. At one point in his discussion Caudwell states categorically that 'poetry is characteristically song', and it might as well be made clear at the outset that when he speaks of 'poetry' he has in mind that most ancient and abiding of literary forms, the lyric. To the extent that this is a weakness in his theory, it is one that he shares with many modern theorists, who, like him, partake in the legacy handed down by the Romantics.

20. *Illusion and reality*, p. 27. Henceforth all citations from Caudwell's book will be noted in parentheses within the body of the text.

21. David Craig (ed.), *Marxists on literature: an anthology* (Harmondsworth, Penguin Books, 1975), p. 55. See also Thomson's pamphlet *Marxism and poetry* (New York, International Publishers, 1946). He has remarked that the two great influences on his work were Engels's *Origin of the family* and Caudwell's *Illusion and reality*.

22. Such an approach to poetic texts is strikingly modern and bears comparison with recent semiotic theory, such as that of Michael Riffaterre in *The semiotics of poetry* (Bloomington, Indiana University Press, 1978).

23. F. C. Prescott, *Poetry and dreams* (Boston, Gorham Press, 1912).

24. *The tangled bank: Darwin, Marx, Frazer and Freud as imaginative writers* (New York, Atheneum, 1962), p. 6. Bertrand Russell commented on the ubiquity of 'evolutionism' in his philosophic essay, *Our knowledge of the external world* (1914). 'Evolutionism, in one form or another, is the prevailing creed of our time. It dominates our politics, our literature, and not least our philosophy. Nietzsche, Pragmatism, Bergson, are phases

in its philosophic development, and their popularity far beyond the circles of professional philosophers shows its consonance with the spirit of the age.'

25. It might be timely to remind ourselves here that although Caudwell changed the title of his book from the original 'Verse and Mathematics', he retained the subtitle 'A study of the sources of poetry', which should remind us that the nature of his project was not literary criticism.

26. Published in 'The contemporary science series' (London, Walter Scott, 1895). Caudwell read it in the 1914 edition. All other titles mentioned in this survey of his sources are listed in the bibliography to *Illusion and reality* unless specifically indicated otherwise.

27. Charles Baudouin, *Psychoanalysis and aesthetics* (London, Allen & Unwin, 1924), p. 111.

28. I. A. Richards, *Science and poetry* (London, Kegan Paul, Trench, Trubner & Co., 1926). Eliot's review, 'Literature, science, and dogma', although critical, described it as 'a book which everyone interested in poetry ought to read'.

29. *Principles of literary criticism* (London, Routledge & Kegan Paul, 1967), p. 184. Original italics.

30. Ibid., pp. 101–2.

31. That Caudwell was not finished with *Illusion and reality* for some time after he left Cornwall is attested by the book's bibliography. The '200 or 300 learned books [he] had drawn on' had been extended to over 500 by the time he submitted the book to Macmillan.

32. Scott Buchanan, *Poetry and mathematics* (New York, The John Day Company, 1929), p. 109.

33. C. K. Ogden and I. A. Richards, *The meaning of meaning: a study of the influence of language upon thought and of the science of symbolism* (London, Routledge & Kegan Paul, 1972), pp. 228–9.

34. In *Problems of Soviet literature: reports and speeches at the First Soviet Writers' Congress* (London: Martin Lawrence, 1935). Caudwell only cites the article, but it must have been in this volume that he read it.

35. Ogden and Richards, *The meaning of meaning*, p. 312.

36. Jane Harrison, *Ancient art and ritual* (New York, Henry Holt & Co., 1913), pp. 49–50. As so often when he found a key text, Caudwell worked extensively from Harrison's short, descriptive bibliography.

37. Ibid., p. 210.

38. Ibid., p. 227. Caudwell, in 'Verse and mathematics', offers a rather flamboyant paraphrase of Sidney in this context. 'The poet who nothing affirms becomes a liar, as soon as, becoming a priest, he doth affirm. Poetry is non-symbolic, and untrue. Religion is symbolic and untrue' (p. 113).

39. See pp. 268–9 of *Illusion and reality* for a graphic representation of this symbolic world.

40. Baudouin, *Psychoanalysis and aesthetics*, pp. 33–4.

41. Henri Bergson, *Creative evolution*, trans. Arthur Mitchell (New York, Henry Holt & Co., 1937), p. ix.

42. Ogden and Richards, *The meaning of meaning*, pp. 25–6.

43. E. Sapir, *Culture, language, and personality: selected essays* (Berkeley, University of California Press, 1958), p. 69.

44. Ogden and Richards, *The meaning of meaning*, p. 328.

45. Harrison, *Ancient art and ritual*, p. 39.

46. Lee Baxandall and Stefan Morawski (eds), *Marx and Engels on literature & art: selected writings* (St. Louis and Milwaukee, Telos Press, 1973), p. 8.

47. For a basic discussion of the transformation of the concept of ideology, the two extremes of which I have given above, see Henry D. Aiken, *The age of ideology* (New York, New American Library, 1956), Chapter 1, *passim*.

48. W. H. Auden, 'Psychology and art', in Geoffrey Grigson (ed.), *The arts today* (London, John Lane, 1935), p. 19.

49. Upward's *Journey to the border* is a fable about such a change of consciousness; from the 'border' of insanity to psychological salvation through commitment to 'the workers' movement'.

50. Alasdair Browne, 'Psychology and Marxism' in C. Day Lewis (ed.), *The mind in chains* (London, Frederick Muller, 1937), pp. 177–8. See also his 'Freud and materialism,' *Left Review*, June 1936.

51. *Illusion and reality*, p. 167.

52. This is not strictly true of Freud. He saw man as a *social* animal, but not, alas, as a completely *socialised* one.

53. 'Freud: a study in bourgeois psychology', *Studies*, p. 184. Caudwell's emphases.

54. Sigmund Freud, *The future of an illusion*, ed. James Strachey (Garden City, NY, Anchor Books, 1964), p. 49.

55. Marx had pointed this out many decades before: 'The abolition of religion as the *illusory* happiness of men is a demand for their *real* happiness', 'Contribution to the critique of Hegel's *Philosophy of right*', 1843.

56. Freud, *The future of an illusion*, pp. 50, 90.

57. Ibid., p. 18.

58. For example the dialectical implications of Freud's theory; the ego's modification of *reality* in the service of the id, as in the following: 'Later, the ego learns that there is yet another way of securing satisfaction besides the *adaptation* to the external world which I have described. It is also possible to intervene in the external world by *changing* it ...'. (*Two short accounts of psychoanalysis*, trans. James Strachey (Harmondsworth, Penguin Books, 1966), p. 111. Freud's italics.)

59. George Plekhanov, *Fundamental problems of Marxism* (London, Lawrence & Wishart, 1969).

60. Ibid., p. 81. Plekhanov is working from Marx's *The German ideology*, where Marx set out to 'demonstrate the development of the ideological reflexes'. He remarks that the ideologues of any given era 'have had to *share the illusion of that epoch*'. Marx's emphases.

61. This title, and other 'periods' of capitalism can be found in the final sections of *Capital* vol. I.

62. Contrast this with the age of Pope (p. 99) where poetry 'is a reflection of that stage of the bourgeois illusion where freedom for the bourgeoisie can only be "limited" .... Hence the contrast between the elegant corset of the eighteenth-century heroic couplet and the natural luxuriance of Elizabethan blank verse, whose sprawl almost conceals the

bony structure of the iambic rhythm inside it.' Generally speaking, Caudwell's 'literary criticism' is better on form than content.

63. 'Contribution' in Robert C. Tucker (ed.), *The Marx-Engels reader*, 2nd edn (New York, W. W. Norton, 1978). *Illusion and reality*, p. 107.

64. See Edgell Rickwood's Preface to *Further Studies*, p. 11.

65. Tucker (ed.), *The Marx-Engels reader*, pp. 4–5. Caudwell had noted these sections of the Preface on the verso of one of the manuscript pages of 'Verse and mathematics' and the text is used as Prologue to his *Further studies*.

66. Tucker (ed.), *The Marx-Engels reader*, p. 158. And see *Illusion and reality*, p. 139: 'Language is the essential tool of human association', etc. And p. 163: 'The construction of consciousness is the socialising of the psyche.'

67. *Illusion and reality*, p. 30.

68. *Anti-Duhring*, Tucker (ed.), *The Marx-Engels reader*, p. 697.

69. Ibid., pp. 715–16.

70. Tucker (ed.), *The Marx-Engels reader*, p. 766.

71. *Studies*, p. 217.

72. Reuben Osborn, *Marxism and psychoanalysis* (New York, Octagon Books, 1974). First published as *Marx and Freud* in 1937.

73. Osborn, *Marxism and psychoanalysis*, p. xii.

74. Ibid., p. 98.

75. Ibid., p. 123.

76. *Modern Quarterly* (Winter 1950–1), p. 22. This article initiated a series of contributions on various aspects of Caudwell's work.

77. Thompson, 'Caudwell', pp. 250–1. Original italics.

78. C. Murchison (ed.), *Psychologies of 1930* (London, Oxford University Press, 1930), p. 267. This sounds like Kornilov's own version of the original German: see the same text as one of the epigraphs to this chapter.

79. Williams, *Culture and society*, p. 266.

80. It now seems certain that Volosinov's texts were produced by Bakhtin.

81. MS 'Verse and mathematics', p. 209.

82. V. N. Volosinov, *Freudianism: a Marxist critique*, trans. I. R. Titunik and ed. in collaboration with Neal H. Bruss (New York, Academic Press, 1976), p. 15.

83. *Illusion and reality*, p. 136.

# 5

## Reality and Illusion: the *Studies in a dying culture*

*But it will be said, bourgeois culture is suffering not from illusion but from disillusionment. Everyone has said it — Freud, Jung, D. H. Lawrence, and the Archbishop of Canterbury. Precisely, for this is the very danger of its illusion, that it believes itself disillusioned. It has shed all the secondary illusions — of religion, God, morality, democracy, teleology, and metaphysics. But it cannot rid itself of the basic bourgeois illusion, and because it is unaware of this illusion, and because this illusion is now stripped to its naked essence, it violently distorts the whole fabric of contemporary ideology.*

Caudwell

*After Blake and Marx, this faculty of dialectical vision has been rare enough for us to regard it with a special respect.*

E. P. Thompson: 'Caudwell'

*What we observe is not nature itself, but nature exposed to our method of questioning.*

Werner Heisenberg

Despite the recognition given to *Illusion and reality* for its heroic attempt at numerous intellectual syntheses, there is a general consensus among commentators on the superiority of *Studies in a dying culture.*[1] George Moberg, in an extensive and insightful review, was an early proponent of seeing the *Studies* as Caudwell's major work. He maintains that Caudwell 'was one of the first important analysts of *capitalist class consciousness*'. Although he has certain reservations — Caudwell's 'historicism' (in Althusser's sense) — Francis Mulhern praises him for his attempt at an 'unitary critique of bourgeois civilization'. As noted in the previous chapter, E. P. Thompson, partly in response to Mulhern's article, has called for a general reappraisal of Caudwell's work, shifting the emphasis away from *Illusion and reality* (Caudwell as aesthetician) to the *Studies* (Caudwell as 'cultural anatomist'). Samuel Hynes, in his introduction to *Romance and realism*, considers Caudwell's method within the broader framework of Marxist literary theory. 'Caudwell will get his due,' Hynes believes, 'when he is seen as what he was — a gifted synthesizer who derived his world-view from Marx.'[2]

Generally speaking, commentators who have wished to defend Caudwell within the tradition of Marxist exegesis have cited sections from the *Studies* as indicative of a less ambiguous stance. E. P. Thompson, for example, has cited the essays in order to protect Caudwell from both the 'mechanical materialists' of the *Modern Quarterly* and the 'idealism' of the younger 'Western Marxists'. It is Caudwell's 'interactionist epistemology', his incorrigible dialectical vision, that allows him to consider the interrelationship of the subject and the object in all modes of being. At times such a vision could take even theory into materiality (the working of the cortex), a position which the Althusserian marxists might find 'vulgar'. Thompson remarks on this aspect of his work in the following way:

> It is one thing to assert, as an abstract proviso, that all matter, society and culture are mutually related or mutually determining; it is quite another thing to examine, or even to argue about, their mediations and determinations; and another thing again to take this argument into the privacy of our own theoretical heads, and to suggest that even Theory itself may be composed of 'the affective "heating" of cortical traces'. This is, presumably, an example of a 'hectic foray' into 'alien territories'.[3]

The importance of Thompson's point here, as we shall see throughout the chapter, is that Caudwell could not regard any aspect of human behaviour except in its *causal* relations with the rest of the environment, whether it be in the abstract field of personal 'liberty' or in the more tangible area of modern physics. He was fascinated by the concept of causality and the concept of freedom: with the concept of freedom *as an aspect* of causality.

It is not my intention in this chapter to discuss the merits of Caudwell's 'orthodoxy' (as if such a concept were ahistorical) but rather my overview has two modest objectives. Firstly, to demonstrate the interrelationship between a range of disparate topics within the structure of Caudwell's overall design, and, more importantly, since this has been a central premiss of my whole survey of his work, to consider these essays — wherever possible — as an individual response to the cultural concerns of the historical period. As with all men, Caudwell's work is the result of personal interest in touch with contemporary concerns; or, as he would have preferred, the subject's adaptation to its social environment.

The *Studies* attempt to explicate, as Caudwell explains at the beginning of his Foreword, the 'bewilderment and pessimism ... of contemporary culture from Einstein to Freud'. He recognises that bourgeois culture[4] has 'achieved much' over the past 50 years:

> Its empirical developments include relativity and quantum physics, genetics, a new insight into the deeper layer of man's mind, the different patterns of social relationships uncovered by anthropology, and hundreds of technicological inventions such as the aeroplane, wireless, motor transport, and electric power. Why, with this proved record, does it despair?

These 'developments', these interests, which as we have already seen, Caudwell made his own, lack what he believed he had recently achieved: a synthetic world-view, a *Weltanschauung*, in which to place such empirical discoveries. We have here, in this Foreword, a reiteration of the sentiments outlined in one of the studies he was to write and one which had great emotional importance to Christopher Caudwell as creative artist. The task of the poet at this juncture in history (1936) must be to attain 'a world-view that will become general' and he must do this by 'destructively analysing all bourgeois culture'. He goes on: 'This book itself would really be a poet's task — a small attempt towards the creation of such a world-view.'[5] The analysis of 'all bourgeois culture' is a gargantuan task, even for someone who worked as rapidly as Caudwell. But if the 'poet's task' was difficult, that of the commentator seems impossible. To attempt to analyse Caudwell's discourses in any detail — if any one man were competent — would take several volumes and it is for this reason that I have elected, as suggested above, to give more of a synthetic account of his work within a historical perspective.

The 'synthetic world-view' which Caudwell chooses for his analysis is of course historical materialism, but within this context he regards as essential for analysis the structure on which the whole edifice of bourgeois ideology is built. This is 'the basic bourgeois illusion [which] distorts the whole fabric of contemporary ideology': that man is 'naturally' free and society binds him in chains. This is for Caudwell the meta-illusion of the bourgeois epoch because it is coincident with its very birth; it is the incubus of 'false consciousness' because it is the very foundation on which bourgeois ideology is constructed. This Rousseauesque conviction was conceived during the 'Renaissance charter of the *bourgeoisie*' which, in its call for 'freedom' from feudal restrictions, replaced an outworn set of social relations. And in this sense the rise of the bourgeois class was a dynamic and positive historical advance. But the principle on which the rise of the bourgeoisie was founded, essential to social progress *for a time*, was given, Caudwell insists, 'the sanction of eternal truth'.

The bourgeoisie has done a thorough job over the past few centuries in disguising social relations, relations between human beings, obfuscating them into relations with commodities, with cash, with capital — with 'things'. In this way, man, although dependent on the social relations in which he finds himself, still remains 'free' because, superior to 'things', it seems he can dominate them and change them at will. This is an illusion, because all these 'things' have been hypostatised out of human relations and it is this realisation which constitutes true freedom.

In other words, such a state of affairs is not one of intermittent manifestation, like a compulsive neurotic tic in an otherwise sound consciousness, but forms the structuring principle of bourgeois consciousness itself. Such 'false consciousness' (this term needs to be scrutinised in the light of more recent work done on ideology) is undetectable to the bourgeois because to be aware of it would be tantamount to transcending that consciousness altogether:

> How can it [this illusion of freedom] appear everywhere in
> ideology, always as the distorting factor, without being
> observed as such? But it is just because it appears everywhere
> in his ideology, like the Fitzgerald contraction, in measure-
> ments of ether velocity, that it cannot be observed by the
> bourgeois, any more than the physicist can observe the
> earth's speed through the ether.[6]

It was Caudwell's task in these studies to step outside bourgeois
consciousness (he had by now moved to Poplar and left his
personal bourgeois world behind) and to analyse those repressed
relations that make beings human, to bring to consciousness the
distorting factors implanted by bourgeois rationalisation. It was
his goal, in fact, to impose reality on illusion.

Another aspect of the bourgeois illusion and the other structuring principle of the *Studies* is the various manifestations in
bourgeois ideology of the separation of subject and object. This
epistemological position is of course allied to the 'common root'
of bourgeois ideology, that of 'freedom'. The bourgeois as subject,
Caudwell believes, feels that he can simply dominate the object,
the environment, because he is ignorant of the necessity of the
determining relations between him and his world. These two
epistemological positions, then — the recognition of necessity in
true freedom and the dialectical determining relation between
subject and object — are the major strands of thought with which
the *Studies* are woven. The two positions are inseparable, but for
analytical convenience (and I believe that this was the rationale
behind the order of publication) the *Studies* emphasise more the
illusion of freedom in bourgeois ideology, while the *Further studies*
concentrate more on the interaction of the subject-object.

The essay 'Reality: a study in bourgeois philosophy' seeks,
among other things, to show how the emergence of the subject-
object dualism arose out of the primary illusion of freedom.[7] This
study, informed by Lenin's *Materialism and empirio-criticism*, the
second of Marx's *Theses on Feuerbach* and Engels's *Ludwig Feuerbach*,
sets out to demonstrate how the philosophical systems of idealism,
mechanical materialism and the 'compromise' of phenomenalism
are the products of bourgeois dualism. The accent is on *praxis* if
any sound epistemology is to be formulated:

> This material unity of becoming cannot be established by
> thought alone. It is established by thought in unity with

practice, by thought emerging from practice and going out into practice. Phenomena are exhibited by the thing-in-itself, and if we can by practice force the thing-in-itself to exhibit phenomena according to our desire, then we know this much about the thing-in-itself — that in certain circumstances it will exhibit certain phenomena ...

  'The point is to change the world, not to interpret it.' Thus the impasse of philosophers is seen to be the impasse of philosophy, and a proof of the impossibility of interpreting the world by thought alone.[8]

The appeal here, as so often in the mind-set of the 1930s, is to Marx's Eleventh Thesis which emphasises the need to change the world, but, typically, Caudwell goes beyond the mere emotional appeal of this slogan and bases his argument on other Marxist writings. In the Second Thesis, Marx had maintained: 'The question whether objective truth can be attributed to human thinking is not a question of theory but is a *practical* question. Man must prove the truth, that is, the reality and power, the this-sidedness of his thinking in practice.'[9] Caudwell had also read Engels's *Ludwig Feuerbach and the outcome of classical German philosophy* as can be seen in his adaptation of Engels's critique of Kantian epistemology quoted above. Scepticism concerning human knowledge, Engels argues, becomes ultimately a practical matter:

> The most telling refutation of this as of all other philosophical fancies is practice, viz., experiment and industry. If we are able to prove the correctness of our conception of a natural process by making it ourselves, bringing it into being out of its conditions and using it for our own purposes into the bargain, then there is an end of the Kantian incomprehensible 'thing-in-itself.'[10]

This essay, 'Reality', as its title implies, is genuinely philosophical. It addresses areas of concern fundamental to the acquisition of human knowledge, particularly in its critique of phenomenalism or positivism, the 'reactionary' philosophy that Lenin attacked under the name of 'empirio-criticism'.[11] But, just as importantly, the essay moves from a consideration of the various aspects of 'bourgeois philosophy' to a system that has no need of illusions, to a philosophy that 'has transformed itself into a sociology'. Caudwell's discourse modulates into the philosophical reality that dialectical materialism implies, the necessity of the unity of thought and practice which was so important to him at the time of writing. Indeed, this study traces the arc of his own becoming, the necessity of his political stance in Poplar in 1936. When one has understood, he tells us, 'the law of motion [of a] society that produces bourgeois philosophy ... one has ceased to be a bourgeois; one no longer stands in one's own light and can see bourgeois culture clearly. One has become a Communist.'[12] Such was Caudwell's understanding.

The new 'reality' which he had chosen and which allowed him to 'see bourgeois culture clearly' was, unlike that of many of his intellectual contemporaries, a practical reality as well as a theoretical one. Not only had he chosen to live in the 'vehemently working-class' district of Poplar, he had chosen to live communally as well. When he moved into 24 Susannah Street it was to share the second floor of a small house with his three comrades, Nick Cox, Ted Roycraft and Ralph Sternberg. Apparently it was, at times, a rather bohemian ménage and other members of the Poplar branch of the Communist Party, who would drop in for discussion periodically, were more than mildly surprised by the lack of 'discipline'.[13] Yet despite the discussions, the camaraderie and his Party duties as outlined earlier, it seems that no one in Poplar was aware of Caudwell's 'synthetic studies ... of modern culture' as he had outlined them, ironically enough, to his 'bourgeois' friends, the Beards. The writer's notebook that he had kept now became one for 'philosophical' entries. Apart from a few personal reflections — selling the *Daily Worker* in Chrisp Street, a few snatches of East End dialect — the extracts in the Poplar notebook reflect in embryo the Faustian nature of his project. He had decided, let us remember, to use a remark from Lenin as his epigraph: that 'the Communist [becomes] a mere bluffer, if he has not worked over in his consciousness the whole inheritance of human knowledge'.[14]

A common theme of the notebook and one which links together the *Studies* is the nature of causality, the interconnectedness of all things in the universe in a process of becoming. There is a section entitled 'The thing-for-us' which is an investigation of scientific knowledge in the light of positivism and which must have been the genesis of the essay 'Reality' discussed above. There is a quotation from Lucretius as 'an anticipation of Einstein'[15] and a modification of Kant under yet another heading of 'Causality', as in the following:

> Kant: 'Everything that happens presupposes something from which it follows according to a rule.'
> I prefer as a formulation: 'Causality implies that the world is a material unity of becoming.' This ensures the mutually [*sic*] determining relation of phenomena. The quest for causality, which is the quest of science (the nature of reality) is therefore simply the discovery of the nature of matter. Since our views of matter are continually being extended (e.g. modern quantum & wave mechanics) our definition of causality is altered.

Another aspect of causality for Caudwell was, as we have seen, the true nature of liberty as being (as he put it in the notebook) 'the enjoyment of necessity'. He had renounced his previous bourgeois 'freedom' not only in theory, but, by joining the Party and living communally with the workers of the East End, he was illustrating his concept of liberty in practice.[16] The study, 'Liberty: a study in bourgeois illusion', although positioned at the end of the *Studies*, is, as its subtitle implies, concerned with the ideological matrix out of which the various manifestations of the bourgeois illusion (the works of Shaw, Wells, Lawrence, etc.) arise. Not surprisingly, Caudwell bases his argument as to the true nature of 'liberty' (which he argues is a relative, not an absolute concept), on the principle of causality. Illustrating the relative nature of what is meant by freedom, Caudwell proposes three individuals: an intellectual (unable to buy a yacht which he badly wants) who could be said to be in some senses free; a 'non-union shop assistant of Houndsditch [who works] seven days of the week', who has no time for culture and has little education; and, finally, there is the unemployed man (plenty of whom Caudwell would have met in Poplar), who is 'free to go anywhere — in the streets and parks, and in the Museums. He is allowed to think of anything — the Einstein theory, the Frege definition of classes, or the doctrine of the Immaculate Conception.'[17] The relative freedom of the intellectual and the unfreedom of the other two men have to be 'causally inter-related'. Just as there are scientific laws to help us to 'attain freedom — that is, the fulfilment of our will', *vis à vis* the physical environment, so also there is 'one scientific analysis of the law of motion of social relations ... that of Marxism'.[18] Caudwell examines this causal nexus both with regard to the large issue of society as a whole ('the causal process whereby bourgeois social relations can change into new social relations without generating a mass of unfreedom') and also with regard to the more 'personal', philosophical aspect of free will. The latter exists only in the sense that we are 'conscious of the motive that dictates our action',[19] which is of course another aspect of causality. Ultimately, and this is an important observation, free will must entail action: 'to be really free we must also be able to do what we freely will to do'. This again brings us back to determinism, because 'free' will becomes part of the determining relations of the environment. It is, in the final analysis, a consciousness of inner and outer necessity which brings personal freedom. And, on a larger scale, it is the recognition of the necessity of social relations which must be brought to consciousness in any attempted reparation of the fragmented or dying culture.

It was such a consciousness that Caudwell believed many of the better-known and influential contemporary writers and would-be 'scientists' lacked. Hence we have those sketches of Shaw, the Lawrences, Wells and Freud, essays which set out to reveal the ideological co-ordinates within which they construct their various remedies for the sickness that is plaguing modern culture. It is Caudwell's view that 'these people must take to themselves the words of Herzen: "We are not the doctors, we are the disease." '[20] The representatives on whom he chose to concentrate would have interested him personally (as poet, novelist and amateur scientist) but, as we have seen already in the case of Freud, these figures were chosen for analysis by other commentators of the period.

It is fitting that John Strachey, whose *The coming struggle for power* influenced Caudwell, should have undertaken to write the introduction to the *Studies in a dying culture*. Strachey, in the third part of his book, 'The decay of capitalist culture', attributed the demise to the fact that such a culture was adapted to an age of 'freedom' and that such a period of 'individualistic freedom is very nearly over'. He makes a broad sweep over the vast 'ideal constructions which the human mind has begotten' — religion, science, literature — and chooses in the latter section to investigate particularly the work of Wells, Shaw and Lawrence. Like Strachey, Caudwell chooses to write on these ideologues because, apart from dealing in literature, they also address socio-economic concerns.

Strachey had characterised Shaw by quoting the words of Lenin

— that he was 'a good man fallen among Fabians' — and Caudwell uses this remark as epigraph to his study 'George Bernard Shaw: a study of the bourgeois superman'. Shaw is a victim of the illusion that reality can be changed through 'pure wisdom', that 'out of debate and ratiocination, without social action [it is possible] to beat out a new and higher consciousness'.[21] This error, which is the result of a 'mind obsessed with bourgeois concepts of liberty', is reflected both in Shaw's rejection of all modern science as 'mumbo-jumbo' and in his artistic productions. Caught in 'the bourgeois intellectual heresy of believing in thought without action', Shaw's plays neglect the essential dialectical interplay of 'being' (man's emotion) and consciousness. His characters are 'walking intellects'. His ideological stance results in a dramaturgy in which 'The actors are nothing; the thinkers are everything.'

> Even a man who in real life would be powerful, formidable and quite brainless — the 'armourer' of 'Major Barbara' — has to be transformed into a brilliant theoretician before (as Shaw thinks) he can be made expressive on the stage ... This weakness naturally shows itself in his proletarians. Like the proletarians in the Army hostel of Major Barbara, they are simply caricatures. Only by being 'educated', like the chauffeur in *Man and Superman*, can they become respectable.[22]

Such thinking (that which is *revealed* in Shaw's plays) betrays a Shavian ideal world, not of communism but, like that of Wells, 'a world ruled by intellectual Samurai guiding the poor muddled workers; a world of Fascism'.

Following Strachey,[23] Caudwell traces Shaw's contradictory position to his 'personal history'. Although an early admirer of Marx's *Capital*, he was an ambitious young man who sought to retrieve the upper middle-class station from which his family had fallen. Though alert (as his writings attest) to the contradictory nature of capitalism, he nevertheless was unable to renounce his bourgeois aspirations. Hence the compromise of Fabianism, 'with its bourgeois traditions and its social responsibility'. Such incompatibility or unsatisfactory compromise is evident in the plays *Widower's houses, Major Barbara, Mrs Warren's profession*, in which the theme of 'tainted money' is dealt with in veiled form. Shaw, like Major Barbara, ends up by marrying 'money, respectability, fame, peaceful reformism and ultimately even Mussolini'.[24]

The first half of the essay on D. H. Lawrence is taken up by some of the questions that concerned Caudwell in *Illusion and reality*. Art forms, because of the 'socially recognised symbols' they utilise, are by definition social, but the dissolution of social values in bourgeois culture (over the past few centuries, but Caudwell chooses the same year as Virginia Woolf, 1910, as being crucial) have led to either vulgar commercialism, or 'art for my sake', such as Dadaism, Surrealism or Steinism. It was to Lawrence's credit, Caudwell suggests, that as a novelist he could see the futility of the 'pure artist', especially at a time when cash relationships and the market seemed more important than relations between persons: 'Lawrence's gospel was purely sociological.' As can be seen from his novels and letters — Caudwell recorded a few of the latter in his notebook — Lawrence was sickened by the decay and deceitfulness of bourgeois social relations and spent most of his life in flight from them. 'There is no repression of the sexual individual', Caudwell quotes Lawrence as saying in a letter, 'comparable to the repression of the societal man in me ... I am weary even of my own individuality, and simply nauseated by other people's.' And in another letter modern relations are described as being 'like insects, gone cold, living only for money, for *dirt*'.[25]

> Social relations, by ceasing to be between man and man and adhering to a thing, become emptied of tenderness. Man feels himself deprived of love. His whole instinct revolts against this. He feels a vast maladaption to his environment. Lawrence perceives this clearly when he talks about the repression of the societal instinct.[26]

But what is Lawrence's 'solution' for repairing the shattered structures of modern social relations? Caudwell believes it is a self-contradictory one, that he 'appeals to the consciousness of men to abandon consciousness'. Lawrence's is a problem similar to Shaw's, in that he finds it difficult to unite thinking and being. If Shaw's programme leads to a form of fascism through dictatorship of the intellect, then Lawrence errs, with the same result, to the other extreme. This is because Lawrence confuses unconsciousness with feeling and consciousness with intellect; but, Caudwell argues, 'they play into each other's hands and heighten each other. Man feels more deeply than the slug because he thinks more.'[27] So, although seemingly at different ends of the spectrum, Shaw and Lawrence meet one another because 'bourgeois intellectuals obsessed with a false notion of the nature of freedom, are by the inherent contradictions of their notion at length driven to liberty's opposite, Fascism.'[28] Shaw and Lawrence are victims of that same incubus that both feeds on, and gives sustenance to, the bourgeois psyche:

> Why did Lawrence, faced with the problem, fail of a solution? He failed because while hating bourgeois culture he never succeeded in escaping from its limitations. Here in him, too, we see the same old lie. Man is 'free' in so far as his 'free' instincts, the 'blood', the 'flesh', are given an outlet. Man is free not through but *in spite of* social relations.[29]

The upshot of Caudwell's criticism of Lawrence (as had been that of most of the radical intellectuals of the 1930s), was that, while recognising the sham of contemporary social relations, Lawrence sought a solution outside them.[30] Yet there are in the novels — and one wishes, if only here, Caudwell had been specific enough to remember Lawrence's own remarks about trusting the tale rather than the teller — allegories or myths of the working man revitalising a moribund class and this suggests that Lawrence had not entirely 'turned his back'[31] on the tenderness in working-class relations.

It was H. G. Wells's singular misfortune to be denied the hard, but at least solid, ground of working-class solidarity. 'Wells', Caudwell tells us, 'is a *petit bourgeois*, and of all the products of capitalism, none is more unlovely than this class':

> It has only one value in life, that of bettering itself, of getting a step nearer the good bourgeois things so far above it. It has only one horror, that of falling from respectability into the proletarian abyss which, because it is so near, seems so much more dangerous. It is rootless, individualist, lonely, and perpetually facing, with its hackles up, an antagonistic world. It can never know the security of the rich bourgeoisie or the companionship of the worker. This world, described so well in *Experiment in Autobiography*, is like a terrible stagnant marsh, all mud and bitterness, and without even the saving grace of tragedy.[32]

Two possibilities are open to someone of Wells's class position. He can shed his 'false bourgeois illusions' and align himself with the proletariat (as in Caudwell's own case) or, 'escape upwards', the 'fierce struggle' which is recorded in Wells's autobiography. But this, in the case of Wells, resulted in a great ideological, if not financial, sacrifice. 'He took the role of popular "thinker", writer of the novel "of ideas" and of "outlines" of science and history, because he had been unable to pursue real art and had been forced to forsake real science.'[33] Like Caudwell, he was heir to all the discoveries of recent time — 'psycho-analysis, early anthropology and comparative religion, archaeology, physics and biology' — but because of his ambiguous class position (and unlike Caudwell), 'he was devoid of any world-view' and could make only an 'eclectic mish-mash' of these ideas.[34] Despite the biting criticism, Caudwell is concerned here with the fate of a man as scientist and artist, a concern that was of crucial importance to himself.

Yet, as in all his work, his reaction to Wells receives further illumination within the context of the ideological struggle of the time. As John Strachey pointed out, Wells had 'shown himself to be a modern encyclopaedist'[35] and his books, from *New worlds for old* (1908) through *The new Machiavelli* (1911) to the three outlines (the last of which, *The work, wealth and happiness of mankind* was published in 1932), constituted in their author's words 'a complete modern ideology'. Wells had written on science, economics and history and had attracted many of the younger intellectuals, including those on the Left, such as J. D. Bernal and Haldane. By 1932 (when Strachey's book was published), it was time to uncover Wells's ideology for what it was, a form of utopian fascism.

Since history is the record of physical and ideological struggle in all man's endeavours, Strachey spends a considerable portion of his discussion on Wells's *The outline of history*: 'For a Universal History is the appropriate definitive expression of the "world view" of a class: it is a sort of summing up of culture which that class has been able to achieve.'[36] While criticising Wells's whole enterprise as the 'spell-binding conception of history', Strachey parenthetically remarks that a 'World history written from the standpoint of dialectical materialism ... has yet to be written.' Caudwell, too, chose to single out Wells's historical *Outline* for criticism and in 'Men and nature: a study in bourgeois history', he attempts to lay the groundwork for a history written from the point of view of dialectical materialism.

142

Wells's *Outline*, Caudwell argues, is defective, not (as some commentators had maintained) because of error or 'neglect of this or that fact', but because it is based on the 'old bourgeois error of knowing producing being, of the freedom and primacy of thought'.

> Wells makes the old bourgeois assumption that men are born, each perfectly free, and that their wants and dreams mould the world of social relations ... Because of this Wells naturally makes the 'logical' deduction that.to change man's mind it is necessary to preach to them convincingly and interestingly, and then all will be accomplished as one desires ... It is doubtful if Wells has ever realised, in spite of his scientific education, that the whole purpose of Marx was to write history causally ... It is because the bourgeois denies causality as Wells does in his Outline, and because the Communist asserts it, and discovers its law, that man in communism can become free. To deny the existence of laws, as the savage denies the existence of physical causality by substituting mythology, is to be the slave of those laws. To assert or discover them, as does the scientist, is to be their master.[37]

To demythologise bourgeois history and to base its study on scientific grounds was Caudwell's intention in 'Men and nature'.

He begins this study by reiterating the central premiss of all the studies, the nature of bourgeois ideology:

> It is not an error in the sense that it can be isolated, as a separate mistake, from every department of culture. It is only revealed on analysis as an unseen force, not explicit in the formulations of that culture, but acting like a pressure from outside. It gives to that culture a characteristic distortion which is not visible to those who still live within the framework of that economy.[38]

It is important to realise here that Caudwell's understanding of 'ideology' is not a simplistic one; such as, for example, the reflection of class desires as manifesting themselves in various intellectual pursuits.[39] On the contrary (and this is closer to Marx's 'illusion of the epoch' theory), the bourgeois ideologues are victims of their own illusions; because, as the above quotation exemplifies, they do not 'fabricate' the various errors in 'every department of culture', but, rather, *necessarily* produce fabrications because of the essential lie that constitutes the 'framework', the world-view, within which they labour.

Thus, it is not a deceptive ploy on the part of Wells, for example, to write history from the point of view of 'unreasonable kings and unscientific statesmen and well-meaning religious leaders'.[40] It is not his fault, as it were, that he sees all the complexity and struggle of human history in terms of personae — the peasant persona, the nomad persona, the educated persona — that is to say, in thought divorced from real active struggle. This is so because of the 'unseen force', the ideological 'pressure' within which the bourgeois historian writes:

> All such ideologies of a ruling class have this in common, that they see thought, consciousness, will (their class prerogatives), not as determined by action or by the outer reality which thought goes out in action to know and change, but as innate — free in the sense in which they regard themselves as free ... It is an illusion common to all class-cultures, and therefore to all ideologies so far produced by history except that of dialectical materialism.[41]

In *The German ideology*, which is a key text in any consideration of Caudwell's work, Marx turns his attention to 'the conception of history' within ideology, and it is here I believe that we will discover the framework of Caudwell's own study 'Men and nature: a study in bourgeois history'. A proper concept of history, Marx argues, would depend

> on our ability to expound the real process of production, starting out from the material production of life itself, and to comprehend the form of intercourse connected with this and created by this mode of production ... a sum of productive forces, a historically created relation of individuals to nature and to one another ...
>
> In the whole conception of history up to the present this real basis of history has either been totally neglected or else considered as a minor matter quite irrelevant to the course of history. History must, therefore, always be written according to an extraneous standard; the real production of life seems to be primeval history, while the truly historical

appears to be separated from ordinary life, something extra-superterrestrial. With this the relation of man to nature is excluded from history and hence the antithesis of nature and history is created.[42]

As Caudwell's title implies, it was his central concern (and the essay is too long and complex to rehearse its various arguments) to heal the breach of the 'antithesis' of which Marx speaks. It is men and nature, the 'interpenetration of nature by man as a result of his struggle with it', which makes history. 'History', Caudwell tells us, 'is the study of the object–subject relation of men–nature, and not of either separately'.[43] Ultimately, history is the story of economic production, of economic co-operation, 'the organization of men in nature' — that is to say, *social* co-operation. But it is just such social relations which bourgeois economy and, as a consequence, bourgeois culture has to deny or veil as its pre-requisite. This is why the bourgeois historian (such as H. G. Wells) can never tell the 'true' story of man's history.

Marx had said that man helps make his own history, but not always the way he wills it. Caudwell could have taken this dictum as epigraph to his study, 'T. E. Lawrence: a study in heroism'. Lawrence is, in the final analysis, a hero *manqué*, because in bringing 'liberty' to the Arabs he inflicted on them the very system he himself had fled: bourgeois social relations. Caudwell's prophetic prognosis was this:

Lawrence felt that he and the British Government had betrayed some of the Arabs. But he never fully realised how completely he had betrayed them all. He had brought into Arabia the very evil he had fled. Soon his desert Arabs would have money, businesses, investments, loud-speakers, and regular employment. But he could not realise this consciously, for he had never been fully conscious that it was bourgeois social relations he was fleeing, and he was not aware of the omnipotent destructive power of the present over the past. He was in fact like a man who, fleeing blindly from a deadly disease to a healthy land, himself afflicts it with the plague.[44]

This study, an essay in the dialectics of historical circumstances and individual action, reflects, perhaps more than any other, Caudwell's response to an issue that was of crucial importance to the consciousness of his time. In this sense 'T. E. Lawrence' might serve as a paradigm for the whole enterprise that was to become *Studies in a dying culture*.

The débâcle of the First World War seemed to have put an end to any possibility of heroism of the romantic and individualistic kind. Lawrence's singular exploits (in the only theatre of the War where such exploits were possible) made of him a myth in his own time. When he died in May 1935, kings paid him tribute and his admirers ranged the political spectrum from Winston Churchill to the young communist theoretician, Ralph Fox. Auden, who had written that 'Lawrence's life is an allegory of the transformation of the Truly Weak Man into the Truly Strong Man',[45] modelled the hero of *The ascent of F-6* on him, and Nicholas Blake (C. Day Lewis) was thought to have used Lawrence's public image for the murdered war-hero in his detective novel, *Thou shell of death*. He seemed to be the archetypal hero for their generation: intellectual, homosexual, Oxbridge-educated; the man of words turned man of action.

Of all the publicity centred on Lawrence shortly after his death, it was most likely Ralph Fox's article in *Left Review* which stirred Caudwell to write his own evaluation.[46] Fox (whose biography of Lenin Caudwell lists in the bibliography to *Illusion and reality*) offers in his essay both a structure and a challenge to any would-be theorists of heroism:

> No one in writing about Lawrence has tried to analyse him as the hero, to see what historical forces made Lawrence possible and also made him such a very peculiar hero and, we may add, such a very uncomfortable one.[47]

Lawrence was an 'uncomfortable' hero as far as Caudwell was concerned, by virtue of the fact that he had not understood those 'historical forces' that went into his making. In the same way that 'a man can only carve a chicken properly if he knows where the joints are, and follows them, so a hero dominates events only because he conforms closely with the law that produces them'.[48] In his pursuit of liberty for the Arabs and freedom for himself, freedom from 'the pettiness and commercialism of capitalism', Lawrence was ignorant of the laws of necessity, of the society of the future. Rather, he attempted to escape into what he believed were the more attractive social relations of the past. Lenin, on the contrary, was aware of 'the joints of the chicken of circumstance' and, with 'the causal laws of society' behind him was able to liberate a people into the future. Caudwell was not the only figure to compare the credentials of Lawrence and Lenin as paradigms of the hero. Among others, Auden, reviewing a book on Lawrence, remarked that Lenin and Lawrence 'seem to me the two whose lives exemplify most completely what is best and significant in our time.'[49]

Even after the war Lawrence fled the 'bourgeois relations' from which 'his soul revolted', and by entering the ranks as Aircrafts-man Shaw he sought a similar ideal to that which he had sought in Arabia Deserta. His 'tragedy' finds its analogue in his very own death. The machine, symbol of the future, attracted him, but intoxicated by its power, the *freedom* that it gave him, he lacked the necessary restraint, the control, and it killed him.[50]

It was not until a year after Lawrence's death that an opportunity for the making of a hero offered itself again. The Spanish War presented a just cause and a theatre of war where individual, courageous action could still be important. It was here, of course, that Ralph Fox and Caudwell himself fell; but, unlike Lawrence, Caudwell would have argued that his going to Spain was as much dictated by historical circumstances as individual will. It was necessary. His understanding of where his 'duty'[51] lay, his decision to take part in what Auden had called the 'necessary murder', was only putting into practice what he preached in 'Pacifism and violence: a study in bourgeois ethics'. I have already commented upon this essay in light of Caudwell's 'practical' experience with Mosley's Blackshirts in the East End. But, again, 'Pacifism and violence' is as much a response to the pressure of contemporary debate as the working out of a personal solution.

After the shock of the First World War, 'pacifism' along with 'unemployment' (both of which were linked for a while under the banner of 'socialism') became watchwords for almost every segment of British society. The 'opposition to war' movement perhaps reached its zenith in 1933 when the Oxford Union resolved not to fight 'for King and Country'. The Peace Pledge Union under the tutelage of Canon (Dick) Sheppard had many prominent propagandists (such as Aldous Huxley) and its membership had risen to 130,000 by early 1937. But, due to the machinations of Hitler and Mussolini, an anti-pacifist faction began to gain momentum around 1935–6, particularly among the young intellectuals on the left.[52] Such was the antagonistic atmosphere when, in April 1936, Aldous Huxley published his pacifist pamphlet, *What are you going to do about it?* Stephen Spender replied in an open letter acknowledging Huxley's sincerity, but finding the pacifist position 'untenable'. Did Huxley really believe that after his World Conference (where the wealth of the world would be more equitably distributed) that Hitler and Mussolini would 'gracefully resign?'[53]

Among Caudwell's papers is his own response to Huxley's 'constructive pacifism' in which he describes himself as 'a rank-and-file member of the profession of novelist' and appeals to Huxley's sensibility as a fellow writer: 'The handing about of colonies from one power to another is not the handing about of lumps of raw material but of real human beings. How could you, a novelist, forget this?'[54] The study that we now have is a general account of the sort of bourgeois ethic that lay at the centre of Huxley's thesis, and although he isn't addressed directly his terminology of the 'haves' and 'have-nots' is. To understand bourgeois pacifism one must understand bourgeois violence, Caudwell argues, and the first section of his essay is taken up by tracing such violence from slavery to imperialism. Violence is an integral part of capitalism: 'the violent domination of men by men'. From the individual case to that of the great powers, it is impossible for the bourgeois to exercise full 'liberty' without infringing the liberty of another. But bourgeois philosophy is unaware of this causal nexus, because it is founded on the bourgeois illusion 'festering at the heart of bourgeois culture' — that true freedom lies in individual action, even if such 'action' is abstention as is the case of the Pacifist. But, as with all bourgeois philosophy, that of pacifism lacks causality:

> No pacifist has yet explained the causal chain by which non-resistance ends violence. It is true that it does so in this obvious way, that if no resistance is made to violent commands, no violence is necessary to enforce them. Thus if A does everything B asks him, it will not be necessary for B to use violence. But a dominating relation of this kind is in essence violent, although violence is not overtly shown. Subjection is subjection, and rapacity rapacity, even if the weakness of the victim, or the fear inspired by the victor, makes the process non-forcible. Non-resistance will not prevent it, any more than the lack of claws on the part of prey prevents carnivores battening on them. On the con-

trary, the carnivore selects as his victims animals of the kind. The remedy is the elimination of carnivores, that is, the extinction of classes that live by preying on others.[55]

The 'causal chain' that led from Mussolini in Abyssinia through Franco in Spain to Hitler's invasion of Czechoslovakia was beginning to impinge on people's consciousness. The early, heady days of the Popular Front with its slogan of solidarity 'against Fascism and war' had come to seem a contradiction in terms. No one epitomised this change of heart more than Julian Bell, who in his introduction to an anthology of statements by conscientious objectors of the First World War, *We did not fight* (1935), maintained that his generation would 'succeed in putting down war — by force if necessary'.[56] He gave up his life in Spain as did Christopher Caudwell, who believed that,

> by abstaining from action the pacifist enrolls himself under this banner ... the banner of the increasing violence and coercion exerted by the *haves* on the *have-nots*. He calls increasingly into being the violence of poverty, deprivation, artificial slumps, artistic and scientific decay, fascism, and war.[57]

It was a mark of Caudwell's urgency and a sign of his belief in the interrelationship of all aspects of the superstructure that he was working diligently on what he felt were manifestations of 'artistic and scientific decay' shortly before he left to fight in the war he and others had predicted. It is also an indication of the consistency of his project that his examination of two seemingly disparate areas, physics and literature, have as their central critical premiss the chronic separation of subject and object. If, in *Illusion and reality*, Caudwell attempts to demonstrate the interdependence of science and art in humanity's symbolisation of its universe, here, in these two book-length studies — *The crisis in physics* (1939) and *Romance and realism* (1970) — he investigates how each branch of the imaginative endeavour is subject to a similar ideological 'pressure from outside', as he defined the bourgeois ideological atmosphere in 'Men and nature: a study in bourgeois history'.

The theoretical constructs of physics may seem the ultimate in objectivity but they too, like the novel, are sign-systems used for the exploration of reality and are, in the final analysis, a product of consciousness. Einstein was aware of this: he maintained that 'physical concepts are free creations of the human mind, and are not ... uniquely determined by the external world'. While agreeing with Einstein that these productions are creations of the human imagination, Caudwell argues that they are not as 'free' as the scientist supposes them to be. Rather, they are the projections of a consciousness which is, in turn, produced by the form of society in which it finds itself. In Heisenberg's terms, the observation of nature not in itself, but as it is 'exposed to our method of questioning'. It is interesting to note that Caudwell is careful — especially at this early date (1936) — to circumscribe the 'reflection' theory with regard to ideological manifestations:

> The symptoms are precisely the same in all spheres of ideology. There is an increasing specialization and technical efficiency inside the different domains of ideology, but this leads to an increasing anarchy and contradiction between the domains. It is not merely that biology separates from psychology, but psychology itself splits up into mutually exclusive disciplines. Hence it is no longer possible to have a synthetic world-view, a living theory in touch at all fronts with practice ...
>
> But in fact this ideological anarchy is only a reflection of the economic anarchy which is the cause of the general crisis. When I say 'reflection' I mean that the same general development has taken place in the sphere of social relations as in ideological categories, because the latter are merely subtilizations, qualitatively different, of the former.[58]

Another example of Caudwell's cautious use of the base/superstructure model can be seen in his study of T. E. Lawrence (p. 25), where he maintains:

> If social consciousness were but a mirror-image, it could change like an image without the expenditure of energy when the object which it mirrored changed. But it is more than that. It is a functional superstructure which interacts with the foundations, each altering the other.

The upshot of Caudwell's critique of modern physics — its particular form of 'epistemological dualism' — is connected in a significant way to Caudwell's other book-length study, *Romance and realism,* which reiterates much of the survey of English poetry that we find between the pages of *Illusion and reality.*[59] The study, however, has more to say on the history and form of the novel. In particular, Caudwell makes some interesting comparisons between the crisis in physics and the contemporaneous experimentation with point of view in fiction. As so often with Caudwell, his own *practical* experience had an effect on the construction of his theory. We will remember that experience had taught him about the difficulty of excluding the self from his only serious fictional experiment, *This my hand.* He wrote that the 'impartiality' he had sought was 'impossible' and that 'the problem of the observer remains the central problem of the novel'. Caudwell's investigation of this 'central problem' is based, like all the *Studies,* on the relation of the subject and the object in epistemology. Although Caudwell does not mention Heisenberg by name, his critique of the novel could be summarised by an adaptation of the scientist's remark which forms one of the epigraphs to this chapter: What we observe in the novel is not some self-enclosed reality, but rather a reality wrought out of the method of narration.

As in much of his work, Caudwell is better at outlining those 'ideological pressures' (as he called them) which help form consciousness and its products, than at any specifically 'practical criticism'. That much of the particular criticism in *Romance and realism* serves only as a series of work-points would not have been denied by Caudwell himself. He spoke in a letter to the Beards of 'the crude outline of "Studies" ', that they were 'only drafts, but with some good ideas'. The 'crude outline' of the history of the English novel betrays its weakness by the fact that the Brontës and George Eliot, for example, are contained in a paragraph each, while Kipling (representative of an imperialistic age) gets five or more pages. Towards the end of the study, Caudwell notes that his brief survey had 'confined itself to the tracing of those chief social changes which produced change in the *form* and *technique* of the novel and poetry'.[60] There is, no doubt, a temptation inherent in such an approach to seek out those texts (Defoe, Kipling) which illustrate fictions as ideological carriers in a simplistic way. Yet, within these limitations, Caudwell often makes innovative remarks on the technique of various writers within the history of the English novel. Commenting on the technical changes in the mode of narration during the modern period, he remarks on the fact that, apart from

Lawrence, the 'major artists' are those primarily concerned with technical innovation. He continues:

> It is also not an accident that these authors, who are to be preoccupied with this epistemological problem of the observer, are each in some way alien to the culture they describe ...
>
> James was an American expatriate. Hemingway, during the most important period of his artistic development, was a member of the American colony in Paris. Joyce and Moore are Irish expatriates. Conrad is a Polish expatriate ... The two women [Woolf and Richardson] are aliens in a subtler sense. Bourgeois culture and art, like that of most older cultures, was and still mainly is man-made. Women therefore who assert themselves, who earn their living, who demand a room with a view, find themselves aliens in a man-made culture.[61]

Caudwell was an early recorder of the fact that many of these emigrés, bereft of a solid world-view, were coincidentally advantaged at a time when point of view — the subject's relation to the object — was in a state of flux: that these novelists wrote the 'significant narrative of their time' in part due to the congruency of an alien viewpoint and a culture undergoing fragmentation. The 'Newtonian' era of the novel (with Defoe's self-contained world as prototype) comes to an end at the close of the nineteenth century when the form that had sustained it for nearly two centuries is subjected to the same 'epistemological crisis' that was 'overtaking bourgeois physics'. Due to various ideological pressures, 'reality', whether moral, scientific, or artistic, could no longer be regarded as 'absolute' and independent of the observer. For complex reasons society was beginning to realise the 'relativity of bourgeois norms', their conventionality rather than their atemporal universality.

The complexity of modern reality begins to render obsolete the old god-like, omniscient observer, and the fictional exploration of reality based on the Newtonian perspective is replaced by a point of view that has its analogue in Einstein's physics. Just as the principle of relativity in physics maintained the closed world of Newtonian mechanics in a disguised and infinitely more complex form, so too the novel moves into 'relativity' in an attempt to keep the author out of his fictional experiment. James and Conrad are the prototypical experimenters with multiple point of view, where 'reality' is seen from different angles by the observer(s) within the novel, in a way similar to Einstein's use of 'tensors', or variable co-ordinates, in physical theory. James is paradigmatic, both in respect of Caudwell's theory of the emigré's privileged position with regard to bourgeois culture and his use of modernist techniques.

> In Henry James' work the epistemological problem is primary; it settles the whole book. Through whose eyes is the 'situation' to be seen? To James the alien, late bourgeois culture is not something whose norms are innate and natural, but one whose norms are accepted and artificial. This attitude excludes the 'normal' observer viewing the world from outside. James' solution takes various forms, and it is always subtle and artistic, never mechanical and imposed ... This formula, which to James ultimately seems inevitable, excludes the absolute observer of Newtonian physics and earlier bourgeois novels (e.g. Flaubertian realism). The observer is now an actor, and this often involves a shift from one observer to another in a story, but it gives far greater subtlety and complexity.[62]

However, as Caudwell himself remarks, this 'subtlety and complexity' results in an inevitable paradox. The modernist novel, in its search for greater objectivity, becomes more *subjective*. James Joyce, who believed himself sitting above his creation, paring his fingernails, is paradigmatic of this modernist 'subjectivism'. In *Ulysses*, Joyce wishes (as if it were possible) to eliminate the observer altogether, thus creating 'the closed world of art by giving quite simply the whole contents of the minds of the actors'. But due to the intricate selection and organisation, the solipsistic nature of such a technique, 'this method in no way excludes the author; it fills the book with him'.[63]

'Bourgeois modernism', as Georg Lukács was to call it some years after Caudwell, suffers from a lack of perspective, the lack of a dialectical relation between a subjective attitude and objective reality that would constitute authentic realism.[64] In short, modernism suffers from what its chief practitioners (mostly all aliens) suffered from, the lack of a positive *Weltanschauung*. In their investigation of the ideological determination of form both men condemn this aspect of modernism, the lack of a necessary 'dialectical unity' (Lukács) between the inner and outer worlds (the subject and the object in Caudwell's terminology); and both of them attack (as a consequence of the latter dichotomy) the inevitable subjectivism of modernism. However, Caudwell's alternative 'perspective', when compared to Lukács's later and more sophisticated critique, is rather a simplistic one. Caudwell's faith in 'socialist realism' as the only method capable of creating a dynamic 'world of values for the observer' was founded on a dream so prevalent at the time, that of the restorative power of the 'proletarian novel'. Lukács, with post-Stalinist hindsight, remarks on the inherent weaknesses of a literary philosophy founded on showing the inevitable downfall of capitalism. Rather than becoming the dynamic force that Caudwell had hoped for it, socialist realism — in a wholly different way to modernism, but just as crippling — reached its own form of stasis: 'it became', in Lukács's words, 'the illustration of an abstract truth'.

This brief discussion of Caudwell's reaction to the modern 'bourgeois' novel represents in miniature the underlying premiss of this whole study of his life and work. It testifies to his unique contribution to our understanding of the ideological matrices of form, while, at the same time, it underscores how he himself was subject to the ideological pressures of his era. His hopes for socialist realism in the novel reflect his desire, a desire held by so many in the decade, for the realisation of socialism in reality. And although his conversion was more conscious, more self-consciously critical, than those of many of his fellow intellectuals, he could not see that what for him was still a living and concrete reality was already becoming, under Stalin, an ossified 'abstract truth'. It seems certain that Caudwell, had he survived Spain, would have found it difficult to sustain the kind of commitment to a cause that, as someone remarked, had become conservative in defending revolution. Caudwell's central, imperative, philosophical position was one that stressed the interaction of subject and object in a dialectic of *change*. In those few hectic days before his commitment took him to Spain, where the counter-revolutionary machinations of Stalin were already at work, he set out the essence of this philosophical position — for the last time — in a letter to his friends, Paul and Elizabeth Beard.

I cannot answer your letter in full, in the present rush. I will only say that like most idealists, you separate subject

from object, and ascribe 'materialism' to the object and
'spirit' to the subject. The result is that the object becomes
so abstract it is just hard matter and the subject so blood-less
and attenuated that it is just Idea. But neither can live
without the other: they exist for us only in their active
relationship where they interpenetrate; and that is life in all
the vivid living of it, with its bony skeleton of iron abstract
laws (the object) and its vivid beauty and tragedy and
accident (the subject).[65]

It is our 'tragedy' that Caudwell, so aware himself of the
fragmentary nature of much of his work, was unable to return to
it, to come back and 'refine' it, as he put it in the same letter.
Nevertheless, his work will be remembered as representative of
'the most heroic effort of any British Marxist to think his own
intellectual time'.[66] It was the intention of this study to offer
documentary evidence to affirm and support such a belief. The
chapter which follows is intended to situate Caudwell, however
obliquely, in more contemporary surroundings, to juxtapose some
of his insights with those of other thinkers, both within and outside
the Marxist tradition.

# Notes

1. The *Studies* have been subjected to arbitrary publication. 'Further'
studies refers not to the sequence of composition, but rather it signifies
a sequel within the publishing industry. Caudwell's vast project has
appeared as follows: *Studies in a dying culture* (1938; 1971); *The crisis in
physics* (1939); *Further studies in a dying culture* (1949; 1971); *Romance and
realism* (1970). *The concept of freedom* (1964) is comprised of some of the
essays from *Studies* and some from *The crisis in physics*.
2. George Moberg, Review of *Studies and further studies in a dying culture*
and *Romance and realism* in *Telos*, no. 12 (Summer 1972), pp. 143–54;
Francis Mulhern, 'The Marxist aesthetics of Christopher Caudwell', *New
Left Review*, no. 85 (May/June 1974), pp. 37–58; E. P. Thompson,
'Caudwell', *The socialist register* (London, Merlin Press, 1977), pp. 228–76;
Samuel Hynes, Introduction to *Romance and realism*, p. 23.
3. Thompson, 'Caudwell', p. 239. He alludes here to the study
'Consciousness', a dialectical exploration of the neuro-physiological bases
of thought processes, an essay that this commentator (along with many
others) feels inadequate to judge. It was Terry Eagleton who had accused
Caudwell of making 'hectic forays into and out of alien territories'.
4. It might be beneficial here to remind ourselves what Caudwell has
in mind when he speaks of 'bourgeois culture'. In essence, his intention

in these studies is to break down, deconstruct, those seemingly 'natural' ways of seeing and to show that in reality they are conventional viewpoints that have their formal origins in a particular ideology. The following definition of 'bourgeois', from Raymond Williams's *Keywords* (New York, Oxford University Press, 1976), pp. 38–9, may help focus attention on Caudwell's primary concern.

> Marx's new sense of bourgeois society followed earlier historical usage, from established and solvent burgesses to a growing class of traders, entrepreneurs and employers. His attack on what he called bourgeois political theory (the theory of *civil society*) was based on what he saw as its falsely universal concepts and institutions, which were in fact the concepts and institutions of a specifically bourgeois society: that is a society in which the bourgeoisie (the class name was now much more significant) had become or was becoming dominant ... different stages of the capitalist mode of production led to different stages of bourgeois society and hence bourgeois thought, bourgeois feeling, bourgeois ideology, bourgeois art.

5. *Romance and realism*, p. 137. The 'book' referred to here is *Studies in a dying culture* of which *Romance and realism* was originally only a part.

6. *Studies and further studies in a dying culture*, pp. xxii–xxiii.

7. See, especially, *Studies and further studies*, pp. 248–9. *The crisis in physics* is largely concerned with this issue also and in this way the two studies complement one another.

8. *Studies and further studies*, pp. 218–19.

9. 'The theses on Feuerbach', in Robert C. Tucker (ed.), *The Marx-Engels reader*, 2nd edn (New York, W. W. Norton, 1978), p. 144.

10. *Ludwig Feuerbach and the outcome of classical German philosophy*, English translation (London, 1935), pp. 32–3. Caudwell has this book listed in his bibliography in the original German edition of 1886.

11. Lenin's book (listed in the bibliography to *Illusion and reality*) caught Caudwell's imagination. Regarding phenomenalism as a form of idealism, Lenin explained the implications of such a system for human knowledge; from its effects on 'common understanding' to those on the 'new physics', which seemed to deny the existence of matter.

12. *Studies and further studies*, p. 237.

13. George Moberg, who interviewed some of Caudwell's old comrades from the Poplar days, remarks on this in his biography.

14. Letter to Elizabeth Beard, 30 November 1935. However, he found what he thought was a more applicable epigraph in Max Planck's *Where is science going?* (1933), although he must have planned and then forgot (in his extreme haste) to use Lenin's dictum as well because he directs the reader's attention on p. xx of the Foreword to the 'quoted words of Lenin'.

15. This appears in *The crisis in physics*, p. 11n.

16. Caudwell's personal reasons for coming to terms with 'freedom' is again a reflection of the debate of the epoch. See, for example, T. H. Wintringham (he fought with Caudwell in Spain), 'Who is for liberty?'

*Left Review,* vol. I, no. 12 (September 1935), pp. 482–7: 'Before we can get further ahead in Britain we must come to terms about the idea of freedom ... I mean all those who want peace, who hate oppression and exploitation, have got to find common ground as to what we mean by freedom' (p. 482). And see Strachey's remarks on freedom, page 136.

17. *Studies and further studies,* p. 196.

18. Ibid., p. 199.

19. Compare Engels in *Anti-Duhring*: 'Freedom of the will means nothing but the capacity to make decisions with real knowledge of the subject.'

20. *Studies and further studies,* p. xix. It is apposite to point out here that Caudwell examines such figures as 'symptomatic' of an ideology that cannot affect any cure, because although they are figures who are 'sincere' in themselves, they are entrapped within the very syndrome they wish to critique. He is not as interested in the work of these men as in what he believes to be the framework of its ideological genesis, and for this reason the reader should not go to the *Studies* for any form of concrete criticism. Spender, therefore, is right, when in his review of the book he remarks negatively: 'He examines not books, but attitudes and opinions ...' See *Tribune,* 23 December 1938.

21. *Studies and further studies,* p. 3.

22. Ibid., p. 8.

23. See *The coming struggle for power* (London, Gollancz, 1934), p. 199.

24. *Studies and further studies,* p. 15.

25. Ibid., p. 58.

26. Ibid., p. 64.

27. Ibid., p. 61.

28. Ibid., p. 9.

29. Ibid., p. 69.

30. See, for example, Douglas Garman (he gave those 'Marxism and literature' classes which Caudwell attended early in 1936), who wrote in his review of Frieda Lawrence's book, *Not I but the wind*: 'The energy he [Lawrence] expended in looking for an acceptable society he might have put into helping create one' (*Left Review,* vol. 1, no. 7 (April 1935), pp. 286–7). 'The young communist intellectual, John Cornford, condemned Lawrence for seeing through the bourgeois society in which he lived, yet refusing to partake in the struggle needed to change it. See Peter Stansky and William Abrahams, *Journey to the frontier: Julian Bell and John Cornford: their lives and the 1930's* (London, Constable, 1966), p. 219.

31. Garman, ibid., p. 287.

32. *Studies and further studies,* p. 76. For a sympathetic yet critical review of *Experiment in autobiography,* see Ralph Fox, 'The open conspirator', *Left Review,* vol. I, no. 3 (December 1934), pp. 87–91. Another review, appearing about the time Caudwell was writing his study, is relevant: 'Nobody loves them but H. G. Wells', *Left Review,* vol. 2, no. 8 (May 1936), p. 408.

33. *Studies and further studies,* p. 83.

34. It was, ironically enough, this exact charge which Maurice

Cornforth levelled against Caudwell's own work in the *Modern Quarterly* debate.

35. Caudwell picks up on Strachey's remark, but argues that Wells, because of his class position, is an encyclopaedist *manqué*. See *Studies*, p. 84.

36. Strachey, *The coming struggle for power*, p. 189.

37. *Studies and further studies*, pp. 86–8.

38. *Studies and further studies*, p. 116.

39. George Moberg (note 2 above) feels that the *Studies* are weakened by the fact that Caudwell minimises, 'at least by implication, the consciously employed deceptive tactics in the bourgeois ideological conditioning of the ruled masses' (p. 144).

40. *Studies and further studies*, p. 86.

41. *Studies and further studies*, p. 120.

42. *The German ideology* in Tucker (ed.), *The Marx-Engels reader*, pp. 164–5.

43. *Studies and further studies*, p. 133.

44. *Studies and further studies*, p. 36.

45. See Samuel Hynes, *The Auden generation* (London, The Bodley Head, 1976), p. 191.

46. Ralph Fox, 'Lawrence the 20th century hero', *Left Review*, vol. I, no. 10 (July 1935), pp. 391–6.

47. Ibid., p. 391.

48. *Studies and further studies*, p. 23.

49. *Now and then* (Spring 1934).

50. As Caudwell points out in his essay, Lawrence was 'fascinated' by the potentiality of the machine. Like Caudwell, he was particularly interested in powered flight. He died, as is well known, after an accident on his powerful motor cycle which he had a reputation for riding recklessly.

51. See the letter quoted in John Strachey's introduction to *Studies*, p. v.

52. The anti-pacifist sentiment invaded the 'poetic' realm as well, as witnessed by this alliterative effort by R. E. Warner (with its not very subtle allusion to Rupert Brooke) which appeared in *Left Review*, vol. I, no. 10 (July 1935), p. 396.

> On lovely levels, whining in a wash of gold
> Pacifists, pale as porridge, are burying bugles,
> Who feel no fight, who are learned liberals.
>
> Blow bugle, blow! Let loose, lungs over the meadows
> to tell these twisters that war is being waged
> cruelly in complete peace and pleasant pastures.

53. Published in *Left Review*, vol. 2, no. 11 (August 1936), pp. 539–41. C. Day Lewis's reply, 'We're not going to do nothing', appeared in the November issue.

54. Part of Caudwell's unpublished paper appeared in *Left Review*, vol. 3, no. 11 (December 1937), pp. 657–61, as a form of response to Huxley's recently published *Ends and means*.

55. *Studies and further studies*, pp. 120–1.

56. Quoted by Hynes, *The Auden generation*, p. 195. See also Stansky

and Abrahams, *Journey to the frontier*, p. 107, on how the advent of the Spanish War changed Bell's outlook, as it did that of many of the younger intellectuals.

57. *Studies and further studies*, p. 126.

58. *The crisis in physics*, p. 27.

59. This is not surprising since, as I argue elsewhere, he was still revising *Illusion and reality* while writing the *Studies*. Compare, for example, pp. 40–50 of *Romance and realism* with pp. 73–83 of *Illusion and reality*.

60. *Romance and realism*, p. 138. Emphases added.

61. Ibid., pp. 99–100. As his editor remarks, Caudwell is confusing Virginia Woolf's *A room of one's own* with E. M. Forster's *A room with a view*.

62. Ibid., pp. 100–1.

63. Ibid., p. 111.

64. Georg Lukács, *The meaning of contemporary realism*, trans. John and Necke Mander (London, Merlin Press, 1972).

65. Letter dated 9 December 1936.

66. E. P. Thompson, in 'Caudwell'.

# 6

## Postscript: Implicating Caudwell

*Social life is essentially* practical. *All mysteries which mislead theory into mysticism find their rational solution in human practice and in the comprehension of this practice.*

Marx

*Language expresses not merely what reality is (what reality is stares man in the face) it expresses also what can be done with reality.*

Caudwell

*Surely, as all Marxists know, there is something intolerable about the use of the accusation of 'vulgar Marxism' to frighten us away from the real issues and to encourage a kind of intellectual discourse more respectable and more acceptable in the university.*

Fredric Jameson

This synopsis of Caudwell's thought is intended to highlight its modernity, indeed in many respects its contemporaneity. By entitling this postscript 'Implicating Caudwell' I have in mind at least two senses of the term: how Caudwell is implied by (or folded within) other discourses and how he is (or should be) 'involved' in them. Such 'implications' need not necessarily be Marxist in their importance, but since historical materialism offers what Fredric Jameson has called 'that untranscendable horizon'

160

in any interpretation of human cultural productions, Caudwell's work can be seen as a contribution that needs to be modified and absorbed within more recent theoretical concerns. We should re-read him in the light of contemporary thought (just as Marx himself on whom Caudwell bases his theory is currently being re-read) and attempt to salvage what is productive in Caudwell's writings rather than, at one extreme, treat him as a Romantic revolutionary who is beyond criticism, or at the other, as a 'vulgar Marxist' who has no place in contemporary debate. For Caudwell *was* concerned with many of the problems which punctuate critical debate today, albeit sometimes in an inchoate and disorganised way, and with a nomenclature that is at times eccentric. He concerned himself primarily with the problem of the subject, the role of language in the structuration of consciousness, and the nature of 'reality' in relation to humanity's imaginary or illusory understanding of it. In short, as was most evident in the discussion of *Illusion and reality*, he was concerned with the symbolic function within the broader ordering of *les sciences de l'homme*. This entailed for Caudwell (as it should for all Marxists) the search for a social psychology wrought out of biological being.

Such an endeavour, involved as it is with the formation of the subject, results in the confluence of those areas of discourse so prominent in modern debate — psychoanalysis, anthropology, and the 'great instrument', language, through which the subject is ultimately constituted. Some of the implications of Caudwell's discourse may have already 'implied' themselves — the social nature of consciousness, the reality producing nature of language, the intersubjective nature of social signs — but this postscript is meant to serve as a prologemena to any further re-reading of his work.

Caudwell's theory of the 'subject' (and this concept needs to be explored in the light of Lacanian theory before the quotation marks can be removed) is comparable to the following post-modernist, semiotic account offered by Kaja Silverman, whose book offers an extremely clear exposition of the historical confluence of many of the strands that led to the contemporary theory of the subject, from Peirce to Lacan.

The term 'subject' foregrounds the relationship between ethnology, psychoanalysis, and semiotics. It helps to conceive of human reality as a construction, as the product of

> signifying activities ... It suggests that even desire is
> culturally instigated, and hence collective ... the term
> 'subject' challenges the value of stability attributed to the
> individual.[1]

Indeed the epigraph to Silverman's book from Benveniste to the
effect that it is 'in and through language that man constitutes
himself as a *subject*, because language alone establishes the concept
of "ego" in reality', accentuates Caudwell's implication in modern
debate. His concept of the 'social ego' as a space where inner and
outer signs meet and dialectically modify one another is essentially
built (as was Volosinov's theory of consciousness) on the foundation of language or signifying practices. That is to say — and
Caudwell argued this throughout his work — a theory of the
psyche, of consciousness, of the 'subject', must be wrought out of
a sociology reliant on intersubjective sign-systems. This is why
Caudwell can maintain that even a sunset is 'a social event'.
Caudwell's 'social ego', then, is a sociologically based, quasi-
semiotic account of the psyche, and just as his concern with the
social nature of consciousness brought him into conflict with
Freud, so now his discourse has to confront, be read alongside,
the work of Freud's revisionists, most notably, Jaques Lacan and
his disciple Louis Althusser. Such a dialogue has important ramifications on the nature of the human subject, its illusions and
realities, its desires and cultural creations.

It is not meant as a gesture of direct or evaluative comparison
if, throughout this summary of Caudwell's cultural theory, I have
frequent occasion to refer to Fredric Jameson's *The political
unconscious*. It is simply that this Marxist enterprise, with its
expansive syntheses — Lacan, Althusser, Burke, Frye, among
others — offers us a contemporary yardstick with which to juxtapose Caudwell's own synthetic contribution to Marxist cultural
theory. Jameson, in what might be called a 'meta-allegory', utilises
the work done by the anthropologists — particularly Lévi-Strauss
— the theory of symbolic action as promulgated by Kenneth
Burke, and the dialectical interplay between 'Desire' and
'Necessity', which in turn brings into play the nature of the subject,
language and ideology. His basic concern is to bring to the surface
the repressed aim of cultural texts, that 'single fundamental theme
— for Marxism the collective struggle to wrest a realm of freedom
from a realm of Necessity'. This is brought about by the unmasking
of cultural artefacts as 'socially symbolic acts' in the great

'collective story' of history. I do not wish to go into Jameson's complex methodology here — with its fundamental Freudian paradigm as revised by the work of Lacan, Macherey, Althusser — whereby, to adapt some words from Stephen Dedalus, history is a nightmare from which the text is unwilling to awake. Through analysis, however, it can be made to reveal the 'absent cause' which at one and the same time brings both itself and the textualisation of the historical situation into being. The grounding for such a notion of textuality is based on Lacan's notion of the 'Real' as that which 'resists symbolisation absolutely' and we shall have more to say on this viewpoint presently. At this stage I am interested in bringing to the surface Jameson's broader vision where a text (and here he is speaking of modernism) is a symbolic act 'which involves a whole Utopian compensation for increasing dehumanization on the level of daily life'.[2] One of Jameson's commentators has expressed this concern in terms that recall Caudwell's central considerations:

> To observe that the world that came into existence with Newton's *Principia* is colorless, then, is to say something at once rigorous and precise. For from classical or Newtonian mechanics to quantum theory and beyond, physics has gained the power of describing the world in abstract or mathematical terms (mathematics being for Jameson the very type of ideality that can operate only through a denial of concrete reality) only to the degree that it is literally colorless, an endless dance of particles ... [This is what] Jameson has in mind when he envisions the first fall out of primitive communism as beginning the process through which the world begins to be drained of its fullness, its vividness, and its color.[3]

Caudwell, too, felt that a splitting of the subject and object, the rational from the emotional, verse from mathematics, led to a similar world drained of its colour. In both Jameson and Caudwell cultural artefacts are looked at, not as static aesthetic forms, but as symbolic acts or practices — in Burkean terms 'strategies' — for resolving or attempting to resolve contradictions in social life. As Caudwell was to utilise the field anthropologists to show how such contradictions are resolved symbolically, so too does Jameson draw on the work of Lévi-Strauss to demonstrate how the primitive through an imaginative act attempts to come to terms with a contradiction in his or her reality.

Caudwell might not have envisaged Necessity as 'the inexorable *form* of events', a sort of proto-narrative, nor could he have thought of history as an 'absent cause' (his historical moment was much too urgently present for such theoretical transcendence), but he would have concurred with Jameson that 'History is what hurts, it is what refuses desire and sets inexorable limits to individual as well as collective praxis.'[4] Poetry, or imaginative experiment, we will remember, is for Caudwell generated precisely as part of that broader contradiction which drives on society — 'the contradiction between man's desires and Nature's necessity'.[5] In this sense Caudwell viewed the function of poetry as helping to shape the desires of man toward 'reality' in the hope of rescuing some 'realm of freedom' from the inexorability of Necessity. Science plays its role too, on the rational plane of causality and the necessity of physical laws in the environment. Conceived in this way Jameson's essay 'On interpretation', with which he begins his book, serves as a counterpart to Caudwell's Marxist aesthetic. The texts that Jameson interrogates, the repressed desires his methodology hopes to bring to the surface, are akin to the desires to alter 'reality' or the historical moment, which Caudwell saw as the genesis and function of the imaginative or symbolic act. But before exploring this hypothesis, we might do well to summarise Caudwell's position within the Marxist tradition as a whole.

## Caudwell's Marx

We have seen that the focal centre of Caudwell's system is humanity's reliance on the symbolic function, if men and women are to become human at all. This reliance both takes place within and contributes to their species development and their adaptation to their environment. The 'philosophical anthropology' which lies behind such a view of human nature is largely that of the early Marx, but it is inherent also in the first volume of *Capital*, where the relationship of labour and imagination are discussed, wherein the result of the labour process is already present at its inception in the *imagination* of the worker, in an idealised form. Sidney Finkelstein, who quotes this passage in an essay which owes a debt to Caudwell, summarises the position thus:

> Art is creation according to the laws of beauty and the laws
> of beauty, if we follow the early Marx, rise out of the process
> of humanizing reality. A work of art is a man-created struc-
> ture, using language ... or any other socially created means
> for exploring inner and outer reality. As such it becomes a
> social possession and a means for educating and transform-
> ing people in their ability to respond to the world about
> them.[6]

This 'humanisation of nature' is the result of a struggle brought
about by a contradiction between man's desires and nature's
necessity. Caudwell's notion of the function of poetry, then, falls
within this broader field of tensions: poetry is generated out of a
wish to 'resolve' the conflict between man's inner being and his
recognition of outer necessity.

Such a vision is derived from and belongs to the classical
Marxist position with its belief in the indissoluble unity of theory
and practice. Caudwell's thought, as outlined in Chapter 4, finds
its co-ordinates in Engels's 'ascent of man' in social evolution,
the Marx of *The German ideology* and the *Theses on Feuerbach*, and
Plekhanov's 'Fundamental principles'. It belongs to the tradition
espoused by Ernst Bloch who emphasised the origins and function
of art in the realm of collectivity, which in turn rests upon the
Marxian supposition of art's role in the humanisation of reality.
As Robert Weimann has remarked (with echoes of Caudwellian
terminology), art is 'not merely a product, but a "producer" of
its age: not merely a mirror of the past, but a lamp to the future'.
He goes on: 'Incidentally it was Karl Marx who pointed out that
art is one of the "besondere Weisen der Produktion" — the "special
forms of production" — in the sense that the work of art can
produce its audience and influence their values and "attitudes".'[7]
Humanity's art forms, in other words, help express its species
essence; the humanisation of nature, the path to freedom — what
Caudwell called making the 'thing in itself' a 'thing for us' — is
brought about by *labour*, including, on the one hand, science, and
on the other, art.

That the core of Caudwell's system relies on a Marxist 'philosophical anthropology' — the Marxism of telos and the human
subject as an agent of change in history — is without doubt.
However, despite the fact that he was 'insulated from much of
Europe' as well as 'intellectually isolated' (Terry Eagleton), there
is much in his writings that bears comparison with those European

theorists who have been grouped under 'Western Marxism', some of whom 're-wrote' Marx in the light of his 'intellectual ancestry'.[8] Louis Althusser is a special case with whom I want to deal later, but those others of the 'school' (whom Althusser set out later to criticise) — Gramsci, Lukács and Lucien Goldmann — illuminate much of Caudwell's work. Lukács puts the same crucial emphasis on the dialectical nature of the subject–object relation for any sound epistemology; that 'in all metaphysics the object remains untouched and unaltered so that thought remains contemplative and fails to become practical', and we have seen the significance of this epistemological dualism for both Caudwell and Lukács as it is revealed in the 'ideology of modernism' and the nature of narrativity. Like Gramsci, Caudwell emphasises a 'reality' only in its relation to man, in praxis, the interrelationship of social co-operation and the natural world. The following two statements (the first by Gramsci), bear close resemblance: 'We know reality only in relation to man, and since man is historical becoming, knowledge and reality are also a becoming and so is objectivity.' Caudwell puts it like this: If causality is to have any meaning for science, it must be within the realm of practical activity: 'the thing in itself becoming the thing for us'. This is because the thing-in-itself 'cannot exist ... We change it — produce qualities — ripples in the water, synthetic dyes, artificial rocks, and sun images'.

> Hence 'naive realism' or materialism is justified not by theoretical arguments but by practice. By continually 'changing Nature', by continually producing effects and phenomena we learn the qualities of matter. Matter is a mere name — as vacuous as not-matter. It is only matter in its causality, in the relations which make *qualities* appear, that becomes rigid and fleshy and really *existent*. In this sense existence is power.[9]

It is perhaps Lukács's pupil, Lucien Goldmann, whose work most aptly bears comparison with Caudwell's. Goldmann evolved his system from the early Lukács of *Soul and form* and *History and class consciousness* and integrated this work with the genetic psychology of Jean Piaget, whose interactionist epistemology also had an influence on Caudwell. Piaget believed that the continual interaction between human beings and their environment produced experiential adaptation, a view which Goldmann recognised as being compatible with a Marxist epistemology. Apart from this Piagetian interactive epistemology, both Caudwell and Goldmann share an interest in the role of biology (to a lesser extent in Goldmann) in the formation of the 'anthropological subject' and the transindividuality of such subjects through the nature of sign-systems, which produce what Goldmann calls the 'collective subject' and Caudwell the 'Social Ego'. The resultant 'cultural creations', including works of art, help create 'possible consciousness' (Goldmann's term), a function which takes its place within the broader adaptation of the subject to its environment. This statement is by Goldmann, but it could be Caudwell: 'Man transforms the world around him in order to achieve a better balance between himself (as subject) and the world.'[10] The two thinkers have much in common in their dialogue with Freud as well. Just as Caudwell had pointed out how the dream was essentially biographical as compared to the poem (or imaginative creation) which has to be turned out in social coinage, so too does Goldmann make the distinction 'between the subject of libidinal behaviour and the subject of historical action and of the cultural creation'.[11] Most revealing is Goldmann's criticism of Freud with regard to illusion and the future, so important to the Caudwell of *Illusion and reality*:

> Further, there is nothing surprising in the fact that Freud's thought, in spite of its genetic character, ignores the future and seems to develop into a two-dimensional temporality: the present and the past, with a clear dominance of the latter. If I am not mistaken, the word 'future' is found only once in the title of one of his books, *The future of an illusion*, which demonstrates that this illusion does not have a *future*.[12]

## The symbolic

For Caudwell the 'life of the simplest tribe' — and unlike non-human species, guided in their development by pure unconscious necessity, by blind biological workings of the organism — must rely on a collective fictionality that can prepare for desires which are not immediately available. A relatively unmediated example of this would be the ritual that ensures the success of the harvest. This is why Caudwell maintains at one point that poetry is 'economic', that these 'cultural creations', as Goldmann terms them, have a real functional role to play in the community. Poetry is a *socially symbolic act*, whereby humanity's desire is channelled in art toward a social function; it is 'symbolised' as social coin and becomes part of a collectivity to be shared. Fredric Jameson (as his subtitle suggests) enlists Kenneth Burke's notion of symbolic action as 'a way of doing something to the world', and this has obvious parallels with the epicentre of Caudwell's theory. Burke's notion, implying as it does, the concept of symbolic action as a modern 'substitute' for ancient collectivity, bears close comparison with Caudwell's thought. Burke's work too has been described as being 'a bewildering number of quarries in no apparent sequence ... an inexhaustible throwing off of sparks'.[13] Burke has described art as 'biological adaptation', he has recruited the anthropological theories of Frazer and Malinowski in order to posit the poet as (in John Crowe Ransom's terms) 'medicine man'. He experimented with a synthesis of Marx and Freud ('Psychology and Economics' as he called it) and enlisted those 'psychologisms' with social emphases, such as Jung, Rivers and McDougall, all of whom are listed in Caudwell's bibliography. Burke's essay, 'Literature as equipment for living', which he termed as a 'sociological criticism of literature', implies in its very title the similarity of the concerns of the two men. He writes:

> Proverbs are *strategies* for dealing with *situations*. In so far as situations are typical and recurrent in a given social structure, people develop names for them and strategies for handling them. Another name for strategies might be *attitudes*.[14]

Striking an attitude toward an experience in the interests of 'human welfare' is of course at the heart of Caudwell's theory. Just as Burke extrapolates the poetic function from the social function of proverbs, so too does Caudwell evolve modern symbolic acts out of the attitudinal significance of ritual for the welfare of the tribe, for the well-being of the Social Ego.

On the very first page of his book, Burke outlines a system which could almost serve as an epigraph to Caudwell's *Illusion and reality*.

> Situations do overlap, if only because men now have the same neural and muscular structures as men who have left their records from past ages. We and they are in much the

same biological situation ... And the nature of the human mind itself, with the function of abstraction rooted in the nature of language, also provides us with 'levels of generalization' ... by which situations greatly different in their particularities may be felt to belong in the same class (to have a common substance or essence).[15]

We have seen how I. A. Richards, working from anthropology, had proposed that the poem (or imaginative fiction) achieved an emotional resolution without overt action and how Caudwell had similarly maintained that the poem, although symbolic and not to be confused with the 'real' world, was still no mere 'phantom aesthetic state' but would have a bearing on any future dealings with reality. Remarking on Burke's theory of symbolic action, Jameson attempts to connect this with — or account for — Althusser's notion of history as 'absent cause', derived as it is from Lacan's 'Real' as that which resists symbolisation. What the text does in fact is to 'bring into being that very situation to which it is also, at one and the same time a *reaction*'.[16] Such an operational device with regard to cultural objects — the textualisation of the 'real' — is essentially what Caudwell outlined as the function of language itself, which he characterised as having a 'tendentious reaction to reality':

It is precisely because language expresses feeling, is a judging as well as a picture of parts of reality, that it is valuable. Language expresses not merely what reality is (what reality is stares man in the face) it expresses also what can be done with reality ... Language is a tool to express what reality is in relation to man — not abstract man but concrete human beings.[17]

Jameson's intricate synthetic web of current theory incorporates Burke's ideas on symbolic action with the myth criticism of Northrop Frye, wherein 'we see literature as a weaker form of myth, or a later stage of ritual ... a symbolic meditation on the destiny of community'.[18] Caudwell's notion of 'squaring the environment with inner desire', a desire which is constitutively social because of the collective nature of the symbolic, bears relation with Jameson's incorporation of Burke's theory and Northrop Frye's move away from 'the Freudian hermeneutic to a quite different interpretation ... conceiving of the function of culture explicitly in social terms'.[19] There is something very Caudwellian in the following remarks by Frye which Jameson quotes to demonstrate the link between desire and society:

> Civilization is not merely an imitation of nature, and it is impelled by the force that we have just called desire ... [Desire] is neither limited to nor satisfied by objects, but is the *energy* that leads human society to develop its own form. Desire in this sense is the *social* aspect of what we met on the literal level as emotion, an impulse towards expression which would have remained amorphous if the poem had not liberated it by providing the form of its expression ... The efficient cause of civilization is *work*, and poetry in its social aspect has the *function* of expressing, as *a verbal hypothesis*, a vision of the goal of work and the forms of desire.[20]

We have here in condensed form the primary elements of Caudwell's theory, that 'social dreaming' expressed in linguistic or symbolic terms gives form to humanity's desires.

Any mention of the subject and desire was, at one time, anathema in any 'orthodox' Marxist discourse, as the debate conducted by the *Modern Quarterly* gives testimony. Yet, as Reuben Osborn makes explicit in his essay on Freud and Marx referred to in Chapter 4 (and the position is implied throughout Caudwell's thought), it is absolutely *necessary* to recognise the workings of desire in order to obtain freedom, in the same way that we must recognise the laws of social relations.

## The subject

In his attempt to subsume or circumscribe as a final horizon those other 'ideological' hermeneutic systems which deal with the inter-relations of the subject and society, the nature of the 'real' and the meta-symbolic system of language which is their 'cohesive bond', Jameson addresses the work done by Jaques Lacan in this area, especially his advance in 'solving' the problem of the individual subject, where wish-fulfilment remains 'locked' within a particular psychobiography. This is analogous to Caudwell's distinction between the dream and the poem, whereby the former is tied to a unique psychobiography and the latter must enter the symbolic, social world of intersubjective sign-systems. Some commentators have remarked on Lacan's contribution to a social psychology that is compatible with historical materialism, mainly due to the fact that his theory is based on the 'motor of all historical movement: contradiction'. Thus the subject according to Lacan is 'constructed from the process of the interaction of the somatic drives with the movement of the contradictory outside'.[21] This is of course nothing new. Such a position was argued by Reuben Osborn in his book *Marx and Freud* (1937) and is implied in Caudwell's theory of art's function as a component within the broader contradiction that 'drives on society', the conflict of inner desire and outer necessity. Indeed, Caudwell's idea of the 'subject', based as it is on the work done by the anthropologists, shares to some extent Lacan's 'socialising of the psyche' and the replacement of the old autonomous cogito with a process dependent on the symbolic. The collectivity which Lévi-Strauss (and after him Lacan), seeks to prove for the unconscious is analogous with what Caudwell set out to demonstrate for the *consciousness* of social beings, their 'social ego'. To oversimplify matters, we could say that Caudwell did not concern himself with the hypothesis of a pre-symbolic humanity, the Lacanian metaphysical notion of the 'true' subject.

A crucial question is whether or not Lacan's notion of the 'subject' *is* compatible with historical or dialectical materialism, dependent as it is on a biological entity rather than what Marx termed the 'aggregate of social relations'. Caudwell believed that what is 'distinctively human in the nature of man's adaptation [is that it is] ideologically and socially mediated, instead of genetically implanted', and that

> Consciousness, in the broadest sense (including therefore the subconscious, which is also the product of modified instinct), is a social product. It is not merely that consciousness has a social component. The construction of consciousness is the socialising of the psyche.[22]

If for Lacan the 'true' or 'absolute subject' is the new-born child (or indeed, as implied at times, a pre-natal, androgynous entity without difference of any kind), then this idea of 'subject' would equate with what Caudwell terms some 'brute' form of life, some hypothetical genotypical or biological entity, without language, or that 'aggregate of social relations' of which Marx speaks in the Sixth Thesis as constituting the 'human essence'. But such an abstract individual is ultimately unknowable, so that just as Caudwell suggests we can only know the instinctual drives (genotypical traits) through their interaction with the social environment and thus must hypothesise or mythologise them as separate entities, so too must Lacan 'mythologise' his so-called 'subject', since 'it' can only be known through the symbolic and social relations into which it enters.

There is a concomitant mythological or allegorical narrative associated with the Lacanian 'subject', no doubt brought about by his own enigmatic style and sibylline methodology. His description of signification — with such terminology as 'caught', 'at the mercy of', 'sacrificed to', 'trapped' — his theory of language and the subject has given rise to a yet more circumspect myth, that of an Edenic 'Fall' into language, into knowledge, and the 'mere' symbolisation of the 'Real'. For Lacan, entrance into the symbolic order, the step that constitutes us as social beings, is seen as a further *alienation* of the 'subject' — the *stade du mirroir* being a previous stage. The entrance into the symbolic order as alienation is in these terms a form of 'banishment' from plenitude, from primordial unity, into a world of difference, division and knowledge, once we have taken one bite of the symbolic or epistemological apple, whether it be simply 'fort' or 'da'. Terry Eagleton's discussion of Lacan in his survey of literary theory is paradigmatic of such a typological or allegorical reading: the child is forced to wander along the metynomic chain, 'severed from ... that inaccessible realm', always searching for the 'lost paradise in the endless metynomic movement of desire'.[23]

Kaja Silverman offers us both a cogent summary of Lacan's position (as far as that is possible) and a graphic illustration of his theory of the 'subject' and the alienating effects of the symbolic. In this Rousseauesque scenario the noble savage is caught, imprisoned, and made to undergo the tortures of culture. Werner Herzog's film *Everyman for himself and God against all* dramatises the acquisition of language by one Kasper Hauser, an *enfant sauvage* who has spent the 30 years of his life existing in a cave without either language or culture.[24] Silverman summarises the Lacanian point of view thus:

> Kasper's entry into meaning ... confines him inside what Fredric Jameson would call 'the prison house of language'

... Kasper is thereafter as fully alienated from his being, and
the world of actual objects, as was Freud's grandson after
he uttered the word 'da'.[25]

What '*actual*' objects are in themselves, without language, outside
the realm of social discourse and signification, is a metaphysical
quandary. What a 'being' is without recourse to an epistemological
faculty, a consciousness and *unconsciousness* formed by a socially
constructed symbolic order, is a heuristic fiction, a metaphor as
intriguing as the movie itself. Kasper Hauser becomes a 'true'
human subject only when he becomes an epistemological being
for whom objects have *significance*. As for the 'Real', it (whatever
'it' is) is epistemologically dead and only becomes an 'object'
when visited by a knowledge-seeking subject. Subject and object,
as Caudwell would have it, mutually define one another. Lacan's
'subject', then, is equivalent to Caudwell's hypothetical 'genotype
or individual, the instinctive man as he is born, who if "left to
himself" might grow up into something like a dumb brute'.[26]
Volosinov, as we have seen, takes a similar position: 'the abstract
biological person ... does not exist at all. It is an improper
abstraction. Outside society and, consequently, outside socio-
economic conditions, there is no such thing as a human being'.[27]

## Language and reference

The key human element here is of course language, the 'great
instrument' in the formation of consciousness. In summarising
some of Lacan's main observations on his 'subject', Kaja Silverman remarks that

> language isolates the subject from the real confining it forever
> to the realm of signification ... Moreover, since language
> speaks no more to the reality of objects than it does to that
> of subjects, it effects as complete a rupture with the *phenomenal*
> world.[28]

Caudwell believed that it is only through 'producing effects and
phenomena [that] we learn the qualities of matter', of objects in
the world. So in this sense language does not *alienate* us from the
phenomenal world; indeed it helps create it out of the flux of
unknowable noumena.

Lacan's notion of the 'Real' as that which 'resists symbolization absolutely' would have sounded to Caudwell like a piece of Kantian idealism. For Caudwell, noumena were a necessary fiction and in practice of no interest to social beings; it is only through humanity's need to make matter — 'reality' — exhibit phenomena that is of importance. The real can only be *real* for creatures whose social fabric is wrought out of symbolic inter-subjectivity. The rest can, and must, be passed over in silence, for otherwise we enter the world of metaphysics. Lacan states his views on the nature of language and reality in the following way:

> For it is still not enough to say that the concept is the thing itself as any child can demonstrate against the scholar. It is the world of words which creates the world of things — the things originally confused in the *hic et nunc* of the all-in-the-process-of-becoming — by giving its concrete being to their essence, and its ubiquity to what has been from everlasting.[29]

As Anthony Wilden comments: 'For Lacan, the interaction between discourse and perception is such that language, and not perception, is or becomes primary.'[30] The uncertainty here of 'is' or 'becomes' points up the problem. It is one thing to suggest as does Cassirer (and Caudwell) that it is the symbolic which provides the structure for ordering reality, that 'language is a mediator in the formation of objects' (Cassirer), and yet another — although this is to stress the obvious — that it is the world of words which *creates* the world of things. Caudwell would want to argue that it is language that *reacts* to the world of things which in turn truly *creates* concepts, symbols, meaning. It is not a question of 'primacy' of language over perception, but a dialectical interchange, an interchange which must find its niche in an already structured symbolic order.

In a recent discussion of the problematic concerning significa-tion — the nature of perception and reference — Robert Scholes has described the issue succinctly when he remarks that 'the problem is not really a matter of the referent but of reference; not a matter of question of whether the world exists but of whether we can perceive it or refer to it adequately'.[31] That is to say, Derrida, Lacan, De Man, and others of that school, accept (like that notable lady) the whole universe, but only as an entity lying adjacent to language, a reservoir for allegory. There is much in Scholes's discussion with which Caudwell concerned himself and with which he would have agreed: the importance of showing how signifiers are arbitrarily chosen, but that signifieds are linked conventionally to perceptual phenomena; that language is not a transparent window, but rather a reaction toward reality, encoding it, encrusting it with meaning, fabricating signs for social beings. Caudwell puts it like this:

> Objects detach themselves as objects from the flux of perception in so far as they become objects for social men. The sun, a mere unrecognised source of phototropism for animals, becomes a socially recognised object for man, ripener of harvest, measure of the working day, clock and compass of the hunter. The field of perception is organised into figure and ground only in so far as figures have a significance for the conjoint action of men.[32]

However, although Scholes sets out to rescue the referential 'human use of language that has been systematically repressed or ignored by structuralist and hermetic theoreticians' (and achieves this end in many important respects), his post-structuralist conclusion is contaminated by the same ideology of language as 'loss', as alienation from some mythical garden of plenitude:

> Human beings become human through the acquisition of language, and this acquisition alienates humans from all those things that language names. The name is a substitute for the thing: it displaces the thing in the very act of naming it, so that language finally stands even *between* one human being and another.[33]

The crucial word here is 'between' and that is why I have emphasised it, because we should understand it in its positive sense, as a link rather than a barrier. It is language's function to stand 'between' human beings, otherwise they would not be human beings at all. We have returned here to the problem of the 'true' subject, to the ideology of Lacanian metaphysics. As far as 'things' are concerned (the very nomenclature reveals the epistemological poverty), we might illustrate the problem here by modifying an analogous statement made by Wittgenstein at the beginning of the *Tractatus*. The world is *not* 'the totality of facts', but of 'things'. These 'things' are epistemological non-entities until they are constructed into 'facts', meaning, by social beings. If anything is alienated in this state of affairs, it is the hypothetical 'thing-in-itself' which is appropriated for human use. What these so-called 'things' are is of no importance and, to borrow Wittgenstein's concluding remarks, we must 'pass over them in silence'.[34]

## Ideology

In the course of subsuming the work of Louis Althusser, especially his concept of history as 'absent cause', Fredric Jameson is forced to confront the problematic of the referent in the guise of the historical process itself. He remarks:

> We would therefore propose the following revised formulation: that history is *not* a text, not a narrative ... but as an absent cause, it is inaccessible to us except in textual form, and that our approach to it and the Real itself necessarily passes through its prior textualization, its narrativization in the political unconscious.[35]

In order to understand the world, in the process of humanising it we must 'textualise' it, turn the 'thing-in-itself' (as Caudwell has it) into a 'thing-for-us'. But Caudwell also remarked that 'words are the money of the ideological market of mankind', and when we enter the symbolic or textual terrain we encounter ideology. For Jameson the text banishes, represses, or confines to the margins its ideological matrices, in a way similar to how history as a sub-text is interwoven into the fabric of its textualisation.

The nature of ideology has never been a simple matter and there have been attempts to rewrite the basic (and at times contradictory) reflections on the concept by Marx, Engels and Lenin.[36] One of the most influential theories has been that of Louis Althusser. Working from the Lacanian revision of Freud, especially the former's concept of the 'Imaginary', Althusser conceives ideology as that system which supplies the illusion of a unified subject, free and independent of the relations which 'really' constitute it and to which it 'subjects' itself. It follows from this theory that ideology is a *necessary* condition for any society, since such representations are needed if the individual is to function within the social structure at all. This idea of ideology as a fabric of representations, rather than a conscious set of practices imposed by any one class for its own economic and political interests, would have caused Caudwell no discomfort in his understanding of the way ideology functions. His conception of ideology is one which sees it as an undifferentiated web, an 'atmospheric pressure' affecting both bourgeois ideologues and the ruling class alike, rather than a simplified version of a conscious manipulation of one class by another. This metaphoric portrayal of ideology as the very air we breathe is used by Althusser when he remarks that: 'Human societies secrete ideology as the element and atmosphere indispensable to their historical respiration and life.'[37] In 'Ideology and state apparatuses' Althusser remarks that 'what is represented in ideology is therefore not the system of the real relations which govern the existence of individuals, but the imaginary relation of those individuals to the real relations in which they live'.[38]

The notion of ideology as a system of representations, or rationalisations, an imaginary or illusory idea of reality as opposed to the 'real' conditions of existence, has the core of the classical position within it. This is implied in Engels's letter to Mehring (among other places) where he speaks of the effects of ideology on the subject, where the 'real motives impelling him remain unknown to him', and it was from such a position that Caudwell set out his ideas on ideology, ideas which cannot be reduced to a simplistic reflection theory, stating as he does the fact that the superstructure is a functional element 'which interacts with the foundations, each altering the other'. Moreover, Caudwell saw ideology and its illusions as essentially a phenomenon inherent within *class* society which would evaporate when 'reality' or scientific socialism imposed itself on the consciousness of men and women. He believed (and here he adheres to the classical tradition) that it was possible to step outside bourgeois ideology (as a *class* ideology) and reveal it for what it is, an imaginary, illusory notion of the individual as a 'totally autonomous' subject in relation to society. Caudwell thought that it was possible to transcend bourgeois class consciousness by revealing the social relations which such consciousness feels itself 'free of', to politicise bourgeois consciousness (as he did his own) which, in the truly

Marxist sense, is the only hope for struggle and *change*. Such a position is incompatible with the Althusserian understanding of ideology, with its emphasis on the individual, necessity and stasis: this viewpoint, coming as it does out of such idealist thinkers as Bachelard and Lacan, is caught up in an individual subjectivity rather than with the transformation of class positions.

Althusserian Marxism, and the psychoanalytically derived notion of ideology so pervasive in the mid-1970s, has come in for some harsh criticism. E. P. Thompson's extensive critique of Althusser, grounded on what he sees as an 'elitist division between theory and practice', not only enjoins us to see Althusserian structural Marxism as a 'stasis' (precluding any sense of class-struggle or change as suggested above), but also as 'idealist' and in the final analysis, ironically enough, as itself an 'ideology'.[39] More recently, Terry Eagleton has summed up the positive attributes of Althusser's thought and its ubiquitous overcompensations (one is tempted to say overdeterminations) with regard to classical Marxist exegesis. Eagleton, writing 'in the tranquillity of historical retrospect', puts the case like this:

> The benefit of each of Althusser's major theoretical concepts was that it sought to correct what could often be convincingly exposed as flawed or false conceptions in other traditions of Marxist thought; but, in almost every case, the alternative formulations offered turned out to be gravely and sometimes equally at fault ... A politically timely anti-humanism, seeking to dislodge the fetishized subject of existentialist, phenomenological and Christianized brands of Marxism by the recovery of the structural character of Marx's thought, fell almost instant prey to a 'structuralist' ideology which marginalized both subjects and class struggles. A fertile, suggestive theory of ideology, which broke decisively with older mechanical models, threatened to expand the concept of ideology to the point where it was emptied of political efficacy.[40]

'Political efficacy' was of course what Caudwell was concerned with both in his theoretical writings and in his life, the practical implications of theoretical premises in the ongoing class struggle that lies at the heart of a Marxist world-view. Nevertheless, there is implied in Caudwell's ideological theory a structuring 'a-historical theoreticism' as well as what Eagleton calls 'vulgarly teleological notions'. For Caudwell the structuring principle of bourgeois ideology, its synchronic aspect, is a false conception of freedom, (in his words) 'the illusion common to all class cultures and therefore to all ideologies except that of dialectical materialism'. But he believed also in a diachronic, historical process which would lead to a less distorted view of social relations, a scientific analysis of society that would dispense with that particular *class* ideology altogether.

Caudwell, as a subject reacting to the given reality of his own historical time was of course unable to step outside the 'ideological atmosphere' of which he wrote. He was unable to escape one of his own fundamental tenets, that the observer can never separate himself entirely from what is observed, contemplate it as an impartial entity. Such an impossibility is summarised by Fredric Jameson in his 'Conclusion', when he speaks of the 'nostalgia for some ultimate moment of cure, in which the dynamics of the unconscious proper rise to the light of day and of consciousness and are somehow "integrated" in an active lucidity about ourselves and the determinations of our desires and our behavior'.

> But the cure in that sense is a myth, as in the equivalent mirage within a Marxian ideological analysis: namely, the vision of a moment in which the individual subject would be somehow fully conscious of his or her determinations by class and would be able to square the circle of ideological conditioning by sheer lucidity and the taking of thought. But in the Marxian system, only a collective unity ... can achieve this transparency; the individual subject is always positioned within the social totality (and this is the sense of Althusser's insistence on the *permanence* of ideology).[41]

This commentary is difficult to understand and seems to reflect a compromise, a juggling act (evident throughout Jameson's book) between post-structuralist notions of the subject and ideology, and classical Marxist premises. 'Collective unities' are made up of individuals (and these unities are *also* positioned 'within the social totality'), and, furthermore, it has been the role of some individuals — Marx, Engels, Lenin — to raise the consciousness, to *form* such a collective unity and approach the kind of 'transparency' needed to combat class ideology.

Some individuals such as Caudwell felt they had achieved that 'lucidity', that moment of 'vision' when the subject could 'think his own intellectual time' (as E. P. Thompson has said of Caudwell) as scientifically as possible. If there are weaknesses in such a belief, Caudwell shares them with the whole tradition of . classical Marxism. Perry Anderson argues that 'the most important responsibility for contemporary socialists may be to isolate the main theoretical weaknesses of classical marxism, to explain the historical reasons for these, and to remedy them'. This is surely what Caudwell deserves; a sympathetic re-reading, an evaluation and correction and modification where necessary, and, most importantly, a place within the tradition of Marxist cultural theory. This rather than the customary patronising talk of 'vulgar Marxism'. Indeed, Caudwell shares certain of these problematic traits with the man who gave his name to the world-view in question. Thus:

> Indeed it was the very range of his [Marx's] general vision of the *future* which in a certain sense induced the local illusions and myopias in his scanning of the present of his own time ... His mistakes and omissions may be said to have typically been the price of his foresights.[42]

If we need to re-write Marx and Engels and Lenin, then we must re-read Caudwell in the light of these revisions.

## Notes

1. Kaja Silverman, *The subject of semiotics* (New York, Oxford University Press, 1984), p. 130. It is a pity that V. N. Volosinov is not mentioned in this otherwise comprehensive volume, a thinker who, like Caudwell, contributed to the concept of consciousness as reliant on 'signifying activities'.

2. Fredric Jameson, *The political unconscious* (Ithaca, Cornell University Press, 1982), p. 47.

3. William C. Dowling, *Jameson, Althusser, Marx: an introduction to the political unconscious* (Ithaca, Cornell University Press, 1984), p. 26.

4. Jameson, *The political unconscious*, p. 102.

5. *Illusion and reality*, p. 158.

6. Sidney Finkelstein, 'Beauty and truth', in Norman Rudich (ed.), *Weapons of criticism* (Palo Alto, Ramparts Press, 1976), p. 57.

7. Quoted in Rudich (ed.), *Weapons of criticism*, p. 20.

8. See Perry Anderson, *Considerations on western Marxism* (London, New Left Books, 1976) for a concise history of this movement in Marxist thought.

9. *The crisis in physics*, p. 130. Italics added.

10. Lucien Goldmann, *Essays on method in the sociology of literature*, trans. and ed. William Q. Boelhower (St Louis, Telos Press, 1980), p. 40.

11. Ibid., p. 93.

12. Ibid., p. 95. Original italics. For a condensed version of Goldmann's method see 'Genetic structuralism' in Elizabeth Burns and Tom Burns, *Sociology of literature and drama* (Harmondsworth, Penguin Books, 1973). See also Goldmann's *Cultural creation in modern society*, trans. Bart Grahl (St Louis, Telos Press, 1976). And for a critical appraisal of Goldmann's work within cultural theory see Raymond Williams, 'Literature and sociology: In memory of Lucien Goldmann', *New Left Review*, no. 67 (May–June, 1971), pp. 3–18.

13. See Stanley Edgar Hyman, *The armed vision* (New York, Vintage Books, 1955), p. 384. Hyman, (pp. 327–85) gives a useful overview of Burke's work. It is interesting to note that Hyman's essay on Caudwell which was present in the 1947 edition of this work is excised from this edition. Perhaps an indication of the political climate in the US during the 1950s?

14. Kenneth Burke, *The philosophy of literary form* (New York, Vintage Books, 1957), p. 256. Original italics. Most of these essays were written in the 1930s.

15. Ibid., p. 3.

16. Jameson, *The political unconscious*, p. 82. Added emphasis.

17. *Illusion and reality*, p. 196.

18. Jameson, *The political unconscious*, p. 70.

19. Ibid., p. 68.

20. Northrop Frye, *The anatomy of criticism*, quoted by Jameson, pp. 71–2. Emphases added.

21. See Rosalind Coward and John Ellis, *Language and materialism* (London, Routledge & Kegan Paul, 1980), p. 8.

22. *Illusion and reality*, p. 163.

23. Terry Eagleton, *Literary theory: an introduction* (Minneapolis, University of Minnesota Press, 1983), pp. 164–85, *passim*.

24. See Caudwell's remarks on the 'brute man', language and society in *Illusion and reality*, pp. 171–3.

25. Silverman, *The subject of semiotics*, p. 175.

26. *Illusion and reality*, p. 136.

27. V. N. Volosinov, *Freudianism: a Marxist critique*, trans. I. R. Titunik and ed. in collaboration with Neal H. Bruss (New York, Academic Press, 1976), p. 15. Quoted more fully on pp. 121–2.

28. Silverman, *The subject of semiotics*, p. 166. Italics added.

29. Jacques Lacan, *The language of the self*, trans. Anthony Wilden (New York, Dell Publishing Co., 1968), p. 39.

30. Ibid., p. 226.

31. Robert Scholes, *Textual power* (New Haven, Yale University Press, 1985), p. 80. See especially the chapters 'The text and the world' and 'Reference and difference' for a clear account of the issues involved.

32. *Illusion and reality*, p. 171.

33. Scholes, *Textual power*, p. 112. Italics added.

34. See the comment by Michael Ryan in *Marxism and deconstruction*

(Baltimore, Johns Hopkins University Press, 1984), p. 22: 'As Marx would have put it, had he lived to be a critic of phenomenology, to privilege perception is to limit oneself to "things", at the expense of the imperceptible social relations that produce them.'

35. Jameson, *The political unconscious*, p. 35.

36. For a brief summary of the different classical positions, see Raymond Williams, *Keywords* (New York, Oxford University Press, 1983), pp. 153–7.

37. Louis Althusser, *For Marx*, trans. Ben Brewster (London, New Left Books, 1977), p. 232.

38. Louis Althusser, *Lenin and Philosophy and other essays* (New York, Monthly Review Press, 1971), p. 165.

39. E. P. Thompson, 'The poverty of theory' in *The poverty of theory and other essays* (New York, Monthly Review Press, 1978).

40. Terry Eagleton, *Against the grain* (London, Verso Editions, 1986), pp. 2–3.

41. Jameson, *The political unconscious*, p. 283. Original italics.

42. Anderson, *Considerations on western Marxism*, pp. 113–14. My italics.

# Appendix:
# Caudwell's Manuscripts

The first part of the lengthy untitled typescript which I take to be that of 'Verse and mathematics', originally some 475 pages (approximately 118,000 words), is missing.[1] The remaining sections are differentiated in the following way: Part II, 'Modern poetry', Part III, 'The method of poetry', Part IV, 'Science and illusion', Part V, 'The psyche and phantasy'. This first version of *Illusion and reality* although different in structure shares many of the concerns of the later book. It takes up the social and collective origins of art and the subsequent evolution of poetry into an 'individualistic, anticollective activity' ('Modern poetry'). It considers the part that poetry plays in humanity's evolution, particularly through the nature of 'phantasy', the peculiarly human faculty of imaginative 'illusion' which helps humanity to symbolise its reality, whether in the realm of science (mathematics) or art (verse). In this version, 'mathematics' stands paradigmatically for scientific discourse, the epitome of agreed conventionality, translatability, resulting in the universal mathematical language of logic. 'Verse', on the other hand, is 'non-symbolic' in the sense that the words 'are not valued as symbols of some external reality, but exist in their own right'. The following will give some idea of the *raison d'être* behind Caudwell's working title:

> Consequently the mathematical word is considered always as imagic of events in the external world, independent of the particular history or viewpoint or position of the person receiving or uttering the word. It is therefore the appropriate instrument for changing the world, and is the chosen weapon of science, the one thing all sciences have in common. But the poetic word, concerned only in being the thing it is, a dynamic psychic act as between poet and hearer, is the appropriate instrument for the changing of psychic contents, not in their view of external reality, but in their internal organisation.[2]

Just as in the published version where science and poetry in their interpenetration symbolise the universe, here it is 'the co-operation and opposition between verse and mathematics'.

Striving for a dialectical relationship between biology and sociology, the Marx of this manuscript takes his place in the explanation of human development beside Darwin and Freud. The conceptual link between biological evolution (Darwin), social evolution (Marx) and the interaction between them (Freud) is Caudwell's notion of the genotype.[3]

> The human genotype comes into the world amorphous and unlicked, and is moulded into shape by the social environment. And it is just because there is this buffer between external reality and the genotype, that social adaptation becomes so much more important than biological adaptation. Darwinism is the law of biological evolution, but on it society imposes a quicker rhythm and new laws; the laws first explained by Marx, but felt dimly by all sociologists worthy of the name.[4]

It is the 'genotype's energy' that, in dialectical fashion, 'drives on the machinery of the social environment', while at the same time it is being moulded by that social environment. There is always this inherent dialectical relationship between instinct and environment that serves to turn the wheels of society.

> Thus the contents of the psyche consist on the one hand of genotypical peculiarities ... and, on the other hand, of social contents, given by the social environment, by the changing ideology of a culture. These contents do not exist side by side in separate compartments, any more than in biology the genotype can ever be considered as existing apart from the phenotype. Each content of the psyche has a genotypical (instinctive) component and a social component.[5]

Despite the fact that these instinctive activities of the genotype can be 'brutal' and 'infantile', they are necessary as 'energy' to help create the social organisation that keeps them in check. In a succinct Darwinian analogy, typical of the discourse in this part of the manuscript, Caudwell remarks that the instincts are *necessary*, otherwise, 'like extinct tortoises, society would perish from the weight of the carapace it had evolved'.

Caudwell's discussion of the various aspects of human evolution and adaptation — biological, psychic and social — are fused in his treatment of the formation of the human psyche and its unique attribute, imagination, or what he calls 'phantasy':

> What is distinctively human is the nature of man's
> adaptation, ideologically and socially mediated, instead of
> genetically implanted. The sign of that plastic mediation is
> phantasy, and just because it is mediative, phantasy presents
> two sides, science and poetry.[6]

We are reminded here of Marx's pronouncements on the instinctive constructions of the spider and the bee in contradistinction
to human artifacts which are raised first in the imagination, an
imagination that plays a key productive role in the advancement
of the species.

It is within this context of the creative role of the imagination
and its 'great instrument', language, that we find an extremely
interesting passage, remnants of which survive in the published
version — see the remarks on Wittgenstein, *Illusion and reality*, pp.
195-6 — but which here, characteristically, have a biological
foundation.

> In our view the conception of consciousness as evolved for
> the purposes of perception is illusory. For pure perception,
> as Bergson[7] showed, belongs to all matter as of native right
> ... Philosophers, destitute of biological knowledge, imagine
> consciousness, in its perceptive form, as a mirror-image of
> reality (or vice versa). But such a mirror-image is un-
> necessary. What would be the biological use of conscious
> perception as a mere duplication of external reality, which
> is bound in some respects to be inferior? Life does not evolve
> useless adaptations. Why evolve a mirror image of reality
> when the original exists? What is its survival value? ... It
> seems to me there can be only one answer, to the peculiar
> form of human consciousness drawn from the distinction
> we observe between men and ants — *phantasy*. By phantasy
> I mean the arbitrary shuffling of the arbitrary images
> obtained by the photography of conscious perception.
> Conscious perception gives us the 'shots'; we edit them ...
> and make the moving film of phantasy. If the film is logical
> — i.e. made in accordance with the orderings perceived in
> external reality, it is scientific or mathematical phantasy. If
> the film is emotional — i.e. made in accordance with the
> orderings natural to the instincts, it is poetic phantasy. Once

again we come upon illusion and reality.

Unfortunately, there are three pages of manuscript missing here. When it resumes, Caudwell is discussing Wittgenstein's concept of a 'perfect' language. Like Bergson, in proposing that language merely pictures the world

> Wittgenstein arrives at a completely false conception of what is a 'good' language. The most barbarous language would in fact be more valuable than Wittgenstein's perfect language for it would contain a feeling element, would be persuasion ... Language is an instrument for the communication of phantasy.[8]

And 'the communication of phantasy' is for Caudwell no mere aesthetic pastime, but an essential inheritance within human evolution. In the same way 'each generation inherits the machines and capital of its ancestors, and all their ideological wealth ... Phantasy, emerging into words, overleaps time and space ... and so everywhere modif[ies] views of reality and affective tones' (p. 238).

Just as in the published version, the imaginative experiment of poetry plays as important a role as the other 'pole of phantasy' (science) in humanity's evolution towards a realisation of its potential. It is not only a question of what man inherits, but what he must, in turn, pass on to the next generation. This is why Caudwell attempts to trace the evolution of art, both in *Illusion and reality* and in 'Verse and mathematics', from its 'matrix' in the ritual of the tribe to what he sees as its potential future. In the 'Future of poetry' chapter of this earlier version the evolutionary paradigm is still paramount. Less concerned with contemporary events and personalities than in the published version where Caudwell was writing as a communist (see, for example, pp. 288–9 of *Illusion and reality*), this section of the manuscript is concerned with what he calls 'the normal historical symptoms of a dying culture'. The following gives an idea of the tone of this concluding section of the manuscript:

> Sometimes collapses of this kind are followed by periods of decay and darkness before a new clan arises to bring order out of chaos ... In view of the widespread power and scope of bourgeois civilization, similar to that of the dying Roman

Empire, one would expect a Dark Ages of this sort, were it not that the analysis of Marx has shown that the proletariat is, by bourgeois social relations, already sufficiently organised to succeed the bourgeois clan in directing the task of social production.[9]

In this text, Milton, Wordsworth and Shelley, whose work in *Illusion and reality* is shown to be symptomatic of 'the bourgeois illusion', are held to be examples of 'evolutionaries, bringing to birth the future in the present'. The future and poetry's role in helping to make it are placed in 'Verse and mathematics', within the extended analogy between the dialectics of nature and that of society as in the following explicit statement.

The class struggle is a biological law, surviving in society; and when, by the dialectic process, it becomes synthesised in the one class, and is therefore classless, society at last becomes completely itself ... Darwin, living in an age when Society's biological struggle was at its bitterest, clearly grasped its prototype among animals, the struggle for existence urging a biological evolution.[10]

In a world where the class-struggle survives, society is not yet Society, but is in a stage of transition from the ape herd ... 'Competition' is, then, the expression of the Darwinian 'struggle for existence' in society itself, from which it must be extirpated.[11]

The ultimate 'evolutionary' philosophy that would rectify this state of 'tooth and claw' struggle was to be, as well, the terminus of Christopher Caudwell's intellectual and emotional quest; his search for a system that would include and unite his 'strong emotional and rational tendencies'. Marxism could embrace and explain those 'biological, psychological ... theories [he had] been forming in the course of [his] reading' and at the same time move society from a state of 'illusion' to a permanent 'reality'. In the typescript from which I have been quoting, he puts it thus:

For a dream, as we see, in its full phantastic construction, is an imaginative experiment, and when it is expanded to take in a whole society, it must take in a whole ideology ... There is only one complete ideology of that nature in the world today, that of communism, the dream of Marx, Engels, and Lenin. It is a huge imaginative experiment, based on the external reality [of] history and the true needs of man expressed in society.[12]

This, then, was Caudwell's first expression of his 'vision' of Marxism's place in humanity's evolution toward freedom. His fellow Marxists who criticised *Illusion and reality* (which seems 'orthodox' in comparison) would no doubt shudder at many of the pronouncements in this version as represented by the passage just quoted. But then Caudwell himself became less satisfied with his first Marxist work. Even from the scanty evidence I have presented here, it should be clear to anyone who has read *Illusion and reality* that 'Verse and mathematics' is not so much a 'first version' as an abandoned project. This brings up an important issue concerning the chronology of Caudwell's thinking and writing and, particularly, the progress toward maturity of his Marxist thought.

For some time it was thought that the *Studies* were written first and that *Illusion and reality* represented Caudwell's last, hurriedly written, work before leaving for Spain. This position is no longer tenable. Apart from intrinsic evidence (*Studies* reflects a more mature voice and a greater clarity of thought) there is, as we have seen earlier in the brief chronicle of Caudwell's activities, sufficient documentary evidence to state categorically that the *Studies in a dying culture* were begun after the completion of the first version of *Illusion and reality*. But the situation is more complex than the positions represented by the following two opposing viewpoints. The first, from David Margolies, dates back to 1969:

> Caudwell had not developed his Marxism sufficiently in *Studies* to make the theory-practice dialectic clear; he has all the ideas for this theory of function but is unable to put them together properly. In *Illusion and reality* his dialectical understanding has improved and he better understands the interaction of theory and practice.[13]

E. P. Thompson, writing in 1977, recognises the fact that 'the relation between *Illusion and reality* and the *Studies* still needs clarification'. However, his insightful essay is based on a 'downgrading' of *Illusion and reality* in order that the 'later work', *Studies in a dying culture*, should take its rightful place in Caudwell's career.

He puts his position in this way:

> Let us, then, enter Caudwell's world from a new direction. *Illusion and reality* is in no respect to be seen as his major work. It was written while Caudwell was undergoing a self-conversion to Marxism, from late 1934 to the autumn of 1935. I do not wish to labour its deficiencies, but will assert these as I find them. Despite an impression gained from the chapter-headings, of massive and complex organisation, it is an ill-organised, involuted, and repetitive book.[14]

Thompson is correct in seeing *Studies* as a more lucid expression of Caudwell's Marxist thought, but much of the 'ill-organised, involuted, and repetitive' nature of *Illusion and reality* may have resulted from the very act of writing those *Studies*. Despite its questionable Marxism, 'Verse and mathematics' (the manuscript I have outlined above), is a more cohesive and organised work, though less rich, than *Illusion and reality*. It was, I suggest, this manuscript that Caudwell wrote while 'under-going a self-conversion to Marxism, from late 1934 to the autumn of 1935'. *Illusion and reality*, the book we now have, was written and re-written well into 1936, at the same time that Caudwell was writing his *Studies* in Poplar. I wish now to outline some of my reasons for this belief.

On 14 November 1935, Elizabeth Beard wrote a long letter to her friend after having just read the carbon copy of the typescript Caudwell now called 'Illusion and reality'. Although she found the book 'good', she had criticisms to make concerning Caudwell's lack of emphasis on the social nature of beauty and that he had not 'come to grips with religion at all'. Caudwell, now resident in Poplar, responded on 21 November, complaining about the length of time Allen & Unwin had had his manuscript without comment: 'If Shakespeare lived today he would include the delay of publishers in his catalogue [*sic*] of life's basenesses and in-justice.' He also attempted to answer Elizabeth Beard's questions, saying his 'treatment of religion was necessarily summary' (hardly the case in the version we have now) and outlined his position on other questions which Elizabeth Beard had intelligently posed. As we have seen he wrote again on 30 November 1935 in these terms:

Dear Betty,
    Thanks very much for your letter. But I shall have to ask

you not to write to me, or discuss these matters with me, because they have a most dangerous effect. As you know, our discussions at Newton [the Beards' farmhouse] on Poetry and the Unconscious resulted in the writing of 'I & R' — 120,000 words of it. After my answer to you on the subject of Beauty, I felt impelled to put on paper all the things I couldn't find room for in the letter. The result is a 10,000 words study on Beauty and the Beautiful ... Reflecting further on the subject of Religion, I was led to that of asceticism, and suddenly saw a most interesting causal connection between the thrift of the Puritan, the asceticism of the Roman Church, of the Roman Republican, of the modern Nazi and Youth movements ... Result, a 15,000 words study. This must now cease! It is interrupting me in my Neccessary [*sic*] work, such as for example, 'Internal Air Mail Contracts of the British Isles'.

We are witness here to the beginning of Caudwell's series of 'studies' on aspects of 'modern culture' which he had for the most part finished by the Autumn of 1936, although he had a draft of most of them by April.

Caudwell's word count of his first two studies is extremely accurate, but the 120,000 words that he ascribes to *Illusion and reality* is much closer to the 475-page or so typescript (approximately 118,500 words) of 'Verse and mathematics' than the 98,000 words (approximately) of the published form of *Illusion and reality*. There is much in 'Beauty' that owes a debt to the central ideas of Caudwell's first book on aesthetics,[15] but the more concise study, with its stress (as he put it to Elizabeth Beard) on the 'importance' of 'the subject–object relation', must have led him — as did the other studies — to reconsider his first 'Marxist' work written in Cornwall.

Caudwell had plenty of time for such reconsideration. Having sent the carbon copy to the Beards, he sent the first copy of the typescript to his agent in London who, in turn, sent it to Allen & Unwin where it remained for months. George Moberg records in his biography the fact that 'almost a year later, Caudwell's old friend Desmond MacCarthy, recommended it [*Illusion and reality*] for publication to Macmillan and Company', who were eventually to bring the book out posthumously in the spring of 1937. This would put the submission of the manuscript to Macmillan at around July 1936, a date by which Caudwell had written the majority of his *Studies*. The notebook that he kept in Poplar contains ideas that he worked up into the various studies, but it also contains at least one entry that he decided to use in *Illusion and reality*. The anarchist joke which appears on pages 112–13 of *Illusion and reality* and the reference to the 'Fascist revolt in Spain' is indicative of how late into 1936 Caudwell was writing his new version of that book. It is not so much, then, a matter of how Caudwell moved from the book he was writing while 'undergoing a self-conversion' to the more mature *Studies*. Rather, I believe he worked on both simultaneously and that the latter's influence may help to explain some of the excrescences and disorganised character of *Illusion and reality* as Caudwell hurriedly wrote it.

There is little enough space to discuss the complexities of *Illusion and reality* as we now have it without going into the intricacies of how the two books may have related in terms of genesis and structure. As remarked upon earlier, there are many differences between 'Verse and mathematics' and the published book, but perhaps the fundamental difference comes from Caudwell's introduction into the published version of the importance of the subject–object interaction and the 'bourgeois illusion' of freedom in all its manifestations. The latter concern comes from the study 'Liberty', and just as the idea of freedom being 'the recognition of necessity' (the epigraph to *Illusion and reality*) influenced the first book, so in 'Liberty' we can find many traces of *Illusion and reality* as in the following, for example:

> Science is the means by which man learns what he can do, and therefore it explores the necessity of reality. Art is the means by which man learns what he wants to do, and therefore it explores the essence of the human heart.[16]

If the reader wishes to see a sample of how the writing of 'Liberty' might have affected *Illusion and reality* he or she should consider the digression on bourgeois illusion that forms the whole of the second section of 'The development of modern poetry'. Again, the excursus on the ideological aspects of religion (pp. 39–44) which makes the next section, beginning 'Poetry then ...', somewhat of a *non sequitur* should be read in the light of the study 'The breath of discontent'.

The 'Introduction' to *Illusion and reality* is primarily concerned with the topics that were currently engaging him in the other essays. The very disciplines that he chose to concentrate on in those studies are listed in the introduction to *Illusion and reality* as a prerequisite for a full understanding of poetry.

> But physics, anthropology, history, biology, philosophy and psychology are also products of society, and therefore a sound sociology would enable the art critic to employ criteria drawn from these fields without falling into eclecticism or confusing art with psychology or politics (pp. 11–12).

There is no doubt that Caudwell believed himself to be writing a more rigorous Marxist version of the book he originally had called 'Verse and mathematics', but one cannot help feeling that his hasty re-writing resulted in a book that is irredeemably flawed. His outline of 'bourgeois poetry' from the epoch of 'Primitive accumulation' to 'The final capitalistic crisis' which takes up Chapters 4, 5 and 6 constitutes an interruptive incursion into the argument from the sources of poetry to its characteristics. Indeed, the major part of Chapter 3, 'The development of modern poetry', which, with its application and paraphrase of *The Communist manifesto* was meant to form the groundwork for the next three chapters, seems an awkward diversion from the interesting discussion of mimesis at the end of Chapter 2 and the re-examination of this concept and its relation to 'illusion' in Chapter 7.

It is indeed unfortunate that such a gifted individual as Caudwell, a poet well-versed in science who felt that he had at last found that 'integrated *Weltanschauung*', both for the living of his life and the explication of his interests, had not the time to integrate the prodigious and rapid reading he continued to do for his *Studies* into a more lucid explanation of the poet's function within society.

## Notes

1. There are a few pages missing in the body of the text, as well as what I assume to be the last two or three pages. The manuscript is lost after the bottom of page 473, but on the previous page (472) it is announced that 'it is time to close our discussion of the future', so that only a few more pages could have remained.

2. MS 'Verse and mathematics', pp. 85–6. Some residual discussion of the relationship between mathematics and poetry can be found in *Illusion and reality*, pp. 130ff.

3. His use of this term is, for the most part, much clearer in the

manuscript than in *Illusion and reality* where such statements as 'the unchanging face of the genotype' have resulted in severe criticism from fellow Marxists.

4. MS 'Verse and mathematics', p. 184.

5. Ibid., p. 192.

6. Ibid., p. 225.

7. Bergson had some influence on the younger Caudwell, but his 'philosophy', along with other earlier influences, is repudiated as typically 'bourgeois' in the *Studies*.

8. MS 'Verse and mathematics', pp. 200–5.

9. Ibid., pp. 404–5. Compared with 'The future of poetry' in *Illusion and reality*, this sounds more like the opinion of a 'fellow traveller'.

10. This is, in part, the essence of Caudwell's critique of Darwin in the recently published study, 'Heredity and development'. Of Darwin's two-part theory, that animals change by adapting themselves to the environment *and* by natural selection, Caudwell objected to the second clause as a 'class theory'. Such a stance reflected the expansionist ideology of Darwin's England, just as in feudal times the theory of nature was one 'in which all species and objects have their places and purposes'; that is to say, the theory reflected the static nature of feudal society. This is a clever essay which bears comparison with Engels's *Dialectics of nature* (which Caudwell could not have read).

11. MS 'Verse and mathematics', p. 445.

12. Ibid., p. 257.

13. David Margolies, *The function of literature: a study of Christopher Caudwell's aesthetics* (New York, International Publishers, 1969), p. 47.

14. E. P. Thompson, 'Caudwell' in *The socialist register* (London, Merlin Press, 1977), p. 234.

15. For example, the distinction and interdependence of science and art in 'social process', the artist's 'mock world', and the 'cognitive and affective elements' in any sign-situation; these are some of the ideas he brought to the essay from his first critical book.

16. *Studies*, p. 228.

# Bibliography

## Primary sources

Works are differentiated here, as in the British Museum Catalogue, under the authors Sprigg and Caudwell. Different editions are cited only if a significant introduction or commentary accompanies the text.

Sprigg, Christopher St John *The airship: its design, history, operation and future*, London, Sampson Low, 1931
—— *British airways ... with many photographs and drawings*, London, Nelson, 1934
—— *The corpse with the sunburned face* (novel), London, Nelson, 1935
—— *Crime in Kensington* (novel), London, Eldon Press, 1933
—— *Death of a queen: Charles Venables' fourth case*, London, Nelson, 1935
—— *Death of an airman* (novel), London, Hutchinson, 1934
—— *Fatality in Fleet Street* (novel), London, Eldon Press, 1933
—— and Davis, Henry D. *Fly with me: an elementary textbook on the art of piloting*, London, J. Hamilton, 1932
—— *Great flights ... illustrated from photographs*, London, Nelson, 1935
—— *Let's learn to fly ... with photographs and drawings*, London, Nelson, 1937
—— 'Once I did think.' ('The ecstasy'), *The Dial*, vol. LXXXII (March 1927)
—— *Pass the body*, New York, Dial Press, 1933. (American title of *Crime in Kensington*.)
—— *The perfect alibi*, London, Eldon Press, 1934
—— *The six queer things* (novel), London, Herbert Jenkins, 1937
—— (ed.) *Uncanny stories*, London, Nelson, 1936
Caudwell, Christopher *Collected poems*, edited with introduction by Alan Young, Manchester, Carcanet Press, 1986
—— *The crisis in physics*, edited with an introduction by Professor H. Levy, London, John Lane, 1939
—— *The concept of freedom*, with an introduction by George Thomson, London, Lawrence & Wishart, 1965. (This includes some of the essays from *Studies in a dying culture* and some chapters from *The crisis in physics*.)
—— *Further studies in a dying culture*, edited with a preface by Edgell Rickwood, London, Bodley Head, 1949
—— *Illusion and reality*, London, Macmillan, 1937
—— *Illusion and reality*, with a biographical note by George Thomson, New York, International Publishers, 1955
—— *Poems*, London, Lawrence & Wishart, 1965. First published by John Lane, 1939
—— *Romance and realism*, edited by Samuel Hynes, Princeton, NJ, Princeton University Press, 1970
—— *Scenes and actions* (unpublished prose), edited with an introduction by Jean Duparc and David Margolies, London, Routledge & Kegan Paul, 1986
—— *Studies in a dying culture*, with an introduction by John Strachey, London, John Lane, 1938

—— *Studies and further studies in a dying culture*, introduction by Sol Yurick, New York, Monthly Review Press, 1971
—— *This my hand* (novel), London, Hamish Hamilton, 1936

## Secondary sources

Acton, H. B. *The illusion of the epoch: Marxism-Leninism as a philosophical creed*, London, Cohen & West, 1955
Aiken, Henry D. (ed.) *The age of ideology*, New York, New American Library, 1956
Althusser, Louis *Lenin and philosophy and other essays*, New York, Monthly Review Press, 1971
—— *For Marx*, trans. Ben Brewster, London, New Left Books, 1977
Anderson, Perry *Considerations on Western Marxism*, London, New Left Books, 1976
Aristotle *The poetics*, trans. Gerald Else, Ann Arbor, University of Michigan Press, 1967
Arvon, Henri *Marxist esthetics*, trans. Helen R. Lane, introd. Fredric Jameson, Ithaca and London, Cornell University Press, 1977
Auden, W. H. 'Psychology and art' in Geoffrey Grigson (ed.), *The arts today*, London, John Lane, 1935
—— Review of *Illusion and reality*, *New Verse*, vol. XXV (May 1937), pp. 20–2
—— *The dance of death*, London, Faber & Faber, 1945. First published 1933
—— *The Orators: an English study*, London, Faber & Faber, 1946. First published 1932
—— *Collected shorter poems 1927–1957*, New York, Random House, 1967
Auerbach, Erich *Mimesis*, Princeton, NJ, Princeton University Press, 1971
Bartlett, F. 'The limitations of Freud', *Science and Society*, vol. 3, no. 1 (Winter 1939), pp. 64–105
—— 'Marxism and the psychoanalytic theory of the unconscious', *Science and Society*, vol. XVI, no. 1 (Winter 1951–2), pp. 44–52
Baudouin, Charles *Psychoanalysis and aesthetics*, London, Allen & Unwin, 1924
—— *Contemporary Studies*, trans. from the French by Eden and Cedar Paul, New York, E. P. Dutton, 1925
Baxandall, Lee *Marxism and aesthetics: a bibliography*, New York, Humanities Press, 1973
—— and Morawski, Stefan (eds) *Marx & Engels on literature and art: a selection of writings*, introd. Stefan Morawski, St Louis and Milwaukee, Telos Press, 1973
Beard, Paul 'Some recent novels', *The New English Weekly*, vol. IX (30 April 1936), p. 52
—— 'Views and reviews: *Illusion and reality*', *The New English Weekly*, vol. XI (30 September 1937), pp. 411–12
Bennett, Tony *Formalism and Marxism*, London, Methuen, 1979
Benson, Frederick *Writers in arms: the literary impact of the Spanish Civil War*, New York, New York University Press, 1967

Berger, John (ed.) *Ways of seeing*, London and Harmondsworth, BBC and Penguin Books, 1976

Bergonzi, B. *Reading the thirties*, Pittsburgh, University of Pittsburgh Press, 1978

Bergson, Henri *Creative evolution*, trans. Arthur Mitchell, New York, Henry Holt & Co., 1937

Bernal, J. D. *The world, the flesh and the devil. An enquiry into the future of the three enemies of the rational soul*, Bloomington and London, Indiana University Press, 1969

Bloomfield, Leonard *Language*, New York, H. Holt & Co., 1933

Bocock, Robert *Freud and modern society*, New York, Holmes & Meier, 1978

Borkenau, Franz *The Spanish cockpit*, London, Faber & Faber, 1937

Branson, Noreen and Heinemann, M. *Britain in the 1930's*, New York, Praeger, 1971

Braun, Stuart 'Three English radical poets', *New Masses*, 3 July 1934, pp. 33–6

Bronowski, J. *The visionary eye: essays in the arts, literature and science*, Cambridge, Mass., MIT Press, 1978

Browne, Alasdair 'Freud and materialism', *Left Review*, June 1936

—— 'Psychology and Marxism', in C. Day Lewis (ed.), *The mind in chains: socialism and the cultural revolution*, London, Frederick Muller, 1937

Buchanan, Scott *Poetry and mathematics*, New York, The John Day Co., 1929

Bukharin, N. B. 'Poetry, poetics and the problems of poetry in the USSR', in *Problems of Soviet literature: reports and speeches at the First Soviet Writers Congress*, London, Martin Lawrence, 1935

Bullock, Chris and Peck, David (comps) *Guide to Marxist literary criticism*, Bloomington, Indiana University Press, 1980

Burke, Kenneth *The philosophy of literary form*, New York, Vintage Books, 1957

Burns, Elizabeth and Burns, Tom *Sociology of literature and drama*, Harmondsworth, Penguin Books, 1973

Burns, Emile *An introduction to Marxism*, London, Lawrence & Wishart, 1971

Camus, Albert *The rebel: an essay on man in revolt*, New York, Vintage Books, 1956

Carpenter, Humphrey *W. H. Auden: a biography*, London, Allen & Unwin, 1981

Clark, Jon (ed.) *Culture and crisis in Britain in the thirties*, Atlantic Highlands, NJ, Humanities Press, 1979

Collingwood, R. G. *The principles of art*, Oxford, Clarendon Press, 1963

Cornforth, Maurice *Dialectical materialism: an introductory course*, vol. 2, *Historical materialism*, London, Lawrence & Wishart, 1953; vol. 3, *The theory of knowledge*, London, Lawrence & Wishart, 1954

—— *Marxism and linguistic philosophy*, New York, International Publishers, 1967

Coward, Rosalind and Ellis, John *Language and materialism*, London, Routledge & Kegan Paul, 1980

Craig, David (ed.) *Marxists on literature: an anthology*, Harmondsworth, Penguin Books, 1975

Crossman, Richard (ed.) *The god that failed*, New York, Harper & Bros, 1949, repr. New York, Bantam Books, 1965

Day Lewis, C. *A time to dance: with an essay, Revolution in writing*, New York, Random House, 1936

—— *Starting point*, New York, Harper & Bros, 1938

—— *A hope for poetry*, Oxford, Basil Blackwell, 1939

—— *The buried day*, London, Chatto & Windus, 1960

—— (ed.) *The mind in chains: socialism and the cultural revolution*, London, Frederick Muller, 1937

Demetz, P. *Marx, Engels and the poets*, Chicago, University of Chicago Press, 1967

Dowling, William C. *Jameson, Althusser, Marx: an introduction to the political unconscious*, Ithaca, Cornell University Press, 1984

Driesch, Hans *The crisis in psychology*, Princeton, NJ, Princeton University Press, 1925

Eagleton, Terry *Marxism and literary criticism*, London, Methuen, 1976

—— *Criticism and ideology: a study in Marxist literary theory*, London, Verso Editions, 1978

—— *Literary theory: an introduction*, Minneapolis, University of Minnesota Press, 1983

—— *Against the grain*, London, Verso Editions, 1986

Egri, Peter 'On Caudwell's lyrical theory', *Filologiai Koxleny*, vol. viii (1962), pp. 23–7

Eliot, T. S. *Collected poems 1909–1962*, London, Faber & Faber, 1969

—— *Selected essays*, London, Faber & Faber, 1969

Evans, A. H. ' "Illusion and reality": Is it a Marxist classic?', *Revolution* Paris, vol. I, no. x (1964), pp. 127–40

Ford, Hugh D. *A poet's war: British poets and the Spanish Civil War*, Philadelphia, University of Pennsylvania Press, 1965

Foucault, Michel *The archaeology of knowledge*, trans. A. M. Sheridan Smith, New York, Harper Torchbooks, 1972

Fox, Ralph 'Lawrence the 20th century hero', *Left Review*, vol. I, no. 10 (July 1935), pp. 391–6

—— *The novel and the people*, New York, International Publishers, 1945

—— *et al. Aspects of dialectical materialism*, London, Watts & Co., 1935

Frazer, Sir James George *The golden bough: a study in magic and religion*, abridged edition, London and Basingstoke, Macmillan Press, 1976

Freud, Sigmund *New introductory lectures on psycho-analysis*, trans. W. J. H. Sprott, New York, W. W. Norton, 1933

—— *Delusion and dream: and other essays*, ed. and introd. Philip Rieff, Boston, Beacon Press, 1956

—— *The future of an illusion*, ed. James Strachey, Garden City, NY, Anchor Books, 1964

—— *The interpretation of dreams*, New York, Avon Books, 1965

—— *Two short accounts of psycho-analysis*, trans. James Strachey, Harmondsworth, Penguin Books, 1966

—— *Sexuality and the psychology of love*, ed. and introd. Philip Rieff, New York, Collier Books, 1968

—— *The sexual enlightenment of children*, New York, Collier Books, 1978

Goldmann, Lucien *Cultural creation in modern society*, trans. Bart Grahl,

Mills, C. Wright *The Marxists*, Harmondsworth, Penguin Books, 1963

Mirsky, Dmitri *The intelligentsia of Great Britain*, London, Gollancz, 1935

Moberg, George 'Christopher Caudwell: an introduction to his life and work', PhD dissertation, Columbia University, 1968

—— Review of *Studies and further studies in a dying culture* and *Romance and realism*, *Telos*, no. 12 (Summer 1972), pp. 143–54

*Modern Quarterly* debate on Caudwell:

    (1) Oscar Thomson 'The poetic instant', *MQ*, L, Autumn 1948, pp. 62–6

    (2) Maurice Cornforth 'Caudwell and Marxism', *MQ*, L, Winter 1950–1, pp. 16–33

    (3) George Thomson 'In defense of poetry', *MQ*, L, Spring 1951, pp. 107–34

    (4) Alan Bush *et al.* 'On Caudwell and Marxist aesthetics', *MQ*, L, Summer 1951, *passim*

    (5) 'The Caudwell discussion', *MQ*, L, Autumn 1951, pp. 340–58

Morgan, Charles *The fountain*, New York, Alfred A. Knopf, 1932

Mukarovsky, Jan *Structure, sign and function*, trans. and ed. John Burbank and Peter Steiner, New Haven, Yale University Press, 1978

Mulhern, Francis 'The Marxist aesthetics of Christopher Caudwell', *New Left Review*, no. 85 (May/June 1974), pp. 37–58

—— *The moment of 'Scrutiny'*, London, Verso Editions, 1981

Murchison, C. (ed.) *Psychologies of 1930*, London, Oxford University Press, 1930

Murray, John Middleton *The necessity of communism*, New York, Thomas Seltzer, 1933

Ogden, C. K. and Richards, I. A. *The meaning of meaning: a study of the influence of language upon thought and of the science of symbolism*, with supplementary essays by B. Malinowski and F. G. Crookshank, 10th edn, London, Routledge & Kegan Paul, 1972

O'Neill, John 'Marxism and mythology', *Ethics*, vol. 77 (1966–76), pp. 38–49

Ortega y Gasset, José *Man and crisis*, New York, W. W. Norton, 1962

Orwell, George *Homage to Catalonia*, New York, Harcourt, Brace & World, 1952

—— *A collection of essays*, New York, Doubleday, 1954

Osborn, Reuben *Marxism and psychoanalysis*, New York, Octagon Books, 1974 (first published as *Freud and Marx*, 1937)

Piaget, Jean *Structuralism*, trans. and ed. Chaninah Maschler, New York, Evanston, San Francisco and London, Harper & Row, 1971

Plekhanov, George *Art and society*, introd. Granville Hicks, New York, Critics Group, 1936

—— *Art and social life*, London, Lawrence & Wishart, 1953

—— *Fundamental problems of Marxism*, London, Lawrence & Wishart, 1969

Pradhan, S. V. 'Caudwell's theory of poetry: some problems of a Marxist synthesis', *British Journal of Aesthetics*, 17 (Summer 1977), pp. 266–74

Prescott, F. C. *Poetry and dreams*, Boston, Gorham Press, 1912

Progoff, Ira *Jung's psychology and its social meaning*, New York, Anchor Books, 1973

Richards, I. A. *Science and poetry*, London, Kegan Paul, Trench, Trubner & Co., 1926
—— *Principles of literary criticism*, London, Routledge & Kegan Paul, 1967
Riffaterre, Michael *The semiotics of poetry*, Bloomington, Indiana University Press, 1978
Rivers, W. H. R. *Instinct and the unconscious*, Cambridge, Cambridge University Press, 1920
—— *Conflict and dream*, New York, Harcourt, Brace, 1923
—— *Social organization*, New York, Alfred A. Knopf, 1924
Roberts, Michael (ed.) *New country: prose and poetry by the authors of New Signatures*, London, Hogarth Press, 1933
Rudich, Norman (ed.) *Weapons of criticism*, Palo Alto, Ramparts Press, 1976
Ryan, Michael *Marxism and deconstruction*, Baltimore, Johns Hopkins University Press, 1984
Samuels, Stuart Raymond 'Marx, Freud and English intellectuals: a study of the dissemination and reconciliation of ideas', unpublished dissertation, Stanford University, 1971
Sapir, Edward *Language*, New York, Harcourt, Brace, 1921
—— *Culture, language and personality: Selected Essays*, ed. David G. Mandelbaum, Berkeley and Los Angeles, University of California Press, 1958
Saussure, Ferdinand de *Course in general linguistics*, New York, Philosophical Library, 1959
Schiller, Jerome P. *I. A. Richards' theory of literature*, New Haven and London, Yale University Press, 1969
Scholes, Robert *Structuralism in literature: an introduction*, New Haven and London, Yale University Press, 1977
—— *Textual power*, New Haven, Yale University Press, 1985
—— and R. Kellogg *The nature of narrative*, New York and London, Oxford University Press, 1975
Silverman, Kaja *The subject of semiotics*, New York, Oxford University Press, 1984
Skelton, Robin (ed.) *Poetry of the thirties*, Harmondsworth, Penguin Books, 1980
Slaughter, Cliff *Marxism, ideology and literature*, Atlantic Highlands, NJ, Humanities Press, 1980
Solomon, Maynard (ed.) *Marxism and art: essays classical and contemporary*, New York, Alfred A. Knopf, 1973
Spender, Stephen *The destructive element: a study of modern writers and beliefs* New York, Houghton Mifflin, 1936
—— Review of *Illusion and reality*, *Tribune*, 23 December 1937
—— *World within world*, New York, Harcourt, Brace, 1951
—— *The thirties and after: poetry, politics, people 1933–1970*, New York, Random House, 1978
—— and Lehmann, John (eds) *Poems for Spain*, introd. Stephen Spender, London, Hogarth Press, 1939
Stansky, Peter and Abrahams, William *Journey to the frontier: Julian Bell and John Cornford: their lives and the 1930's*, London, Constable, 1966
Starr, Albert 'Psychoanalysis and the fiction of the unconscious', *Science and Society* (Spring 1951), pp. 129–43

Storr, Anthony *Jung*, London, Fontana/Collins, 1975

—— *The dynamics of creation*, Harmondsworth, Penguin Books, 1976

Strachey, John *The coming struggle for power*, London, Gollancz, 1934

Symons, J. *The thirties: a dream revolved*, London, Cresset Press, 1960

—— *The detective story in Britain*, London, Longman, 1962

—— *Mortal consequences*, New York, Harper & Row, 1972

Sypher, Eileen 'Christopher Caudwell: the genesis and function of literary form', PhD dissertation, University of Connecticut, 1976

—— 'Towards a theory of the lyric: Georg Lukács and Christopher Caudwell', *Praxis*, no. 3 (1976), pp. 173–83

Thomas, Hugh *The Spanish Civil War*, Harmondsworth, Penguin Books, 1977

Thompson, E. P. 'Caudwell' in *The socialist register*, London, Merlin Press, 1977, pp. 228–76

—— *The poverty of theory and other essays*, New York, Monthly Review Press, 1978

Thomson, George *Marxism and poetry*, New York, International Publishers, 1946

—— *Aeschylus and Athens: a study in the social origins of drama*, London, Lawrence & Wishart, 1949

Tillman, Frank A. and Cohn, Steven (eds) *Philosophy of art and aesthetics from Plato to Wittgenstein*, New York, Harper & Row, 1969

Tindall, William York *Forces in modern British literature*, New York, Alfred A. Knopf, 1947

Trotsky, Leon *Literature and revolution*, New York, Russell & Russell, 1957

Tucker, Robert C. *Philosophy and myth in Karl Marx*, New York, Cambridge University Press, 1961

—— (ed.) *The Marx-Engels reader*, 2nd edn, New York, W. W. Norton, 1978

Ullman, Stephen *Semantics: an introduction to the science of meaning*, Oxford, Basil Blackwell, 1977

Upward, Edward *In the thirties*, London, Heinemann, 1962

—— *The railway accident and other stories*, London, Heinemann, 1969

—— *The rotten elements: a novel of fact*, London, Heinemann, 1969

—— *The spiral ascent*, London, Heinemann, 1977

Volosinov, V. N. *Marxism and the philosophy of language*, New York, Seminar Press, 1973

—— *Freudianism: a Marxist critique*, trans. I. R. Titunik and ed. in collaboration with Neal H. Bruss, New York, Academic Press, 1976

Watson, George *Politics and literature in modern Britain*, Totowa, NJ, Roman & Littlefield, 1975

Webb, Sidney, *et al. Socialism and individualism*, New York, John Lane Company, 1911

Weintraub, Stanley *The last great cause: the intellectuals and the Spanish civil war*, New York, Weybright & Talley, 1968

Wellek, René and Warren, Austin *Theory of literature*, Harmondsworth, Penguin Books, 1966

West, Alick *Crisis in criticism*, London, Lawrence & Wishart, 1937

—— 'On "Illusion and reality" ', *Communist Review*, 7–13 January 1948

—— *One man in his time: an autobiography*, London, Allen & Unwin, 1969

Wharton, Fred 'Christopher Caudwell's "Illusion and Reality" ', *Science and Society* (Winter 1952), pp. 53–9

Wheelwright, Philip *Metaphor and reality*, Bloomington and London, Indiana University Press, 1968

Wilden, Anthony *System and structure: essays in communication and exchange*, London, Tavistock Publications, 1972

Willet, John (ed.) *Brecht on theatre*, New York, Hill & Wang, 1977

Williams, Raymond 'Literature and sociology: in memory of Lucien Goldmann', *New Left Review*, no. 67 (May–June 1971), pp. 3–18

—— *Culture and society 1780–1950*, Harmondsworth, Penguin Books/Chatto & Windus, 1976

—— *Marxism and literature*, Oxford, Oxford University Press, 1977

—— *Politics and letters: interviews with New Left Review*, London, New Left Books, 1979

—— *Keywords*, New York, Oxford University Press, 1983

Wilson, Edmund *The shores of light: a literary chronicle of the twenties and thirties*, New York, Farrar, Strauss & Young, 1952

Wimsatt, William K. and Brooks, Cleanth (eds) *Literary criticism: a short history*, New York, Vintage Books, 1957

Wittgenstein, Ludwig *Philosophical investigations*, Garden City, Anchor Books, 1966

—— *Tractatus logico-philosophicus*, London, Routledge & Kegan Paul, 1969

—— *Culture and value*, Chicago, University of Chicago Press, 1980

Wojcik, Manfred 'In Defence of Shelley', *Zeitschrift für Anglistik und Amerikanistik*, XI (1963), pp. 143–88

Wollheim, Richard *Art and its objects*, Harmondsworth, Penguin Books, n.d.

—— *Sigmund Freud*, New York, The Viking Press, 1971

Wood, Neal *Communism and British intellectuals*, New York, Columbia University Press, 1959

# Index